GYULA ILLYÉS

PEOPLE
OF THE PUSZTA

Translated and afterword by G. F. Cushing

CORVINA KIADÓ

Title of the Hungarian original
PUSZTÁK NÉPE,
Nyugat kiadás, 1936

Second, revised edition
© Corvina, 1967
ISBN 963 13 0594 5
Printed in Hungary 1979
Franklin Printing House, Budapest
CO 1684-h-7981

CONTENTS

CHAPTER ONE

Taking bearings. A puszta in Transdanubia.
The character of the inhabitants

I was born and bred in the country, but for a long time I knew scarcely any more about village life than if I had been a city child. The world and mentality of the peasants was known to me only by hearsay. I was born on a puszta and lived there until my teens.

The Hungarian word *puszta* does not refer only to the romantic wide-open stretches of endless steppe re-echoing to the thunder of Petőfi's steeds.* In Transdanubia, which lies west of the Danube, the word has no such connotation, for the simple reason that this type of land does not exist there. West of the Danube, *puszta* means the whole conglomeration of farm servants' dwellings, stables, sheds and granaries built in the middle of a large estate and often reaching the size of a village. This cannot be called a *tanya*,** for a *tanya* contains one or two families only, while the puszta frequently shelters one or two hundred families. The puszta has a school and church, or at least a chapel which is usually attached to one wing of the manor-house. So there is a manor-house also, in the middle of an extensive and delightful park, with its tennis-court, artificial lake, orchard and majestic avenues of trees.

---

* Sándor Petőfi (1823–1849) sang the praises of the Great Plain in many of his best-known lyric poems.
** *Tanya* is an isolated farmstead typical of the Great Plain, where villages are infrequent.

7

Round all these runs a superbly-wrought high iron fence, which in its turn is surrounded by a muddy ditch reminiscent of some time-honoured castle-moat. After the big house the most elegant building, and one which may indeed be even more imposing, is the ox-stable. Then comes the farm manager's house, which in accordance with some long-lost tradition is almost everywhere surrounded with cypresses and pines. Somewhat less ornate than the manager's house is the bailiff's. The chief mechanic lives in an even plainer house. These are usually detached buildings. The farm servants' quarters have no pretensions to beauty whatsoever—and by farm servants I do not mean cotters; the Hungarian word *zsellér*, cotter, refers to the farmhand or day-labourer who, worn out in service, has been forced to find a house in a nearby village. The farm servants live under one roof in long, low, single-storey houses like slum tenements on the outskirts of a city. The living quarters are separated from each other only by thin walls. The slum-like long houses are so divided inside that there is a common kitchen with an open range between each pair of rooms. According to a law enacted at the beginning of this century, only one family may occupy one room. This law is now observed in many places, but there are quite a few where it is not. In the heart of Somogy county I have seen several farm servants' houses which did not even have chimneys; the smoke from the common kitchen escaped through the door, and several families lived together in each room. What this really means can be imagined only when we realise that farm servants tend to be quite prolific. Generally there are six or seven in the family, and even today some families consist of ten or twelve members. The houses are scattered at random among the stables and barns. In front of them and behind them are arrayed the pigsties and hen-houses belonging to the farm servants. These are built just a few paces away, so that they can keep an eye on the domestic animals they are allowed to keep as part of their payment in kind. According to the ethnographers, these outhouses are still constructed on the architectural principles once common in the original Central Asian homeland, out of a few bits of wood plastered with mud and straw. On most pusztas there are three or four long farm servants' houses, a separate one for the ox-drivers and a separate one for the coachmen, who according to the traditions of puszta society are in a higher class, though neither their work nor their pay is any different from those of the ox-drivers. Surprisingly, it is not the swine-herds who form the lowest class, as one might have expected from village traditions, but the workers in the tobacco-fields.

Almost half of the arable land in Hungary is cultivated by the farm servants on the pusztas. In morals, customs, outlook on life and even in the way they walk and move their arms, they differ sharply from all other social strata. They live in utter isolation, more hidden away and cut off than any villagers. They work all day, Sundays included, and in consequence hardly ever stir from the puszta. To reach them on their home ground, as I have often said, is a more difficult task than to study a tribe in Central Africa, owing to the long distances, the bad roads, local Hungarian conditions, and not least to their primitive suspicion of strangers. It was only after the First World War that they began to receive notice in literature. They live in a curious, airless but somehow invigorating community, materially and spiritually alike. This community possesses many traits which give it the kind of homogeneity more often to be found in the factory than in the village. But even so, it is very different. It is a world apart; not only the vocabulary, but even the dream-world of its inhabitants is unique, and this is only natural.

I still remember the stark, palpitating astonishment that gripped me and held me captive for weeks when at the age of eight or nine I first entered a village. The streets, the houses built side by side with streets in between, the markets whose purpose I could not possibly comprehend, all filled me with endless amazement and terror. Days later they still had to force me to go back there; first they used threats and then they took me by the hand, so petrified was I by the mad din of traffic, with all those carts, people, cattle and children in such a narrow space. Up to that time I had never seen two houses deliberately built in line, and now I could not take my eyes off all those houses with their terrifying orderliness and congestion. The regularity, discipline and secrecy of prison corridors have the same depressing effect on the soul as these streets had on me, with their fences, gateways and the houses crouching behind them. And since this village happened to be inhabited by Germans (it was Varsád in Tolna county where my parents had sent me on exchange to learn some colloquial German), I believed for a long time that all this was a German invention which they had introduced into Hungary. My guess, we now know, was more or less correct. I found German difficult to grasp. No doubt this was largely due to the depression I felt at the prisonlike atmosphere, mixed as it was with a kind of terrified amazement.

At home, as I have already stated, only the manor-house was fenced in. Here I must add what seemed so natural and obvious that I had previously forgotten to mention it—that when they passed along that fence, the people of the puszta were not allowed to make a noise or sing or, in accordance with some ancient decree, enjoy a smoke. These orders were enforced, of course, by keeping the youth under constant discipline and frequent chastisement. In my youthful mind, dogs too were associated with the idea of a fence and all its accessories. The farm servants could keep dogs only with special permission and for specific reasons. This was partly because they might have damaged the estate property—though it is difficult to imagine what property, since by now deer never dared to approach the puszta—and partly to prevent them from inciting the numerous pure-bred dogs that flocked round the big house to degrading attachments. So when I saw houses in the village sternly fenced in and guarded by snarling dogs, it is easy to understand why I gained the impression that in each of them there lived a count, or some other powerful human, haughty and unassailable, unsmiling and arrogant; in this notion too, as appeared later, I was not far wrong.

Either by instinct or because I felt a sense of shame, for a long time I did not consider the people of the pusztas as an integral part of the Hungarian nation at all. As a child, I was unable to associate them with those heroic, warlike and splendid Hungarians about whom I was taught in the puszta school. In my imagination the Hungarian nation was a distant, happy people, amongst whom I should dearly have loved to live. In my dismal surroundings I yearned to be among them as if they were legendary heroes. Every nation has a splendid image of itself; I took this image for reality and pursued it ferociously, having to discard more and more living Hungarians in the process. Much later, when I was abroad in Germany and France, I began to come to my senses, and this experience, despite my supernational principles, was painful and humiliating.

When I asked foreigners who had travelled in Hungary for their candid opinion of us, they always saw the simple sons of the Hungarian soil as a submissive, quiet folk, ready to doff their hats and come smartly to attention; this led them to believe that they were somewhat downtrodden and probably not lacking in hypocrisy either. . . This characterisation caught me unawares, astounded me and made me blush. What kind of Hungarians had these foreigners met? I came to realise that all the visitors had enjoyed the truly proverbial hospitality of the big country houses and had observed the folk around them as they passed by. To them these represented the Hungarian people, and they were exactly the same social stratum that I know. I know their virtues and I know their ills. Their virtues are known to all; I shall talk of what is not so well-known.

Nothing, believe me, is more remote from the inhabitants

of the puszta than that proud arrogance which is generally believed to be characteristic of the Hungarian race and which, in any case, is typical of the gentry throughout the world. It also exists among all the independent smallholders in the world, and thus among Hungarian smallholders too. The people of the pusztas, as I well know from my own experience, are a servile race. The people of the pusztas are submissive, but this is no calculated pose nor has it any ulterior motive. In their glances, in the way they jerk up their heads even at the cry of a bird, it can be seen that their submissiveness is inherited, it seems to run in their blood after a thousand years' experience. Of the various theories concerning the origin of the Hungarians, none has struck me with greater force and certainty of revelation than the latest one, which states that the Hungarians came here not with Árpád, but as the mute baggage-carriers of Attila, if not even before him. At all events it was due to their unwarlike nature that they were neither driven out nor slain with the Huns or the Avars. It enabled them to stay alive and enter the service of Avars and Franks after the Huns had departed—indeed they served every master who happened to be thrust upon them. Finally they entered the service of Árpád's tough, self-assured Turkic warriors, who moulded a state out of these taciturn, hard-working people. They yielded all they had to their noble conquerors, even their exquisite Ugric language—a normal historical process in the relationship between conqueror and conquered.

Certainly everything fine and good that may be said of servants is true of the people of the pusztas who in language, customs and looks even today preserve their ancestral characteristics virtually intact, no matter where they may be found in the country. They have not intermarried with other folk, not even with the neighbouring villagers, chiefly because nobody has wanted to intermarry with them. They are undemanding and so obedient that there is no real need to give

12

them orders; they sense their master's thoughts by telepathy and fulfil them, as is right and proper for servants whose father, mother, great-grandparents and even great-great-grand-parents have served the same kind of masters in the same place. Instinctively they know all the family customs; they will undertake any work, and when they have finished their job they will slip out of the room without any bidding, just as they slip out of life and out of history itself. There is no danger that they would be surprised by, say, the right of secret voting. There is no secrecy greater than theirs; it enables them to sense, even at distances as far as from here to Paris, their masters' wishes, demands or fatherly advice. These they follow just as they always have done in the past. If they had not done so, they would not be where they are now and would not be in service still. True, they have to be goaded to do the work in hand, but is this opposed to their inherent instinct to obey? Is it not an essential peculiarity of any social stratum that it is compounded of opposites? This is why these folk cannot be properly known at first sight and must be viewed cautiously from every angle. The true servant is servile in great matters. The arm may be slow, but the spirit is quick to obey.

My instinct tells me and my conviction strongly supports it, that even in the early days of *cuius regio, eius religio* no force was needed to make them realise immediately the more salu-tary and profitable features of whichever Christian creed their master happened to adopt in accordance with his frequently changing views. I am convinced that as soon as they heard of their master's secession or reconversion they fell in with his views and of their own free will, with the bailiff at their head, marched off singing in fervent procession to the Calvinist or Roman Catholic church and *vice versa*. However painful and shameful it may be to confess it, I dare not be either proud or assured of the faith I inherited. I know why it was handed down to me from the seventeenth century, after the noble family owning the estate had changed its creed several times. It was from this family that the Budapest firm of Strasser and König took over the puszta when I was a child. If the principle of *eius religio* had remained in force for another three centuries —a mere nothing in the eyes of eternity—I should certainly find myself discovering Semitic traits in my face, which my friends now tell me is Mongoloid; and what of my soul proper, my psyche?

This naturally does not imply that these folk are stupid. They are clever and keen-scented, and their historical premonitions are quite astonishing. Like all shrewd serfs, they are without doubt basically cruel and thirsty for revenge. When they do take revenge, they know no God and no limits, as is shown by their last rising, the rebellion of Dózsa.* This same rebellion proves how quick they are to learn; they have never forgotten the terrible lesson they learnt then, and have always had second thoughts about meddling in 'the affairs of the gentry', as they call politics. The experience of the centuries works admirably. Not a sound can be heard from the pusztas. True, there are other reasons for this besides mere shrewdness. Experts have demonstrated conclusively that a town-dweller may well find the food and clothing situation among the people of the pusztas simply inconceivable. So it is, but neither the chattering of their teeth nor the rumbling of their stomachs can be heard, directly or indirectly. They have no representative in parliament, no party, no newspaper, nor even a friend to plead their cause, though it is obvious that the fate of the whole country rests on the shoulders of those who hold the land in lots of ten thousand acres apiece. But is it not the prime task of Atlas to remain immovable? And is it mere chance that the member of parliament who refers in the House not to the conditions of these folk, but merely to the situation

---

* The peasant revolt of 1514, led by György Dózsa, which was quelled with the utmost severity and led to the enactment of the harsh laws embodied in the code of István Werbőczy *(Tripartitum)* in 1517.

of the farm managers rarely gets back there at the next election?

It is impossible to find better material from which to create a state, for the people of the pusztas have the greatest respect for authority. Undoubtedly this respect is the result of their training, which is so traditional and so thorough that today it runs deep in their blood and has so permeated their nervous system as to become almost instinctive. Those who regard this as their most primitive trait are quite correct. In my own family I was frequently astonished to hear the count who owned the estate given his full title even during the most confidential and intimate conversations. I still possess a letter from one of my cousins who attained the rank of bailiff. One fine day, for no reason the count dismissed him from his post. The letter describes the shocking event without frills; it uses the most spontaneous expressions of righteous indignation against the count, but retains an eerie respect for his title. 'Now it is quite plain,' one paragraph begins, 'that His Excellency the Count is a rotten beast and a stinking cur.' I well remember the reproachful looks I once received when, once again in the intimacy of the family circle, I was talking about the young gentlemen who were visiting the manor-house. They were friends of the count's daughters, and I called them simply 'that Wenckheim' and 'that Wimpffen'. Suddenly the faces around me displayed disquiet and annoyance. I soon learnt that the most familiar expression permissible was 'the honourable Mr Laci' or exceptionally 'the honourable Laci'. They are not fastidious in giving homage. Famous names and social rank do not count nor is it true that newcomers or social climbers are received with ridicule. At the beginning of this century quite a few Jewish families acquired estates in our part of the country. On the day after they had moved in, they received exactly the same apprehensive respect as their predecessors. It was as if at the moment that they drove through the pseudo-baroque gateway they had become magically transformed into different people, as indeed they had. For simplicity's sake the domestic servants probably had their own names for them, but in their presence—and this is what really matters—they addressed them with the same stammering respect as that given to the previous landlords.

This respect is shown at all levels. A distant relative of mine, who was about my age, succeeded in reaching secondary school by a series of marvellous and unexpected developments. After a great deal of floundering and confusion, for like many other village boys, he too had been destined for the priesthood as the sole means to social advance, he became a magistrate. Then, since he was diligent and had a truly phenomenal capacity and ability for study, he rose rapidly to a high post in the judiciary. When I was in my teens, I once happened to be present when he was visiting his parents. His own father and brothers, who were ordinarily loud-mouthed overseers or foremen on the puszta, hardly dared to utter a word at table. His mother, deeply touched and full of astonishment, kept glancing at him as if he were a divine messenger from another world. To me the most surprising thing was the behaviour of the young man himself. He accepted their homage and regarded it as quite natural. Following his deep-rooted instinct, he too had a high regard for himself and behaved accordingly. He ate and talked as he would have done at a county banquet. It was only later that I recalled with a pang of shame that I too had assumed his style. My heart warmed to his brilliance and I played out the shoddy scene while the onlookers followed it uncomprehendingly but perhaps for this very reason, with reverent joy.

I had even closer experience of reverence for lesser authorities and its reaction. My family is a model for puszta families who climb the social ladder. Those who got on in the world did so before my very eyes, or if they were already well up the scale, they had not yet shaken off all the marks of their former environment. Spread over three generations, my family

16

contains representatives of the highest and lowest degrees attainable. The majority, of course, are still impoverished labourers, landless farmhands and estate servants, but we also include an innkeeper, a chauffeur, a teacher and even a medical student. These provide a human ladder which I may climb up or down at will in order to study the various strata of society. The highest rung was reached by an uncle of mine who became chief clerk of a nearby county. He was the brains of the family and the pride of us all; we never ceased to mention his name on every possible occasion to folk of our sort. He was the powerful protector to whom we went with all our various troubles. He owed his advancement both to his outstanding ability and to the fact that he was a 'son of the people'. At election-time the voters enthusiastically gave their votes to this former barefooted lad and then glanced up at him in enchantment; they knew that the gentry liked him too and that he stood up to them.

Once when I was still at school I was passing through the town of D., and went to visit him at his office. I approached his room along the broad corridor of the town hall. Opposite the office door, on the well-worn red tiles by the wall, I saw ten or twelve Sunday-best hats, caps and lambskin kalpaks neatly arranged side by side on the floor. I stopped and almost burst out laughing in my first surprise. Just then a man from the puszta came up from the entrance, took off his hat and without looking for a peg (though there are always pegs in peasant houses everywhere), placed it beside the others on the floor as if it were the most natural thing in the world.

'Pegs?' said one of the assistant clerks when I asked about it later. 'Whatever next? They're so spoilt already that you can hardly cope with them.' He told me why the peasants had to leave their hats outside. When they clear their throats, in their nervousness they are liable to spit into their headgear, and this had once caused a rather highly-strung inspecting official to be violently sick.

In my uncle's room, standing close together like the hats outside, was a delegation of elderly farm servants from a neighbouring puszta. These 'spoilt' folk stuttered and stammered their way through what they had to say, and I suddenly realised that I too had caught their awkward nervousness.

My uncle did not so much as glance at them. He kept his eyes on his writing-pad and scribbled on it with his pen. This he did certainly from kindness or at least from experience, for if unwittingly he looked towards whoever was speaking, the words would immediately die away into a series of gulps. It was an obscure case of some burial fees which they had paid out and wanted to recover from the town council, whose ultimate responsibility it was to bury the person or persons concerned.

They did not get the money and were told so briefly and forcefully. They went out straight away, quickly, humbly and with polite words of farewell. As they were on their way out, I caught sight of a distant relative of ours, a cousin of my father's, who bowed to my uncle even more deeply and submissively than the others. I felt so confused and ashamed that my only thought was to get outside as quickly as I could. I collected the crown he usually gave me, by way of saying good-bye I kissed his hand and scurried out. In my confusion I lost the money in the next street. Maybe I threw it away unconsciously; perhaps I ought to be proud of my action now, but at the time I went through all my pockets for hours in search of it, reaching the verge of tears in my greed.

Was I then identifying myself with the people of the pusztas, even through such a slight reflex action of the spirit? I was still far from it. Those who set out from the farm servants' dwellings to become human beings regularly cast aside and forget their origins at first, like tadpoles becoming frogs. This is the road of progress and there is no other. Those who desert the air of the pusztas must acquire new hearts and lungs, otherwise they die in their new environment. And if they

18

ever want to get back there, they must compass the world to do so.

I myself went through the stages of this agonizing metamorphosis and only after the sixth or seventh stage did I become enough of a man to tackle the puszta. Once again I tried to breathe its air, I threw away the aristocratic signet-ring which at one stage of the metamorphosis had been put on my finger by the topmost stratum of the family with some little ceremony and obscure explanations. In nature there are only leaps and bounds, so naturally reassimilation is not free from excesses. I had to find my way to the very shore of the Atlantic, where I gave a fiery address at a meeting of the Negro dock-workers in Bordeaux, before I finally realised what it was that had launched me on my way. Only then, after all my reluctant home-comings, when I had felt not only the stables and farm servants' tenements but even the sunset on the puszta to be bleaker and emptier than anywhere else, was I able to return to my spiritual home. Only then, freed from a fanatical enthusiasm for peasants and from that passion for home found in great reformers, could I survey the landscape and take a dispassionate view of it all. The valleys and hills knew me better than I knew them. It was rather like meeting an old ox-driver and addressing him as a stranger; he listens with knowing winks to what one has to say and then suddenly reveals himself as the Uncle Pali or Uncle Mihály one knew as a boy. I am always suspicious of those who harp too much on their 'roots', especially before they have displayed their fruits. When storks return in the spring, they fly straight as an arrow across whole continents, then circle for hours over their old nests before they finally settle down. What holds them back? They examine every twig in the nest. This is how I came back too and examined the haunts of my childhood: to what end will become clear.

19

CHAPTER TWO

The spirit of the region. The homeland of the puszta folk.
My birth-place

In the eyes of modern literary historians, a birth-certificate from Transdanubia is an excellent recommendation. By some remarkable and hitherto unexplained misunderstanding, Transdanubians are blindly and unaccountably credited with cultured, refined and stable minds, the wise moderation of the Latin-Catholic spirit and all the optimism and clear vision that accompanies it—in short, they are credited with all the brilliance of the west that irradiates this part of Hungary. The simple reason for this is that here the sun sets later than anywhere else in the country. For a time I made capital out of this unexpected gift without batting an eyelid. I gladly accepted all the eulogies of those outposts and repositories of western civilisation, the towns of Transdanubia. And then one day my conscience pricked me and I began to feel like an impostor when I was congratulated, because I knew no Transdanubian town whatsoever. Up to the age of ten I had only once visited a town; on that occasion I went to the hospital at Szekszárd with a splinter of metal in my eye after Aunt Varga, the local repository of culture at home on the puszta, had been unable to remove it with her darning-needle, burdock leaf, and various ointments. So let other writers praise the Latin-Catholic spirit, the citadels of serene wisdom, the towns where happy citizens play the 'cello. Let other writers extol the virtues of the country-mansion on whose veranda the master of the house notes down

20

the year's labour services in the back of his Horace. In the region of which I am writing, you can travel for a couple of days without seeing so much as a town. It was as windswept, empty and vast as Levedia.*

The countryman who starts talking about his homeland sooner or later gets round to his home county, his native heath, his village and finally the yard, the kitchen and the two-windowed room where he learnt his mother-tongue. Thus unconsciously he works back through the history of a word and recreates the primitive times when *ház* (house) and *haza* (homeland) had the same meaning. My native land is the region round my house, and as I grow up it gradually extends to include ever wider circles, like the ripples from a stone thrown into the water. It may overcome whole worlds and may even reach the stars, when the old home has disappeared for ever.

When I recall my birth-place, I too think of a little house in the country. But I can remember only the house with its two tiny rooms and the earth-floored kitchen in between. The yard stretched as far as the eye could see. When I first struggled over the well-worn threshold, the infinite world lay at my faltering feet. The house stood on a hill. Beneath it in the valley lay the puszta, which conformed to the usual pattern. To the right lived the steward, the farm foreman, the mason and the wheelwright; in the same block of buildings were the forge and the wheel-shop. To the left were three or four rows of long farm servants' quarters, then there was the manor-house among its age-old trees, then the farm manager's dwelling. Immediately opposite was a large cart-shed in Empire style, behind which on a little rise stood the granary and ox-stables. And all around lay the endless fields, speckled with the white smudges of distant villages.

* The region between the Don and the Dnieper where the Hungarians were living in the early 9th century.

21

The original inhabitants of the puszta would throw longing glances towards these villages, wondering when and in which of them they might drop anchor for the last time, after a lifetime of tossing to and fro, which I know has been going on now for a thousand years. Every one of them regarded the puszta as merely a port of call, and those who were able to acquire a tiny patch of land on the edge of a village declared that this was where they hailed from.

It was something of a disgrace to be a puszta-dweller; it implied having no roots, no native land and no fixed abode—which of course is true.

Those who could find no patch of soil to call their home attached themselves to the village where their fathers or grandparents had had their dwelling or their grave. The people of the pusztas belonged nowhere, nor could they do so. The owners of the estate usually possessed several pusztas and could transfer the farm servants from one to another as they wished from year to year, or even in the middle of the year. For example, one of the Esterházys' farmhands might find himself at home on a puszta in Tolna, Sopron or Somogy or wherever the Esterházys had estates, provided he remained in their good books. If you want to know where a puszta-dweller comes from, you do not ask him where he lives or even less where he was born, but who his master is. My own family had served mostly the Apponyis, then the Zichys, Wurms, Strassers and Königs and their relations—for the landed gentry were apt to exchange their servants with their relatives; thus a clever cowman, a good-looking coachman or a deft-fingered gelder would be transferred or even presented to one of the relations, this being regarded by the servants themselves as a mark of special distinction. So we wandered from place to place, sometimes taking all our odds and ends, our collapsible hen-houses, our hens and the cow; sometimes it was only to visit relatives, a brother or sister-in-law who had suddenly been snatched away after living nearby for five or six years. Sometimes we drove all night and all morning in the wagon, but we were never away from a puszta, and felt at home everywhere. The house where I was born did not belong to my father, but in the land of my birth I received an unrivalled inheritance. I can call half a county my own.

My homeland and my world are where the River Sió, trickling from Lake Balaton, finds an unexpected partner in the River Sárvíz from the north. They do not join forces immediately, but wander side by side the whole county through, two or three kilometres apart, almost arm-in-arm, winking coquettishly at each other like dreamy lovers. The two streams share one bed, so large, fertile and wide that it might be called a family-size double-bed. On either side the gentle slopes and peaceful hills are adorned with colours that would not be out of place on the walls of a serene and cheerful home. Up north is Sárrét and down south Sárköz, where almost every village name begins with Sár-. This is my part of the country. Behind me, but only at arm's length away, is the delightful district of Völgység where, 'donning the countenance of youth', Vörösmarty's soul wandered dreaming a whole life through, 'burdened with gentle bonds of flowing golden hair'.* Our fields of flax were on the soil of Sárrét, but our hen-houses on the hill behind the house were in Völgység.

Perhaps it is immodest of me to claim all this as my birthplace, for Sárbogárd, for example, is well to the north in Fejér county, and Sárpilis is a long way south in Tolna. Yet I am glad to call it all mine. On my native heath I am like an impoverished monarch in his kingdom: he may not possess a scrap of land there, but in care and affection it is all his. In allotting me my birth-place, Fate prompted me to share myself and my affections with this region, for according to the official register I was born at Sárszentlőrinc.

* Mihály Vörösmarty (1800–1855), the celebrated romantic poet, recalls his youthful love in these lines from 'Széplak'.

It was a pleasant surprise to discover this among the details on my school-report one year, and I was far more proud of it than of the ivory rosary I had won as a prize. The first time I ever went to Sárszentlőrinc was when I walked there on my own two feet; I was born in fact at Felsőrácegres puszta. In the course of time, the puszta is attracted to first one, then another of the distant villages and to this day cannot decide which to love the best. So it bequeathes its newly-born babies to various villages. This explains how my mother, who was born in the same house as I, was officially born at Pálfa. The postal address is Simontornya, and the nearest station, across the 'island', is Vajta. I confess that this mixture delights me. I should be only too pleased if these villages would desist from their traditional knife-battles (nobody knows their origin—perhaps they date from some prehistoric quarrel in Central Asia), and would one day compete honourably with each other over me, as once the seven Greek cities did over Homer. Apart from the villages I have mentioned, Kajdacs, Bikács, Uzd-Borjád, Cece and Ozora might enter the lists, not to mention Kisszékely and Nagyszékely... and then Szilasbalhás, but there is no need to go further afield.

At Felsőrácegres even the ancient Romans... but I will not go into its history. The farm servants knew nothing about the history of the puszta except a few shreds of legend. The Turks came here and have remained in their memory as if they had disappeared only at the beginning of the last century. They were followed by the destructive Serbs who burnt everything. There were traces some of the *kuruc* too.*

The Hapsburgs left no remains. After that the professional rulers who had disappeared into the clouds seem to have yielded their place to an outlaw captain or two. Bandi Patkó had been a good captain. Then came the counts, and then the Jews,

---

* Soldiers in the armies of Imre Thököly and Ferenc Rákóczi II, who led insurrections against the Hapsburgs in the late 17th and early 18th centuries.

or in other words the tenant-farmers. This was all that was known of local history. In a distant part of the puszta known as the 'stinking corner' on the bank of the Sió, a cattle-shelter had been erected on the ruins of a church dating from the Árpád dynasty. Here too old chalices had been discovered, and gold coins from the time of the Mongol invasion.* We may well believe that Rácegres, like all the Transdanubian pusztas, was once a flourishing place. Today it is a warm, cosy little hollow in the folds of the hills, sheltered from storm and tempest; even figs grow there. From it rise the sounds of piglets and babies squealing, oxen lowing and bailiffs grumbling, to the outside world these are the only signs of life. It is invisible even to the traveller who passes right by it, or rather flounders above it in the sea of sand which forms the main road from Simontornya to Sárszentlőrinc, flanked by tall gleditsias. From outside the puszta is hidden by a thick barrier of leaves which seal it off as hermetically as the lid of a pot. From the road a steep narrow track leads down to the puszta.

Running up this same steep narrow track from time to time, I would peep at the outside world, at my native land, at Europe. The highroad was already a foreign world, dangerous and forbidden. Once or twice a week gipsies, tradesmen or wedding-parties would go past. On the other side the count's pinewoods stretched into the far distance, with the cattle-pastures in the foreground. Just like the gophers who poked their curious heads out of the holes down there in the pastures, the bolder ones even standing on their back legs to see further, I would push my head out of the security and warmth of the little valley; I would sniff the air curiously and observe the country round, longing to go ever further afield. This is how I remember those days.

When I think of the count's estate and five or six villages, I realise now that around my cradle Fate had laid enough history

* 1241–42.

and enough of Hungary to study for life. My gaze ranged over the towers that gleamed out from behind the hills and woods. In my imagination I conjured up the pusztas and villages that crouched beneath them, as I discovered them one by one. To me each one was different, each one was a separate world, another story-book, with strange folk, customs and legends. Like good textbooks, they entertained me while they taught me folklore, history, Hungarian syntax, social sciences and a lot of other subjects that were not mentioned in the puszta school. Now as I recall this open-air school, I realise that today I am being examined in what I learnt there.

Sometimes I would pass through two or three villages in search of a calf that had strayed into the outside world. I went to see relations for name-days, weddings and funerals. My father's trade would take us sometimes six pusztas away. Later I was driven on by my own wanderlust. All in all, I came to know the countryside in every detail like the back of my hand. Came to know it? What did I see in it then? Beautiful hillsides, single wheatfields that stretched as far as the eye could see, fields of tall maize like forests where one might get lost for hours before reaching the far side, thickets of broom and willow by the misty rivers, and here and there a village or two, to which at first I cautiously gave a wide berth, like the wild beasts of the field to whom I felt more akin than to human beings. But the hills, woods and lush river-valleys were part of nature and not part of me. They did not take root in me, or even if they were alive to me, they had nothing to say to me yet. It was only when I had heard their story and read about them that I really got to know them. Like photographic plates dipped in developer, the scenery took on light, shade and colour within me under the exhilarating influence of some shepherd's fantastic exploit, the legend of an outlaw, or some historical event. I well remember how it all began.

One spring morning I was squatting on the doorstep, avidly and all unsuspectingly reading a ponderous tome that my grandmother had borrowed from some itinerant tradesman to brighten up the winter feather-plucking. All of a sudden I was overcome with fiery excitement and an indescribable ecstasy of joy filled me, body and soul alike. The blood rushed to my face and I had to get up. I read that Petőfi, Sándor Petőfi, had lived for years here in Sárszentlőrinc and had attended the secondary school there. It was not Sárszent or some other Szentlőrinc, but that village just behind the poplars across the way... 'From September 28th, 1831, he studied at the Lutheran secondary school at Sárszentlőrinc in Tolna county, and in the summer of 1833 he completed the first-form syllabus there...' In a flash Sárszentlőrinc was transformed before my eyes; it began to sparkle and scintillate with golden light. Had lightning struck it, had the Virgin Mary suddenly appeared at one of its wells (a relatively frequent occurrence then in those parts), had a divine miracle occurred, nothing could have clothed the village with more merit or excellence. I jumped up and set off there just as I was, barefoot and bare-headed. Two hours later, dusty and panting, I stood at the end of the lovely broad village street which is almost wide enough to be called a square. The old school was a simple, reed-thatched, single-storeyed peasant-house, not different from any of the others, except perhaps that the side facing the street was somewhat longer. It was situated on the edge of the village, as if it had come to greet me in my enthusiasm. I looked in wonder through the tiny windows and in a trance paced the little room whose clay floor felt deliciously cool to my bare feet. I was not at all disappointed. The spirit of Petőfi irradiated everything, even the cobbler's bench, for a bootmaker lived there now. 'This was the latch he lifted and these the very eaves beneath which he used to stand'—yes, it was all true, and I struggled to hide my tears. Here was the gate through which he went, and the very road where I was now walking he had trodden too. Perhaps he had even gone out to

27

Rácegres—why not? His friends would certainly have tempted him out there. I looked around on the green landscape. Later, whenever I considered the nature of true patriotism, my emotions of that morning would flood back in me. Leaping, whistling and running, I returned to the puszta to read more of the book. On the next page I read that he had also been in this district later. He had visited Cece and Ozora, and had written a host of poems there in Borjád. I was so exasperated that I nearly wept. If I had not been so impetuous, I might have gone on to Borjád, which lay just beyond Sárszentlőrinc.

The landscape suddenly grew in beauty; it acquired colour and developed a soul. Poems gleamed like swallows as they circled round it. A divine radiance shone on the miserable ox-carts as they lumbered out of the puszta, their rotting sides and wheels thick with dung; it lit up the tubercular beasts and drivers who were mere bags of bones. They moved on in brilliant clouds of poetry, thanks to Petőfi who had sung of them. Here in Borjád he had written 'The Four-Ox Cart', whose mood has for ever charmed moonlight nights for me. Whenever the moon rises, I feel that I am in the middle of the nineteenth century and seem to smell the scent of hay, even in winter.

> 'It was a glorious night. The moon rode high
> And wandered pale through jagged cloudy peaks,
> Just like a widow who, bowed down with grief,
> Her husband's grave within the churchyard seeks.
> A mercenary breeze roamed fields nearby
> And purchased from the grass its sweetest scent,
> As with their waggon down the endless road
> With sluggish tread four oxen slowly went.'

Here too he wrote 'The Magyar Nobleman', which also affected my emotions for a lifetime, giving them a much more dangerous bias than the former poem.

From then onwards, whenever we drove through Sárszent-lőrinc and Borjád, I was seized by the kind of agony one feels at confession or at examinations: it seemed as though the poplars beckoning from afar were expecting some solemn confession of faith from me. We often went that way to Kölesd where my mother's younger sister lived with her husband, also on a puszta, of course. But my reading soon mingled harsh sounds and scents with the idyllic peace of the glimmering Sió and the whispering trees that arched above the road; to me it meant the clash of steel and the reek of blood. Very soon the journey to Aunt Katica's merely implied that we should be crossing a battlefield in both directions. It was an incredibly lengthy tract of ground for a destructive battle which, we now know, was more like a massacre than a regular engagement. I sat on the plank which served as a seat, with the inevitable present of a newly-baked cake in my lap, while the clatter of the wheels drummed into my ears the barbarous din and meandering rhythms of a wild charge. I knew of this from a poem which made me feel not only the historic event itself, but also the boasting of the warriors, the flashing swords, the prancing horses and the destructive despondency of the age as well:

> 'At Kölesd, at Kölesd the battle began,
> And I was there too, to the front line I ran;
> To the front line I ran and I hacked my way through;
> Like a reaper the grass, so I scythed and I slew.'

The rich smell of the warm cake tickled my nostrils and the sound of my parents talking buzzed in my ears, but I was far away. All my senses were held in thrall by the sounds, scents and visions conjured up by the lines of verse.

I have never read a more thrilling and expressive battle-poem. Its dramatic brevity and the genuine bloodlust that pulses behind its words are proof that neither this nor the other similar verses could have been written by Thaly, who was a poor rhymester when he wrote under his own name; this is also the view of Babits, who has a delicate poetic instinct.*

> 'When bold Ádám Balogh raised high his keen blade,
> Then young László Sándor brought up his brigade.
> "Let no German bullets your courage dismay,
> And never, my lad, your heart's terror display,
> And never, my lad, your heart's terror display." '

Or was it only in me that it aroused such feelings, who like all other children quivered with battle-fever as I leaned against my mother's arm, either from some secret desire for revenge or from a feeling of oppression? Every time we made the four or five-hour journey, all along the rustling reeds I relived the appalling encounter right up to the scene which even today makes me see the swamps running with blood, the wounded gasping for breath, their faces distorted by their shrieks:

> 'And in Sió's thickets a great scream arose,
> And through Simontornya the shrieks of their foes...
> His infantry slew them, his horsemen pursued,
> And the meadows to Szekszárd ran red with their blood.'

After the victory the *kuruc* generals praised the peasants who had risen and distinguished themselves chiefly in pursuit of the enemy. At the first hint the sons of the pusztas burst out of their reed hovels like wild beasts, spurred on by some secret desire

---

* The Battle of Kölesd took place on September 2nd, 1708, and was commemorated in a poem of the same title published by the historian Kálmán Thaly as a genuine '*kuruc* song'. It later transpired that Thaly had himself written a large number of them, including this one. Mihály Babits (1883–1941) was an outstanding Transdanubian poet and critic.

for revenge and by their sense of oppression. Wielding their flails, they charged the enemy, none of whom in the end survived to tell the tale.

In later history they gave further proof of their warlike spirit. In October 1848, it was the men of this region who trapped the Croatian forces of Róth and Phillippovich at Ozora. On that occasion they won praise from Görgey, who was no lover of the non-professional militia. 'The heights on my left as far as the Sió,' he writes in his memoirs, 'have been occupied since last night by the Tolna militia. There is no doubt that in the successful outcome of this campaign chief honours are due to the commander of this force.' But he also reprimands them. The militiamen immediately fell on the weapons of the Croats so that each of them, 'in memory of this great and glorious day, might acquire at least a good rifle.' Perczel was able to recover only twelve antiquated cannons, for they had taken even these away. To commemorate the great day? Up to 1847 anyone who allowed them, the non-nobles, to have a sword, rifle or even gunpowder, was given twenty-five strokes of the rod.

In the *kuruc* wars urban Transdanubia took the loyalist side; in the revolution of 1848 it was cautiously pro-Austrian. This country region, however, remained faithful to the spirit of rebellion which as always represented the true spirit of the nation. The area of the Sió and Sárvíz, that marshy valley which curls twisting in a narrow band from the Danube up to the Balaton, always glinted firm and ready to strike, like a sword drawn from its sheath, whenever the winds of freedom began to blow. This it is only proper to say, but I am afraid it was also ready to strike whenever there was a chance of shedding blood freely, of opening the flood-gates of pent-up bitterness, or of taking revenge, the Lord alone knows for what cause. Are the serfs so warlike then? Indeed they are: the people of the pusztas make excellent soldiers. At the beginning of the First

31

World War, the 44th Kapos Infantry Regiment was wiped out four times in as many months and four times rose again. The sons of the puszta did not seek to save their own skins. In their heroic defiance of death, only the Bosnians, of all the peoples in the Austro-Hungarian Monarchy, could vie with them. Such is the impartial judgement of German experts on this subject. I myself have frequently listened with amazement to stories of their exploits. The eyes of haggard, hollow-chested estate wheelwrights and carpenters who became tongue-tied in the presence of the cook from the manor-house, began to sparkle as they told the tale of how they had crawled under the barbed-wire towards the Russians, how with bayonet between their teeth and home-made spiked club in their right hand, they had leapt down perilous ravines upon Italians, French, Negroes and anybody else who happened to be in their way. How often have I seen the long-bladed knife gleaming out of the top of their Sunday boots—for they take their knives with them even when they are off to a dance. And here let me record, in case it has escaped the notice of the ethnographers, one of our local proverbs, of which I know two variants. One runs: 'Even in church it's a good thing to have a knife'; the other is: 'A Hungarian never goes out without a knife—not even out of the back door.'

But I am talking of the environs of the puszta, of the villages. I feel, however, that the subject I have just mentioned cannot be avoided, for each village has its own characteristic method of fighting, without which no description would be complete. In Pálfa, for instance, they struck at the face, while the men of Simontornya grew dumb when the fight began and wielded their knives in eerie silence as if they were performing a ceremonial rite. According to specialists in anatomy, the method used in Ozora displayed a profound knowledge of that subject; there they stabbed the crook of the neck, piercing between the bones into the artery. It is interesting to note that nowhere did they aim below the chest or at the stomach. Those who take such matters into account may regard this as a national characteristic, for some nations are known to prefer the stomach. The reason, however, lies in the method of holding the knife. The thumb is extended firmly upwards towards the end of the haft, as I was carefully instructed by my friends who minded the geese. With such a grip it is possible to strike only downwards from above. In Rácegres they favoured the yoke-pin as well as the knife. This is an iron rod about half a metre long, ending in a ball about the size of a child's fist. It was used for striking, like a club, but it was also hurled. Such were the ways in which I began to discover the soul of the region, which is also mine.

CHAPTER THREE

The separate world of the puszta. Private property.
Unifying forces. Two ambitious families

·

It is not my intention to give here an account of my own life. I do not feel that I have reached so high a plane that the scenes I have left behind me can be used to give delight or direction to others. My only aim is to depict the character of a certain stratum of society; if I include my own experiences here and there, it is merely to illustrate my theme. Any recollections I unearth simply help me to descend into that deeply-buried scorching stratum, which apprehensively hides its whirling world from all outside scrutiny and even from the impartial light of day. From experience, I know that others may well acquire some knowledge of it, but only those born in it can truly understand it. I should also like to defend it.

There is good reason for this sensitive withdrawal. If the people of the pusztas were to give the slightest hint of the peculiar order in which they live, they would be compelled to renounce it all and turn against themselves, for their pattern of life is so utterly different from that prevailing above them. This nether stratum is a warm mud-bath, above which there howls an alien, freezing wind. Those who break away from it do so in one or two years, during which their minds and nerves develop from, say, primeval humanity to the condition of an assistant caretaker. If those who stay there should poke out even their little finger, they draw it back immediately, shivering. This world is a wild one, its principles and morals have become cooled and hardened like the earth's crust; now, we may as well admit, they are merely formal, having lost all but the tiniest spark of life. It is a dangerous world, with its own laws, customs, concepts of private property and love-life. Who could possibly find his way around in it? One must be born to it.

If we consider first the most obvious subject, private property, here the puszta, though it may not admit it, holds views which differ completely from those demanded by the laws of the land. I do not consider myself competent to judge which view is the more just and humane. The attitude of the puszta is at all events more original, conservative and antiquated. It preserves the tradition of some age-old community whose concepts of 'mine' and 'thine'—as regards either land or love—were not so sharply defined as they are today. The large estates of one or two (and not infrequently ten or twelve) thousand acres are not divided into small plots. The enormous fields of wheat and rye are cultivated in common, and the huge green and gold tracts roll away as far as the eye can see; they are as boundless as the sea and sky. Faced with this sight, the simple soul feels only the strength, the blessing or the recalcitrance of the earth and, in the absence of frequent and appropriate warnings, is apt to forget that the common labour is performed to order, while the harvest profits one man only. From the time of Árpád, the experience of the puszta folk has been that nature pays badly. If one does not die of hunger, then things are going well; such is the lore of the centuries. Whether all the extra wheat which could be made into more bread or even cake is carried off by hail, by the Tartars, by the count, or by the count's man Schlesinger is a mere detail of the whole problem. In brief, they work and cultivate the land, and if starvation does not force them to give up the ghost, they do not feel like asking why their portion of it is so shockingly small. On the other hand, it is difficult to get out of their heads the idea that the land with which they struggle is first and foremost their business, that nature is, well, nature and belongs to everybody. They have a great *penchant*,

35

as one of the estate managers' wives once put it to me, for letting the produce that passes through their hands stick to their fingers. 'They must be treated like bees,' went on the lady with a charming smile. 'You must take away from them to make them work on. If they had everything, they would pound the zither all day and warm their backsides in the sun; for all they cared, the weeds could grow up waist-high in the sugar-beet.' This is indeed likely—if they had everything.

But they have nothing and so they work; meanwhile, where they can do so, they thieve like magpies. Social scientists would say that they are still motivated by some atavistic clan-spirit, a spirit which, as I have said, prompts common distribution of what is acquired in common. This, however, grows weaker every day.

I was able to feel it at its height. I also felt—painfully catching my breath— the power of the other order of things. I was well on the way to manhood when it impinged on my life and began to teach me its ways. When, for instance, the Swabian at whose house I was staying to learn German once sent me to get some fodder, I went out with the innocence of a new-born lamb and collected the green maize leaves which lay scythed in the neighbour's garden. There were maize leaves in his own garden too.

It was only after the third clout on my head that I realised that I had been stealing.

'Well, doesn't it belong to the estate?' I asked indignantly. Things which belong to the estate or to the count are everybody's; and everybody grabs what he can before he touches what is his own in a mood of rash extravagance.

I went through precisely similar scenes at my grandparents', where I rounded up the village teacher's pigeons, and at my uncle's, where one afternoon I was accompanied home by the watchman from somebody else's vineyard. It occurred again at the station at Vajta, when I followed my parents on to the train carrying a huge railway lantern. When I was in the first form at secondary school, I tried to take a live goat from the village pasture and present it to the lady of my heart who had a passion for goats. Unfortunately when I had dragged the stubborn quarry on to less dangerous territory, two kids broke away from the herd and with despairing bleats rushed after their mother. I took a long time to learn.

If we consider how families have amassed fortunes in the course of history, or have enriched themselves during the machine-age, the ethics of my family's acquisition of worldly wealth may be censured only on the grounds that lesser results are less easily justified. My father's father was a shepherd, a head shepherd. This will raise a smile among those who have some faint appreciation of what this occupation meant after the *Ausgleich* of 1867. He was head shepherd to Prince Esterházy and afterwards to the tenants.

He was the last person to be able to explain to me or, presumably, to the Prince, the precise arrangements governing his occupation. When asked about them, he would embark on complicated explanations and talk for hours about breeding, one-year-olds, seven-year-olds, wool-scouring, tegs, tail-docking and allowances for staggers. In the end he would either declare that he owned nothing and was a penniless servant, or that really every sheep belonged to him and only out of the goodness of his heart would he drive an occasional one up to the manor-house. The truth of the matter was that besides his yearly payment in kind he had a direct income in proportion to the increase in the flock. The first flock that he had taken on for the Prince when he was a young man gradually increased in size as the years went by, and there were times when he had as many as five or six shepherd boys serving under him. In some years he had five thousand sheep. He was a power in the land, like a ruler at the time of the great migration. How many sheep could Árpád have had? To his honour I may say that grandfather possessed no arrogance of wealth; it was rather the chieftain's pride and the arrogance of freedom that he bore in his straight back and thrust-out breast. Those were the good old days. He received a certain share of the wool. He had to report on lambings. As verification of the death of a sheep, he merely had to hand in the skull, then later the hide too. Even more recently, the gentry discovered that sheep may be milked too, and acquired a taste for their cheese, which until then had merely been some kind of peasant mush. The world had taken a fearful turn for the worse.

But by that time grandfather had a vineyard in the neighbouring village, a house and plot of land in the chief town of the district, a son in the county administration, another son in his own inn, a daughter also keeping an inn of her own, a daughter married to a master-cooper, yet another daughter whose husband possessed his own threshing machine and yet another son... the Lord alone knows what he possessed then. He even had his own altar inscribed with his name in gilt letters in the church of a nearby village. All this he owed to grandmother, for he himself was contemplative and peaceful by nature; he liked to hum tunes and whittle away at wood. He liked comfort and as long as he kept a donkey, would sit side-saddle on the fat beast, leaning his right hand on the animal's head as if he were in an armchair. This was how he travelled all his life.

It was grandmother who saw to it that this branch of the family prospered. Grandfather always called her grannie; incidentally he made us call him gaffer and grandmother gammer but these appellations were so peasant-like, that even though my tongue got round them then, I find them difficult to write now. Grandmother was tall, half a head taller than grandfather; she was dark and stern-looking. She came from somewhere in Upper Somogy, but also from one of the Esterházy pusztas, of course. It was she who brought into the family the stature and iron determination of a grenadier. She too came of shepherd-

38

stock, though I was never able to discover more precise details. Occasionally she would mention her grandfather, a certain László Börcsök, who was 'a rare handsome man' and had seen the world; every year he took the silver dollars to the Prince in Vienna, all by himself. Of all the ancestors I have never seen, this Börcsök lives most vividly in my imagination. I can see his slender figure and dark, lively face and hear his brisk speech. I see him as he leaps down from his saddle in front of an inn and fingers his pistols as he steps into the bar. According to grandmother, my elder brother was the very image of him. He was stabbed to death at the age of twenty-nine on October 3rd one year in the eighteenth century. On this day, as on so many others, grandmother mourned his memory, praying and fasting from dawn to dusk, for she was incredibly devout. We children had to join her devotions and pray loudly for the salvation of the soul of the late lamented Börcsök, for he had gone—to purgatory, we hoped—without the last sacraments. Such is the power of tradition.

What sort of a woman was grandmother? How did she get on with grandfather? I was scared stiff of her. I remember most of all her icy feet, poor soul, which my cousins and I clasped in turn as she lay in her coffin, so that she should not return to haunt us.

Much later when grandfather divided his days with minute precision between singing litanies and swilling down liquor, he turned to me after a long silence spent in front of a press-house and slowly, haltingly muttered the answer to a question that had been put perhaps fifty years before. 'I had a girl from Gyulaj recommended to me, and another one from Pula—one of them had sent me her kerchief. Her father kept his own flock of sheep. "That's the kind of girl for you, János," they said. But she wasn't. A servant's lad should not go to his in-laws' house, where he'll only get under their feet; let him go under his own roof. I could have found a better-looking girl than this Náncsi, but she would bring the clean linen out to me even a day's journey off before we were married. I didn't regret it,' he added, suddenly jerking his head up and fixing his clouded eyes on mine. At that time grandmother had been dead for ten years; it was the first time that I had heard her Christian name. The simple name transformed her magically into a living being, a muscular young girl and a stubborn bride. In her lifetime she had been more of a guiding spirit in the family, the directing genius of tenacity, ruthless economy and ambition.

What was there for her to economise on? Not long ago I came across a contract of employment that had belonged to grandfather. It raised his yearly wages from fifty to seventy forints, in recognition of thirty years' faithful service.

Grandmother instilled her religious fervour, which went far beyond mere bigotry, into her husband and children. Certainly she would not have sinned against her conscience for the world. No temptation could have made her touch anything that belonged to someone else. Whatever she laid her hands on, she did so with a perfectly clear conscience and without the least sense of guilt. Grandfather lived three pusztas away from us, a good half-day's ride in the cart. From every visit there, we returned laden down with rich gifts—often this was the only reason for our visits. But it was always on the edge of the puszta that we picked up the live or slaughtered sheep and pushed it under the hay on the rack with the utmost secrecy. For fear of the bailiffs or the head shepherd? No, it was because of grandmother, whose conscience would never have allowed her to connive in the removal of anything from the puszta. Inside the puszta, however, she was like a dowager empress and regarded everything as her own.

She lorded it over the folk there too. The smiths, gardeners, storemen and watchmen all obeyed her blindly, fetching and making whatever she ordered at the expense of the estate. Her authority was not due to her husband's power but was, so to speak, based on democracy, for she convinced everybody that she was cut out for it.

My maternal grandmother was another such figure, though compounded of different forces. I regard it as more than pure chance that both sides of my family were commanded by women who directed the campaign. In the stifling atmosphere of this primeval world, which preserved so much of the warmth of tribal life, it was the women, the mothers, who ruled over each family group.

They did not rule by oppressing the menfolk. The men would roam for weeks in the fields; even in winter they did not sleep in the house, where most of them did not have a sleeping-place anyway in the dark hole which had a family living in each corner. They slept in the estate stables to keep an eye on the animals by night too. They may well have been scared away from home also by worry—the endless complaints, the weeping and wailing, the birth of children and their almost as frequent death; all these were women's affairs. And the women shouldered their burden with grim determination, like she-animals. Compared with their life, the men's was as free as a bird's. Everything at home depended on the women; if a family went up in the world, it showed the strength of the woman behind it, if it declined, it showed her spinelessness.

My maternal grandmother was a genius.

I use this word quite dispassionately and in full knowledge of its meaning. If my paternal grandmother wanted to secure her dominion over the swift currents of the future by erecting bastions of money, and would have sacrificed the health and perhaps the life of herself and her warriors for a farthing, my mother's mother put her trust in the power of the human spirit. She was an educated woman with an astonishing factual knowledge; not only in the puszta, but even in the district and perhaps in the whole county there were very few who had read

41

more than she. She had been a servant-girl from the age of nine, serving a butcher, an innkeeper, a clerk, and a Jewish grocer until finally she spent four years as head chambermaid to a director of the Kőbánya brewery. Here she learnt that life could be different from that led by her parents. It was here too that she met my grandfather and with an unquenchable, almost idolatrous, lifelong passion immediately fell in love with his unusually handsome features, his politeness, his distinguished name (he was called Lajos), and, I believe, above all with his utter helplessness. Grandfather had been discharged from the army at that time, but had not returned to his native village; he was working in the factory whose director employed grandmother, for he was a wheelwright.

Whenever grandma mentioned her husband's occupation, even when she was very old indeed, she paused for an instant and glanced round her audience severely. I too bow to the defiant strength with which every member of the family except grandfather clung to this title. For grandpa was indeed a wheelwright, even if he had learnt the craft only when he was a grown man. He came from Gyulavári in Békés county; when he was sixteen, in the time of the 'Great Drought', he enlisted in the army for eight years as proxy for someone else, for the sum of seventy forints; there seemed to be little future for him on the land anyway, and there were eleven brothers and sisters at home. He was so short that after he had been recruited, his mother had to pin up his white uhlan cape so that he could walk in it. In the cavalry regiment he was scared of the horses. I was very surprised to hear from him that in those days they scarcely ever saw horses where he came from, beyond the Tisza; they used cows for ploughing... He was sent off to the stud-farm at Kisbér, where there were fifteen hundred wild stallions. For three years he groomed and fed them, moving amongst them with a trembling heart. Then he happened to meet a young blacksmith from Tolna, who took pity on him. They became friends, and what a friendship that was! If only I had the power and ability to give but an inkling of it! They spent their whole lives together, and when he was seventy-two and half-blind, grandfather set out one morning almost out of his mind to cross the frontier into Muraköz, then occupied by the Serbs, to touch the wooden grave-post he himself had carved and see whether it was still intact. It was this young smith who got him away from the horses into the workshops belonging to the stud-farm; here he rapidly took to carpentry and never changed his trade again. This smith was loud-mouthed, hot-headed and violent, the very antithesis of my grandfather, and after they had been demobilised, he dragged him off to Pest, a town which was then beginning to boom. There they went from factory to factory, for they would only agree to be employed where there were vacancies for both a smith and a wheelwright. The young smith looked after grandfather and cared for him until he handed over his responsibility to my grandmother, laying the foundations of the match with his approval, the loan of a bed and ten forints. This was all he could afford, because he himself got married at the same time; it could not have been otherwise, because they did everything together—even their children were born at the same time. The only difference was that the blacksmith married into a job on his native soil when he took as a bride the daughter of the smith at Rácegres. Two months later my grandparents were also on the puszta there. The former wheelwright, smitten by the merciless ordinance of fate, was struck dead by lightning and thus left the way open for them.

Thus my mother's family also began life like a little shoot, a tiny green speck in the ground, which does not reveal even to the expert whether it is to become a nettle or an oak. The seed, however, was excellent. Grandfather, who hitherto had been blown about like thistledown before the wind, was now securely staked and began to strike deep roots in the familiar soil, he gained a new zest for life and made daring plans. With the right woman at his side, he blossomed out and found rich fulfilment in life. In the turmoil of 'free' competition in the outside world, he would surely have perished, but here in the rich black mould of a static society, in the nether world of poverty and servitude, his peaceful nature, soft-spokenness and Calvinist inflexibility acquired a reason for their existence and became roots of nourishment. A swarm of bees landed on a tree in front of the house, he took them in a sack and though he had never kept bees before, some three years later extracted forty kilos of honey with an extractor of his own make. Grandmother of course sold it to the last drop in the heat of the moment. He was a taciturn man with a ready smile, who never uttered a harsh word but once refused to accept an important official communication because on it his surname, which happened to be identical with that of an old aristocratic family, was wrongly spelt. Again, without a word and in cold fury he hurled the spoke of a wheel he happened to be making full in the face of a gardener who in the course of a lengthy flood of swear-words cast the usual aspersions on one's mother —his mother, on this occasion. For he never swore. It is still the most astonishing thing to me that one never heard any swearing or filthy language in his house, which is to say the room and corner of the common kitchen which was his. Round about the puszta seethed and frothed with obscenity, and ideas were always expressed in the coarsest fashion, but at his threshold and windows they died away. Later we, his grandchildren, who had been brought up in this coarser linguistic atmosphere and at the age of five knew all there was to know about parentage, the functions of the body and the relationship of the sexes, went through an instinctive change whenever we entered the wheelwright's shop. Like dogs coming out of the river, we shook off our usual world of ideas and its expressions. For a long time I believed that grandfather did not even know these words. His accent was different from ours; he spoke in the dialect of the Great Plain, where perhaps these words were unknown. Only once did I hear him utter a curse: 'I wish he'd been burnt to death when he was a day old,' he said of one of his sons-in-law. His eyes were gentle as he said it, but his mouth was grim.

My grandparents even took a newspaper, or rather went to fetch it every other Saturday from the Calvinist minister in a nearby village, who for a couple of eggs would hand over all the papers he had collected. Originally the daily paper they got was *Unity*, whose large pages were excellent for covering the beehives in the winter; then it was *Hungary*, for the minister was a great follower of Miklós Bartha.* Who can recall the *Illustrated Family News* and the *Housewives' Journal*? The loft was full of them, bound in yearly volumes according to the bookbinding lessons included in them. I can still remember who József Prém was.**

If somebody bought a book in a distant village, grandmother would know all about it two days later. She would do everything in her power to borrow it, enlisting the services of the egg-collectors and rag-and-bone men, with whom in any case she was very friendly. When a French governess arrived at the manor-house, she struck a bargain with her to give me lessons every evening in exchange for some needlework or sewing, although at that time there was no thought of my going on to secondary school. So at the age of eight I conversed in French behind the ox-stable.

Yet at that time grandmother was beginning to decline. She had already sent her fledglings from the nest. When did she read? Nobody knows. She worked from dawn to dusk, for in addition to the land due to them by contract, she cultivated other plots as a sharecropper. With her four daughters she hoed and weeded even on Sundays and holidays. For she was an atheist, and knew what that meant. In any case there was no church on the puszta. Unfortunately she regarded the printed

* Opposition politician and writer (1847–1905).
** Author, reviewer and editor (1850–1910).

word as gospel truth. Once she read that caraway-seed soup was good for children's blood, so for four years we breakfasted on caraway-seed soup, detesting the nauseating stuff, though milk was available if not abundant. She also read that children should always be kept occupied. So we never had a free moment. She read further that draughts do no harm and that virtue brings its own reward. She believed everything and looked towards the future with invincible faith, for even then the most gloomy articles ended with a ray of hope. It was she who drew the moral from novels and tried to learn from the fate of the young count who had lost all he had on horses. My mother would tell of how they educated themselves in the evenings while they were knitting stockings. One of them would read aloud while the others plied the needles. Knitting, in any case, was her passion, to which she introduced not only the girls but also the boys. 'You don't know what you may have to do for a living,' she said, and sat me down there too. I know how to knit socks and I can scallop edges too—you should just see me! Her first aim was to educate her daughters, all of whom received fantastic names after heroines in novels.

This, however, was really beyond her means. The eldest, my Aunt Elvira, was sent home after the first two months from a nearby convent, to the good-natured amusement of the whole countryside; she brought an explanatory letter which my grandmother immediately tore up. But she did not give in; the girls must not grow stupid there on the puszta at the back of beyond. She found places for them as maids and sewing-girls and instructed each of them what to look out for and what to guard against. Moving from place to place, the girls watched and examined everything like spies, then exchanged experiences at home and discussed them with a healthy air of superiority. Certainly Switzerland could not have offered them a more excellent and practical finishing school. Each of them would have had a brilliant future if they had followed their mother's advice in choosing a husband, and if they had not exercised the

46

independence which she had nourished in them first and foremost in love, in their selection of a groom. They even had money; each of them on their eighteenth birthday received a bankbook with fifty forints in it.

Where did all this come from? I ask again. My grandfather received twenty forints per year in cash. As for his payment in kind, which consisted of corn, a vegetable plot and the right to keep animals, it was just sufficient to keep body and soul together, if that. Let me repeat that the whole family lived in one earth-floored room and shared the kitchen with the farm foreman's family. They were poor as church-mice, and by urban standards should have gone begging. When the men talked of an evening, my grandfather would sigh for the good old days of the free serf-world. Their situation now is by no means as bright as these words of mine couched in literary style paint it. Nor do they regard themselves as heroes in their struggle with Fate, for they cannot see any proof of it. They are simple, struggling folk, farm servants who to the eye of the stranger are no different from all the other servants. They share the same lot, and had I not written about them here, they would have been indistinguishable from the mass with which they are identified and from which they will never break free. I was brought up in their environment.

Yes, there is no doubt that they were somehow different from the other inhabitants of the puszta, but neither they nor the people of the puszta felt it. On no account did grandfather ever mention before strangers something of which he might boast— that his mother had been the daughter of a Calvinist minister whose large family had reduced him to poverty. My grandparents lived in close alliance with the rest of the poor puszta folk, an alliance that was silent, hence indissoluble. It was an alliance that nourished them also and made it possible for their children somehow to break away, at the cost of decades of privation and hard labour. They, the old folk, deliberately clung fast to this nether world, for they felt its upholding strength. It was indeed strong.

Typhus broke out in the family, and grandfather, grandmother and all their children took to their beds. Finally the doctor from the neighbouring village went out to see them. It was not the new doctor, who cured with powders, but the famous old one who prescribed wine, and the whole county loved him for it. The old man ordered wine for every disease Szekszárd for coughs, Homoki for stomach-ache, light Schiller for heart-disease and a mixture of wine and mineral-water for adolescent troubles—all by the bucket. I must add that all his patients recovered; at least the number of deaths amongst them was lower than among those who went to the other doctors. For typhus too he ordered Szekszárd, a heavy red wine, and a quart of it for each of them at a price which they could not possibly afford. Fortunately there were a few barrels of it in the estate cellars. That night, after the doctor had staggered off and the helpless family was convulsed more with cares than with fever, there was a knock on the window and the steward without saying a word took the water-pail out of the kitchen. And for three whole weeks—grandmother wept as she told the tale forty years later—every morning and every evening without fail he brought it back full of wine. They were cured by it too; only their hair fell out, but even that grew again later.

A plague began to wreak havoc among the pigs, but the vet was not called out. Their two sucking-pigs died of it too. They were just getting ready to bury them with much weeping and wailing, when the swineherd appeared and told them to take one of the corpses up to the estate sties. So they did, and cunningly exchanged it for a live one. The spirit of justice, however, refused to allow such machinations and cruelly struck down the changeling too. But the swineherd was not to be outdone and, changed this corpse also. So it went on through three or four similar disasters until justice gave in. There were still four hundred pigs in the estate herd.

48

All this, of course, meant compensation. Out of the estate wood, grandfather happily fashioned tables, chairs and soldiers' boxes for the labourers. For one of them he even carved a pipe-rack, for this was what he had set his heart on, and it had to be exactly like the one belonging to the parish priest at Pálfa, even though the recipient possessed only one Sunday-best clay pipe and normally preferred to chew his tobacco. Grandfather naturally worked for the bailiffs and managers too; he had to buy their indulgence. Yet even among them there were some 'good Hungarian folk', who showed their sympathy with the servants by beginning to thunder their disapproval a hundred yards away from where the work was going on, so that by the time they arrived there they might find everything as it should be. The servants saw through the mask and realised that there was a heart of gold behind the flashing eyes. When one of them, an old bachelor bailiff, died, they wanted to erect a marble gravestone to his memory. Later they had second thoughts and, after collecting money for eighteen months without getting enough for what they considered to be a worthy monument, they spent it all on a funeral feast and for two days ate and drank to his memory. Of course, not all officials were like that.

Even those who were inclined to be 'understanding' soon became quite helpless. Production began to shed its feudal form—or the patriarchal form which had been maintained here and there in the midst of feudalism—and take on the ideas of capitalism. On the feudal lands there began to appear steam ploughs and with them the modern, educated staff required by rational farming. They addressed the servants politely but treated them as coldly and ruthlessly as machines or factory-workers. The puszta became big business. The marshes were drained and the forests uprooted. But the roots of the soul were deeper and continued to resist.

CHAPTER FOUR

The encounter: two hostile families and two pusztas meet.
Religious belief on the puszta. The old folk

My parents would never have got married, I am sure, if there
had not been so many obstacles in their way. From the moment
they first saw each other, everything conspired to prevent a
further meeting, or so I have heard. From the very outset they
had to contend against their surroundings; instead of getting to
know each other, they had to gauge the thoughts and intentions
of stubborn parents, brothers and sisters-in-law in order somehow to outwit them. It was this prohibition that welded my
parents together. Both of them had grown head and shoulders
above the world of the old folk; they felt themselves to be new
creatures and wanted to act according to their own ideas.
Doubtless they also gained not a little pleasure from the battle
itself and from the permanent and vivid proof that they were indeed different. They were 'head over heels' in love, though they
had scarcely seen one another. Later I heard it rumoured in the
family that at this time my mother, who was sixteen, had attempted to commit suicide, while, my father had struck one of his
elder sisters. Though both of them talked freely about their
youth, there was never any mention of this period of their lives.
Like all parents, they were ashamed of the passion which had
brought their children into the world, and kept it secret from
them. Yet they did come together in the end; the circumstances
can be guessed from the fact that my father carried my mother
off to the end of the world, to Őzehalma puszta in Szolnok

county, an incredible distance away. They came back only after the birth of my elder brother, when the two families had patched up the quarrel a little. They came to settle in Rácegres almost opposite the house where my mother's parents lived surrounded by their children and an ever-increasing horde of grandchildren, for the other daughters had all married locally.

I am telling their story in detail because such alienation is rare among the people of the pusztas. They are all alike and if occasionally they rub each other up the wrong way, they quickly settle down in peace again, like so many grains of sand at the bottom of a stream. What was it that caused these two families, despite their mutual curiosity, to draw in their horns angrily when they first met? Both my mother's and my father's parents had the same aim in life: advancement. My grandfathers were so alike and so similarly fashioned that they might easily have taken each other's place in life. Later they did more or less become friends. So what was the dividing-wall which still stands almost intact between the two families, even in the third generation? If their mutual dislike ever flared into an open quarrel, it turned on the question of religious belief.

Religion on the puszta? Where even though a chapel was finally built—and it was a Jewish tenant who had it erected—it was remarkable if a service were held once a quarter. Religion among the people of the puszta, who at the very most offered sacrifices to superstition? It is true, my father's parents were fanatical Catholics and my mother's parents were numbered among those Calvinists who, in their vague belief that there must be some superior being or principle that keeps the world going, came near to atheism. And my father's brothers also brought into the family wives who crossed themselves merely for the sake of appearances and who did not hide their views about priests and church ceremonies, if they were mentioned in conversation. When she heard them, my father's mother would shake her head smiling, with her eyes closed, since she could not automatically set a seal on her ears.

51

And in our house in particular... When she visited us, she brought a rosary for each person in the house. A yard away from the door, she stopped, clasped her hands together and began to pray, peering with one eye at the door as if she were waiting for the moment when the devil slipped out. We all stood silently in front of her, like soldiers ordered to give evidence; we pretended to pray and patiently waited for the end of the scene which, we suspected, was put on just for our benefit. At last she would sigh, straighten up and offer her hand to be kissed, just as she may have seen it done at the manor-house; then with head held high she would sweep into the house in front of us. Next came the torture; we would follow her round dumbly, glancing at each other. Why did we feel this sense of guilt? In the kitchen and in our room there was much more order and taste than at her house in Nebánd—but even this made my mother feel ashamed. Grandmother gazed at the patterns on the earth floor and we blushed. She looked round the room and without saying a single word made us horrified to realise what was missing: there was not a single religious picture on the walls. (Apart from my mother's framed myrtle-garland, we could boast only portraits of King Matthias and Ferenc Rákóczi and a picture entitled 'Árpád Made Leader'.) After a single glance of hers, we felt that the lace curtains at the windows were a glaring proof of depravity. In general, whatever she looked at immediately became transformed by magic into a sign of sin. One feels the same during a house-search.

In her own way, however, she was very kind-hearted. From the heights to which she knew she had been raised by her wealth and her children's success, she looked down on us benevolently, but in the end we were all roused to wrath by her perpetual indulgence and everlasting forbearance. Probably she regarded us children too as living signs of guilt, the irreparable proofs of my mother's passion and my father's transgression. But by now she patiently put up with everything; she gave a

52

great sigh and let her glance rest on my mother's beautiful face. To the very last she remained a stranger to her.

Obviously grandmother regarded her as a temptress, as most selfish mothers regard their daughters-in-law. 'János might have done better for himself,' she sighed piously, managing to cram a quiverful of pointed allusions in this one sentence.

In his youth, my father may well have been very different from her other children. He was straightforward and contented, a helpless soul in their eyes. The desire to get on in the world which they instilled into him had not yet taken root. He had no desire whatsoever to get away from the puszta—a characteristic which broke out again in him at the end of his life—and they even had to drive him with a whip to school in the nearby village. It was not that he was afraid of study; he had a good brain, but he felt that beyond the line of poplars that marked the edge of the puszta anybody could have stripped him of his boots, as he put it. He wanted to follow in his father's footsteps as a shepherd. But by the time he had grown up, grandfather himself was kept on more as an ornament than as a working head shepherd; more land was being ploughed up, the sheep diminished in numbers and the old world was coming to an end. So for a long time he merely vegetated on the puszta. He was apprenticed to the blacksmith on the puszta, but this man hardly knew anything more about his job than the gipsies at the bottom of the village. Nor did he take his teaching seriously, and the pupil was allowed to wander abroad all day long, which he did, and went wherever his varied and increasing interests took him. The result was that he learnt all the trades it was possible to acquire there. He was as good a bee-keeper, wood-carver or gardener as he was a blacksmith. (Even later, when he had a permanent job, he always spent his free time on Sundays trying his hand at various different crafts; he made cupboards, wove nets, carved pipes out of wood and even tried his hand at veterinary surgery—he was quite simply a master at trepanning sheep's heads.) All this general knowledge and interest would have fitted him to be steward, or granary overseer and in time perhaps fore-man of the puszta. When first there was talk in the family of such plans, he left home with a quite surprising desire to work. In those days agricultural machinery was beginning to come into general use on the pusztas. He gazed at the machines and wandered round them longingly, but only certificated mechanics were allowed to touch them. He envied these mechanics and thought them the most distinguished folk in the world; most of them did not speak Hungarian, nor did they want to in their superiority. The examination could be taken only in Budapest. So after he had made his escape from the puszta, he went there and in a few weeks took the fireman's examination. Then he went on to learn about other machines. For a couple of years he served on various pusztas in Transdanubia, but he never stayed anywhere for more than a month or two. He kept circling round the old puszta and gradually approached it. During his travels he happened to arrive at Rácegres, where there was a vacancy for an assistant mechanic.

My mother's parents did not take to him, chiefly because he asked to marry my mother after he had known her for five weeks; the only dowry he sought was a bicycle, because he would himself make all the furniture they needed! He was happy and interested in everything, but could suddenly turn silent and melancholy, which earned him the reputation of being haughty and bumptious. He never sought contact with his own parents, but always boasted that he came from a distinguished family. 'The son of the head shepherd from Nebánd'—I could still feel years later the scorn my mother's relatives put into these words. He was a young man who wanted to please and impress. In Rácegres, however, these inclinations did not meet with approval. They were puritans, and to them frankness did not imply that one should pour out one's heart to its very depths, with all its light and shade, and even enjoy doing it.

My mother's mother walked over to Nebánd to warn the shepherd's family to take the boy away somewhere else, since he refused to give up his plans. Even if she had wanted to, she could not have offended them more deeply. Apart from the fact that this was the first they had heard of their son's intentions of marriage, to be told in addition that he was not wanted...! Who did not want him? A beggarly wheelwright and his family? An upstart, 'wood-whittling' farm servant? It was a Sunday, but they did not offer grandmother anything hot to eat.

True, my father was hasty not only in the choice of trade, but also in his opinions. After a little wrangling, he left Rácegres, but he had given his word. He returned to his parents. By then the family was flying high; the girls had all married and gone to villages, while the boys without exception wore boots. My father was the black sheep of the family, of whom nothing out of the ordinary could be said. Even though they treated him gently, they certainly looked down on him somewhat. He too noticed it from time to time, and protested angrily that he was being ordered about. Everybody wanted to give him good advice, even his younger sisters, one of whom already had fillings in her teeth which gave her boundless self-respect and a superior tone. They overstepped the mark when they wanted to marry him off and found a suitable, stylish shepherd's daughter for him. (I knew her too. When I was nine or ten years old, one day in the market my paternal grandmother suddenly tugged at my shoulder as we met a well-built woman. 'Shake hands with Aunt Zsófi—she was nearly your mother.' Dumbfounded, I looked up at her towering figure and she snatched me into her arms and covered me with kisses, asking me question after question, as if she had been a real relation. During the short time we were together, I became truly attracted to her.)

While this was happening to my father, they tried to find a husband for my mother too. There was no lack of suitors, for the girls were all highly esteemed. This was the time when my mother attempted to commit suicide, or so it was said. My father appeared on the puszta and behaved with such politeness and humility that my mother's parents, who on principle were unwilling to interfere in their daughter's affairs, shook him by the hand in recognition that he was now her acknowledged fiancé.

A month or two later a stranger spoke to my mother one evening as she was drawing water from the well, and asked her if she were the girl concerned. They talked for a little while. It was my grandfather, my father's father, the shepherd. But however much my mother invited him in, he would not enter the house of his future relations by marriage. 'See here, my girl, I've brought ten forints with me. I thought if I liked the look of you I'd give it to you straight away to seal the engagement,' he said and pressed into her hand a twenty-crown gold piece. My mother accepted the money and burst into tears, for she had suddenly come to love the stranger during this biblical scene. They fell silent. 'I'll give you the other one too,' my grandfather said at length, 'for to tell you the truth I brought twenty forints with me. But don't say a word about this to anybody.' My mother never spent the money; she sacrificed it to the national cause in 1915 at the time of the 'gold for iron' campaign.

My mother was beautiful. She had the fresh beauty of a young girl, with a slightly Mongol face but a clear, fine skin; all her life she had an innocent, childlike air. When we were children, and she took us to a strange place, everybody regarded her as our sister. We were accustomed to this and were ready for the subsequent misunderstandings, from which we got endless amusement. On these occasions she too became a child and entered into the spirit of it with us. She is no longer alive. Sometimes when I am looking at illustrated papers, my heart misses a beat at the sight of a 'Sárköz bride' or 'Women outside the church'. It is her glance that looks at me, her smile that lingers on the unknown face, as if parts of her being were living on independently. Often the whole face is mysteriously

56

hers, as if she had gone not to the grave, but to the Hungarian region in the south of Tolna, a place where, to the best of my knowledge, she had no relations at all.

Undoubtedly my father, who was inclined to be boastful—he would make much of the tiniest thing that pleased him and proclaim its virtues far and wide, in the belief that his delight would thus infect the whole world—led his wife into his parents' family with head held high. He might not have done much to improve its lot, but which of the sons had got himself such a bride, with her outstanding beauty, refined spirit and cleverness? This, he may well have felt, made up for everything. At Nebánd, the sturdy sisters-in-law and sheep-dogs of brothers-in-law sniffed suspiciously at the young, fragile bride while all the time they outdid each other in friendliness. My mother's fate was sealed.

All this I know from vague hearsay. When I began to take notice and think for myself, the silent battle between the two families was already in progress, and I took it to be as eternal and natural as the division of the day into two parts and twenty-four hours; that by day it was light and by night dark. The two families could not understand each other; they were made of different stuff—this I accepted and it did not occur to me to seek the cause for it or to put a stop to it. Each family was a separate country, with its own customs and utterly different races; I could even define their geographical boundaries exactly. Simontornya and Igar, for example, where my father had relations, belonged to Nebánd; north and east of this began the territory where my mother's family held sway. Naturally even the sky above them was different. Over one it was full of martyrs and saints, angels peeped from behind the clouds and in the moon at night Cecilia played the violin; the other sky was more sober, with only sunlight or rain to fall on the crops. We were in between.

The two opposing poles spread their own opinions, intentions and gossip quite separately. This caused no trouble as long as they kept each to their own circuit. But where the two met and the live wires crossed, showers of sparks flew, crackling and spluttering. In the end, wherever else there were contacts, no harm was done, but in our little family circle the fuses blew. Over us the air was always heavy and full of the tension of approaching storms and the stench of discharged lightning. Whether we liked it or not, we became used to it.

As I have said, the prime cause of trouble was the salvation of our souls, and particularly the children's. We were all baptised Catholics, and a lot that meant. 'Say the *Ave Maria*,' said grandmother to me one day when the family was all together and before I could get a word out she glanced meaningfully at her son. Indeed, I knew nothing about it at all. My mother blushed and in her helplessness put on an awkward, apologetic smile. She did not know the Catholic prayers either, and though she had received from her mother-in-law a beautiful prayer-book with an ivory cover, there were so many prayers in it that even if she picked a couple at random and learnt them, making us study them at the same time, she never found the right ones. My father knew these prayers well and even if he did not say them, he expected his children to know them too. He felt them to be part of proper conduct. His religious feelings, if he ever thought about them, may well have rested on the view that 'there's no knowing'. But apart from whether he himself believed in God or not, he felt it his paternal duty to teach his children religion, as did every father at the time. And first and foremost on utilitarian grounds. For if folk are not afraid of anything, they will steal and rob, and what will then become of the world? In those days even the priests argued on these administrative grounds for the existence of God. The family council—in other words, grandmother— arranged for us children to spend some time at Nebánd or Ozora, the village where my father's relatives had begun to settle as they left the puszta. There was a proper elementary school there too, not one of the puszta sort. At first my mother gladly welcomed this plan, like everything else that broadened her children's knowledge. But later she had every reason to protest against it in her own way.

At Nebánd we were subjected to a mild form of exorcism. Then we were initiated into the faith—not the Catholic faith, as I myself thought at the time, but that of the puszta, which differed somewhat from it. I showed myself highly receptive. A delightful fairyland opened up before me. At home with my parents we were never told fairy-tales, because my maternal grandmother thought they were only useful for frightening children. And whenever, in accordance with her other main principle, we were engaged in some useful occupation like shelling beans or making rag-carpets, where we could talk to each other, she would tell us about her life as a servant-girl for our instruction. Later, when she grew older, she would often tell us about how she came to know grandfather. Now at Nebánd, a half-naked figure of Christ welcomed us in the kitchen; He was in a heavy gilded frame, floating in the air above His grave without any visible means of support, and with a huge wound in His chest. He was flying to heaven, to His Father, who was an immense eye in the middle of a coloured triangle. Thirstily I followed Him into the intoxicating world of miracles. My acquaintance with holy men and women led on to devils, dragons and witches. At night ghosts sat outside the door. In the cattle-well at Rácegres only frogs had their lodging, but at Nebánd a water-sprite would keep poking his head out of it, especially if I thought about him before I set out there. I interpreted the statement that God sees everything and is everywhere as 'everything and everywhere at Nebánd' for a long time. It was a magic world. At Nebánd by night wizards roamed, the cows predicted wars by giving gory milk, the liveried coachman, after limbering-up with enormous swings of his arms, hurled the hatchet to the heavens

59

from the middle of the sheepyard and thus averted the hailstorm. Between a couple of curses the women would mention the dear Jesus and their faces would light up as if they had stepped out of a cellar into the sunlight.

There was no church on the puszta and only one or two old maids went into Ozora to mass; even then they went very rarely, when it was fine. But this did not lessen the air of piety at all.

Almost every day when it grew dark three or four elderly women would squat in the kitchen with my grandmother. Was it really their thirst for faith that drew them there, or were they trying to find favour with the head shepherd's wife, to whom they had to go so often to borrow a little flour or salt? Or was it to sip not only the little glass of brandy with which my grandmother regaled them, but also the sweet savour of gossip, so delightful at all times and places? There they crouched on tiny footstools round the stove, whose light grew stronger as the twilight deepened, and lisped or sang endless litanies while they husked maize; grandmother got them to do this not only so that they should be usefully employed, but so that their hands might have some exercise—for if they had nothing to occupy them, these old hands, accustomed to endless work, soon grew stiff. This was the school in which I had to drink in the Word. The old women knew this too; it is probable that they knew every detail of my parents' marriage and had also been informed why I was there amongst them. My soul was on its way to perdition and at grandmother's request they gladly undertook to rescue it. Who does not love to teach? They vied with each other as they poured into my soul all that they had amassed in fifty or sixty years of religion, miracles, the hereafter and supernatural powers. They took me with them during the day too. One of them, called Aunt Mári, took me particularly under her wing.

Their instruction, of course, soon ran on to dangerous ground. The words of the Virgin Mary as recorded in the Bible became muddled in my mind with those that she address-

60

ed to the wife of the herdsman at Kula when she appeared to her on the top of a tree in the forest at Tamási. The words of the confession ran into those of the spell for blisters. And did not Aunt Mári call on Saint Joseph when she threw three bits of glowing wood into the pot of water? If they sank to the bottom, they really cast the evil eye on the grandchild, the cow or even the mulberry tree in front of their house; if they did not sink, they had no effect. (They always sank.) Did she not call on him when she dropped lead into water and from the shape of it recognised unmistakably the person who had frightened the epileptic baby? Even grandmother would set a hen only at noon when the distant church-bells were ringing, or when the swine-herd was driving out the pigs, and if possible she would take the eggs out of a man's old hat. On Fridays, for which she had a special epithet whose meaning I have never been able to discover, she would never do this anyway, because the chickens would all have been born with twisted legs. We awaited Whitsuntide not only with the Christian devotion appropriate to the great festivals, but with a bottle of rainwater caught on Trinity Sunday as well; to wash in it is a sure aid to beauty, particularly if one drinks red wine afterwards.

Even at home we always used to trick the new cat with a mirror, so that it should believe that it was not alone in the house and try to find the other cat that it saw there, but what was this compared with the things they knew at Nebánd? A girl brought a wild pigeon to Aunt Mári, who took out its heart, dried it, and ground it to powder; with it one could tame a boy. She took the tape from a pair of pants and various bits of hair and dug them into the heaviest soil she could find in the river bank, so that the boy to whom they belonged should feel just such a weight of love for her protégée. What else is there to say? Aunt Mári's married sister took the footprint of one of her enemies out of the mud and wrapped it up in rags, then hung it in the chimney, because so long as it hung there the enemy would be tortured by stomach-pains. I think it is still there today. I was made to sprinkle holy water round the bed of a woman in childbirth, because this operation required the services of a male who had had no intercourse with the opposite sex. They knew everything at Nebánd. Do you want to rid yourself of a lover of whom you have grown weary? Put three pins in the place where he goes to relieve himself. The best cure for warts is the undertaker's rope. I left the puszta with an ever-growing fund of knowledge. When I was eight, I was informed that I should marry the daughter of a man in soldier's uniform and that I should have three children.

I prayed a great deal and returned to Rácegres like St George all ready for the fray. I was determined to sacrifice myself; I had a hazy idea of converting my mother's family which, according to the folk at Nebánd, was irretrievably on the road to hell. Did they receive me with an air of superiority? They did not receive me at all.

Grandfather stretched out his hand for me to take (he thought kissing was effeminate and kissing hands uppish) and looked at me gently. 'Well, what's that round your neck, lad?' he asked with the glimmer of a smile. There was no irony in his words, nor surprise, nor even interest, but they went straight to my heart. I slipped away and without a word took off the ribbon with the medallion of the Virgin Mary on it; I had demanded this in my overenthusiasm at Nebánd, as a talisman against the flames of Gehenna, but even there it was only suitable for girls to wear.

I was surprised and confused by the equanimity with which they faced certain perdition. I had supper with them and was seized by a sudden excitement; I wanted to shout aloud in desperation, as one shouts to somebody walking on the edge of a precipice: 'Grandad, you'll go straight to hell!' But I kept silent and my tongue remained numb, as in a dream. This eerie boldness of my grandparents was also dreamlike. At this time my mother was cooking food appropriate for fasts, as far as she could tell from the complicated ecclesiastical prescriptions;

doubtless she was afraid of the folk at Nebánd and did not wish to burden her soul with the fate of her husband after death. At all events we refrained with stern determination from eating meat on Tuesdays and Fridays, not that this was any great hardship, since we never ate meat on other days either, with the possible exception of Sundays. We only had to keep ourselves from eating the scraps left after a pig had been killed. But two houses further along my grandfather would calmly slice the piece of bacon he was holding between his fingers. Brushing his moustache aside, he swallowed the gleaming white pieces of meat, the very embodiment of mortal sin. I looked in horror on this tempting of providence and tensely waited for him to go up in sulphurous flames or at least to be choked by the bacon as a kind of deterrent miracle, of which I had heard a lot, even from the lips of priests. I was worried about him and anxious for his fate, because I loved him more than all the folk at Nebánd put together. 'You'll grow out of it,' he said, when at the end of a theological argument I was driven to confess that I was a Catholic and said so somewhat provocatively. I told him all the awful things they laid at the door of heretics like him. He listened with interest, but as far as I can remember, did not make any direct retort. 'They're peasants,' he said and deep within me I felt him to be right, though they owned ten times as much as he did, and could count craftsmen and even a county official among their ranks at the time.

But the other reformers in the family were on the warpath. By the time the subtle theological arguments of old had reached their level, they had become coarse, as in the time of the itinerant preachers. The dispute about the immaculate conception had degenerated into obscenity and their dissent had even turned them away from Mary; they spoke of her with scorn and disrespect, for she belonged to the Catholics. For a time I kept silent, then unobtrusively I went over to their side. When I next visited Nebánd I arrived a pagan once more, or rather worse than a pagan, an apostate. What an amount of whispering, coaxing, threatening and angry outbursts was needed to wash me clean and to swing my spiritual balance in their direction once again! Like the pointer on a pair of scales, I swung between the two pusztas as my visits grew ever more frequent. I had a foot in two camps and only realised it when it was too late to change. I was articled, so to speak, to both of them. In the tension between them my sympathies, my behaviour and even my general attitude were all torn in two. Even today I often feel the wound. They taught me that of two opposing sides both might be right; they taught me to discover and take into consideration all truths, which is the most perfect labyrinth. Unwittingly they taught me real Christianity: that we can love our enemies. Before a battle I always have to fight against myself.

The folk at Nebánd lived only for their faith and for the future. On the left and right, these two blinkers kept them from straying or becoming needlessly restive, and from the sudden and dangerous leap from being beasts of burden to true humanity. My mother's family, as it went up in the world, began to acquire information not only of the future but of the past too. They got to know things which had no direct bearing upon them and without which they could have managed quite happily. The spirit of the family, like a cell exposed to light, took on shape, developed and began to feel around. They knew about their Hungarian homeland, about politics and almost had a political viewpoint. Fortunately if some more weighty idea about public affairs dropped in their midst like a meteor from the skies, it was always fifty or sixty years late in arriving, and immediately became petrified and idolised. They mourned the martyrs of Arad,* for example, and had an undying hatred for

* The generals of the Hungarian revolutionary army, executed at Arad on October 6th, 1849.

64

the Hapsburgs. In Nebánd they had no idea that there was a homeland outside the puszta, or rather that even in the air above the puszta the vibration of the homeland could be sensed.

Which branch was right? At the time when I was getting to know in due order what my name was, whose son I was and that my folk were farm servants, at long last I understood that I was also Hungarian. It was my mother's family which, in its own way, of course, informed me of this special, additional and comforting fact. The kind of homeland in which they might have participated unfortunately signified merely a tradition, a past in whose brilliance and honour practically everybody might share alike. They knew something of the past. My mother's father had been four years old in 1848 and remembered the Cossacks galloping through his native village to stamp out freedom. Grandfather deplored this. In his imagination, the stamping out of freedom was the great 'if', the obscure turning-point and blind twist of fate without which everything would have been different in the world, perhaps even including the poor man's lot. My father's father was seventeen in 1848. I had already heard about the child-heroes of the revolution, and excitedly waited for my next visit to Nebánd to demand an account of how he spent those stirring times.

He had spent that time in the forest at Tamási. 'They were grabbing soldiers in those days, Hungarians and Germans alike,' he said haltingly, when at last he had run to earth in his memory the years I wanted to hear about, 'so we went off into the forest. We made bread too, because we took flour with us.'

He had spent the whole of the revolution and the confused period that followed it in the woods, in very pleasant company; even sixty years afterwards he still smiled at one or two amusing incidents. They had made little huts and hunted wild boar with matchets; nobody cooked better stews than grandfather. They had their own patrol and various ways of signalling danger. At night they would creep back to the pusztas. Once they had even outwitted a band of gendarmes. My eyes began to sparkle; had they been outlaws?

They were not outlaws. True, it was such folk as these who became outlaws as a result of unfortunate mishaps, and had they struck such bad luck, they might have been in this category. They were peaceful shepherds, who also undertook the pasturing of swine. Were they scared of being soldiers? No. Grandfather simply did not want to go to 'foreign parts'. If they had arranged to fight at the end of the puszta, he would gladly have taken his part in it. He had almost offered his aid to Görgey, but unfortunately he had arrived too late and turned back. He spent two winters in the forest, but which they were he could not remember, because he had not the slightest idea when the revolution broke out, nor indeed that it had broken out at all. All he knew of the Croats was that they might be chased. He went into the woods at Dombóvár, and since even two years later it was still not safe on the puszta for young men of military age like him, he came out at the other end, at Ozora, where his mother came from. 'For in those days all the lands were the same to shepherds,' and they would go six counties away to look for a wife, not like the farm servants or the 'peasants bogged down in the mud'. It was then that he turned up at Nebánd. 'I was just as much of a shepherd lad there as I had been at Nosztány or Gyulaj'—where he never returned, not even for a visit. Instead, his parents came to him when they had grown too old for further service. 'And nine brothers and sisters of mine stayed on there.' (Later, when I was in that district, I looked for them. Not one had remained there.)

He related this story quite unconcernedly. It never occurred to him that half of his fugitive existence, when Kossuth was seeking recruits, had been cowardly and the other half, when the Austrians were enlisting soldiers, heroic. The recruiting authorities of both opposing armies followed almost on each other's heels in the villages, and one might be a hero one week and a coward the next. Grandfather merely sat there in the

66

forest, not bothering to weigh it all up; he regarded it all as something to do with the gentry, and had already given up trying to make sense out of such matters.

He was well-balanced, a model of the so-called cool-headed Hungarian type. He expressed his thoughts with such terrifying objectivity that they seemed to become real objects that could be touched, like a soup-plate or a shepherd's pipe. One could not contest them, but only observe them. He would gladly talk by the hour, but the words of the person he happened to be talking to did not have the slightest effect on him. He would not accept ideas, but only experiences. He had no flashes of inspiration or invention, only experiences. He did not agree with anything my mother's father did, but he would talk for hours with him after he had committed the great act of 'betrayal', the real one, which made the family rise up in anger. This happened when he suddenly came to love my mother. I was old enough to recall the occasion when, surrounded by his many daughters and daughters-in-law at Nebánd in some family gathering, he unexpectedly declared in a quiet voice that my mother was worth more than all of them put together. They gazed at him in horror. It had taken grandfather ten years, ten years of observation and examination, to make up his mind. He did not mind the half-day he spent in coming to us, that very evening he trotted over to our house and from then onwards turned up every week.

'What on earth has come over the shepherd?' mumbled my mother's father when his relative by marriage was making his way home after that first visit, enveloped in a cloud of dust as he spurred the one-eyed grey donkey to a trot at least as far as we could see. He looked for some intrigue in every step the folk at Nebánd took. All the same, when grandfather next appeared, he wandered across to our house to see whether he was slipping something into his pocket. Thus they became friends. Not long afterwards the old man from Nebánd visited his daughter-in-law's parents and set foot in their house. But usually they withdrew to the little garden where much of the space was already taken up by the beehives which later proved a certain source of income to grandfather when he had grown too old for service. The guest pulled off his big boots and was given slippers. They chatted. Sometimes a bee would fly buzzing between them and without exception circle round the nervously flapping guest as if it scented the stranger in him. The host would smile deprecatingly; he was never stung by the bees. He felt superior on every count.

What did they talk about? The shepherd gave a long and endlessly complicated lecture on, for example, the difficulty of stamping out wireworm in sheep. My mother's father would describe at equal length how the peasants of Gyulavári lived in his youth. As a rule each of them described things of which the other could not see any use whatsoever. They would listen attentively to each other and even ask questions about details that were not clear to them. Sometimes they would accidentally bring out expressions to each other's detriment: for example the guest said once of somebody's character, 'He was an honest man, even if he was a Calvinist.' And the Calvinist host nodded and the conversation would go on without any awkwardness.

Yet religion was the one topic where they were liable to clash head-on. Even here, however, they never came to an open rift. Frequently they had some hard things to say, but they always did so calmly and impersonally, like truce-bearers of two opposing camps who merely say what their party expects to be said and lose their own views in those of the mass. My father's father, for example, instinctively regarded Hungary as the property of the Catholics, into which the Calvinists had somehow pushed their way later. My mother's father raised his eyebrows: 'What?' And he came out with the Calvinist line which, as we know, proclaims precisely the opposite with almost equal claims. 'What about Kossuth? And Petőfi and János Arany, and Csokonai, Berzsenyi, Kölcsey, Tompa, Jókai, Kálmán Tisza, Dezső Szilágyi, Miklós Bartha and ...'* The constant stream of names fell from grandfather's lips like hammer-blows; most of them he had noted from some ecclesiastical calendar for just such an argument. Were not these folk Hungarians? Everybody worth his salt in Hungary was a Protestant! Nebánd listened, defeated and silent. He knew nothing at all about the list of notables, but suspected something fishy behind it all... He sipped the questionable brandy which his host himself had concocted out of cloves, horse-radish and fermented honey according to the recipe in the *Beekeepers' Gazette*, and whose peculiar flavour made him feel even more uneasy. He tried to find another more realistic theme.

'When I got to Tóti...' he began, dragging up at random a thread from the tangled skein of his memory, and the day was saved; for the next couple of hours the floor was once more his.

They accepted me as an audience for their conversation. My glance flitted like a restless bird from one old face to the other; their features had been similarly carved by a common lot. I waited for them to clash and, like militant angels of the faith, fight out the battle of the soul in my stead. But I was not brave enough to interrupt their talk and inspire them to a clearer defence of their viewpoint. I had the confused feeling that there was something greater, and this was the difference in religion which bound them together through heaven and hell. Once the conversation turned to religious processions. 'They're for the womenfolk,' said my mother's father scornfully, and his relative by marriage, the traitor, nodded in agreement. They were men.

Like old folk in general, they would bring the distant past to new life. I lounged there with them and became so full of their talk that these tales, always far brighter and truer than reality, became more rooted in me than the actual events of my childhood. For instance, there was the exceptional year when they

* All well-known poets except for Kossuth and the last three, who were politicians.

were building the embankment for the Budapest–Fiume railway across the pusztas; I know so many tales and adventures of this period that for a long time I believed it had all happened in my own age. The period when my parents were young and the nineties remain indistinct to me, but I know my way around before the *Ausgleich* of 1867. I should not lose myself in Kaposvár as it was in the sixties when grandfather from Nebánd once drove twenty-four sheep there to be slaughtered, and spent the journey-money on a week's spree with some swine-herds from Ukk... That's why I sometimes feel three times older than I really am.

CHAPTER FIVE

*The past of the puszta folk. Peasants, landless serfs, and farm
servants in history. Their descendants on the past*

The past, of course, was always better than the present. At
first I listened with enthusiasm to the old folk as they talked,
then with the customary superiority of youth, I doubted them.
Later, however, I thought they were right: the past they talked
about was indeed better.

How many shirts has a hired farm-lad today? When grandfather from Nebánd got married he had in his chest six
ordinary pairs of wide trousers, six pairs with fringed edges
and six round-necked shirts. In addition he had two pairs of
top-boots, a real silver cane and a sheepskin cloak which would
still be good today, had it not been struck by a chance flash
of lightning and burnt up together with the wooden arm
of the well where it had been left. What do the people of
the puszta eat nowadays? In grandfather's time the farm
servants' wives took lunch out to their menfolk in wooden
bowls so enormous that they could hardly keep their heads
upright under their weight. Around eleven o'clock a long
caravan of women would leave the farm servants' dwellings.
The sheep-dogs would raise their heads a good mile away as
they sniffed the paprika stew whose scent floated like a glimmering ribbon through the thousand smells of the fields. For
in those days there was everything. There was even fish.
'There were no poor folk then.' The beggars rode in carts.

The only thing lacking was lamp-oil, for that cost money—and there was no money in those days either.

Truth to tell, however, there was no real need of money. Grandfather was satisfied. 'That's what the world of serfdom was like,' he mused—an age which by his reckoning lasted up to the eighties and whose passing he mourned with sad shakes of the head. This disturbed me. Was grandfather not glad that serfdom had disappeared? 'Ah, those were the good old days,' he sighed and recalled summers and autumns full of merriment, while I was astounded to calculate that these had occurred during the sad years of national oppression. 'Well, grandfather, weren't you emancipated?' I asked. He looked at me in astonishment. He knew nothing about the struggle for the freedom of the press, nor had he ever really thought about the ending of villein services, tithes and feudal dues.

The name of Kossuth caused grandfather's heart to stir as little as that of anyone else on the pusztas. Kossuth, 1848, liberty—all these were regarded as the concern of the village-folk, just like parliamentary elections, when carts going from one parish to another sometimes rattled through the puszta, with loud songs, much flourishing of national flags and wine-bottles. True, Kossuth forgot them too. In general everybody forgot them in every age until it had become a custom. Not only the statesmen of all times, but the scholars too passed them over. Thus there are even fewer 'genuine' details of their past than of their present. What were their origins? I could no longer be satisfied with the words of the old folk, who as a rule could only say of their grandparents, 'He was a very poor old man, God rest his bones,' but usually could not say where the poor old man had been buried.

'The serfs were liberated'; for a long time I pictured this in the same way as I did the Hungarian nation. It had happened somewhere afar off, in some happy land, and certainly not where I was living. The serfs had got their land, had become their own masters, and were free citizens of Hungary... How was it then that as far as my eye and imagination could see, the lands in all directions around me belonged to unknown potentates whose power was kept more secret than that of the medieval war-lords? At very rare intervals their emissaries visited the manor-house in a coach-and-four. The common people, stiff with fright, bowed to them and whipped off their hats; they looked neither independent nor free... Why had these folk not been emancipated? Feverishly I began to look for the mistake, and after much trouble I came upon it. What I found, I discovered largely by my own instinct; there were scarcely any guides or sources to follow. The people of the pusztas and the mass of landless serfs who are of the same stock spring up in Hungarian history like the disappearing streams in the Karst, and cause considerable surprise—nor is it a pleasant one. Has anybody written their history, the history of those who cultivate half the land in Hungary? I am not aware of anyone who has. For years I plodded through excellent books, but only rarely did I come across some dim traces of them in a passing reference or two. I questioned expert economists and sociologists, but it became clear that they knew scarcely as much about these people as I did, whether in the past or in the present. My memory at least retained one or two odd details. I should not be surprised if this present book were the first to attempt a general picture of them—I say this to excuse the deficiencies of this initial effort.

Even the best-equipped investigators of the past of Hungary see scarcely any more differences between peasant and peasant than does the town child who observes and knows the people through the windows of the train. Up to the selfless, glorious liberation of 1848 there were nobles and peasants...—this is more or less the view taken even by the well educated. Yet it is certain that during the reign of Matthias Corvinus* a

* 1458–1490.

landed peasant looked down on the 'landless puszta serf' and despised him at least as much as he himself was despised by his landlord, if not more. At times perhaps the landed and landless peasants were united, as for example when a peasant revolt was forcibly suppressed, in common misery; this unity, however, resembled the fusion of various races overwhelmed by common trouble after their country has lost a war. Otherwise the distinction between them is as great as that normally found between those who possess land and money and those who do not.

The farm servants were in the same condition under our distant ancestors. The form of servitude, of course, varied considerably, but usually changed for the worse. In general our forebears who conquered Hungary were free as long as the land was free, that is, until someone happened to occupy it with every intention of staying there. The tribes who settled in the country did not occupy the whole area, if only because they were too few in numbers to do so. They left wide strips of free land between them, partly to act as frontiers and to guard against quarrels, and partly—very wisely—as reserve land, for they expected to increase. It was these lands, representing about half the area of the country, that Stephen* suddenly declared to be royal lands, in other words his own. This was the first real seizure of land and it occurred because the tribes were still farming their own lands in common, with their shepherds, Asian artisans and a few agricultural slaves. If only they had suspected that in this way the free zones would immediately be turned into clamps of iron! Some of them had their suspicions. It is probable that Koppány** and his followers wished to defend not only the old pagan religion but their ancestral freedom too when they drew the sword in the yery area where the events of this book took place. They were

* First king of Hungary (1001–1038).
** Pagan war-lord who fought against Stephen for supremacy.

74

defeated and in accordance with the practice of the time, those who remained alive were branded as slaves. It is known that the lands which were still free then were declared to be the property of one or two knights. So are the servants here the offspring of the one-time wild pagans? I try to find in myself the pale shadow of the passion with which our forefathers (whose memory is still accursed in our school histories) flung themselves upon the armed missionaries of German Christianity. Perhaps there is some dim trace there.

This process went on in other parts of the country too, but without armed conflict. Out of the royal lands came ecclesiastical and baronial estates, and the same happened very soon to the common tribal lands. And what happened to the folk who had first occupied them? Kálmán* attempted by decree to resettle the peasants who had been banished from their land —not very successfully, as can be seen from the situation today. Even those who were able to hold on to their family dwellings, whether large or small, came under the power of the great lords and church dignitaries. Two centuries later in Hungary 120 great lords rule over 520 villages, and this excludes the extensive possessions of the Church. Now since there were certainly more than 120 who took part in the original occupation of Hungary, a great proportion of the descendants of those early heroes were already on the downward path to serfdom, with its unlimited varieties of servitude. By the thirteenth century farm and domestic servants had already taken the place of the weekly servants in the houses of the nobility. These are the first visible ancestors of the people of the pusztas. The rest were landed serfs in the more distant parts of the vast estates, on land that they had either received or retained in return for various services. A great part of them, like actors waiting to take part in a crowd scene, had already been allotted the role of serfs.

* Coloman Beauclerc, king of Hungary (1095–1116).

Although there was land in plenty, in the fourteenth century there already appeared beside the landed serfs the *inquilinii*, who had no land and no house of their own; in Hungarian they are said even today to 'live on other folks' backs'. A considerable proportion of the fields round the villages inhabited by landed serfs became manorial land or *praedium*— a telling expression.

But we find the landless serfs and servants in the villages also, where they lived like slaves alongside the landed peasants. 'The feudal dues were most burdensome in the slave-villages,' writes Acsády*; the lengthy deed of the Abbey of Dömös in 1138 reflects this in all its severity. According to Knauz, this abbey, founded by the unfortunate Prince Álmos, younger brother of King Kálmán, owned at that time not fewer than 57 villages, some of which were quite well-populated. Thus there were 70 houses in Cuppan, 66 in Scer, 62 in Geu, 53 in Lingu and 35 in Tamach. Even then several families were to be found in each house—in Simur, for example, the deed mentions 7 houses but 21 heads of families. Judging by their names, all the serfs were Hungarians, who according to the deed answered to the following: Sleepy, Liar, Rubbish, Remnant, Bull, Scurfy, Wolf, Black, Friday, Saturday, Clever, Jew, Ass, Cock, Whitsun and so on. These names, if nothing else (for they were certainly never chosen by their owners), show that the ancestors of the landless serfs and servants were under continual supervision, goading, cursing and threats at a time when the monasteries were engaged in a great cultural drive. They had to supply the fathers with fat pigs, oxen, sheep, geese, hens and rock-salt and last but not least with mead; the village of Geu, for example, and the neighbouring parishes each had to send an average of 25 butts every year, which amounts altogether to no mean quantity. In Lent they gave them 30 fat fish or, if they

* Author of a history of the landed serfs in Hungary (1906), from which this passage is quoted. See also footnote on page 79.

were unsuccessful with their nets, money instead. The deed declared that no slave could be made free or *vice versa*. From the many writs and complaints still surviving, it is clear that nowhere were the slaves and landed serfs so exploited as on these monastery lands. The method, taken over from the more advanced West, was quick to take effect. In the twelfth and thirteenth centuries the cries of woe are solely against the monasteries, but later with the decline of the Middle Ages, almost perfect similarity can be observed among the shouts of misery aimed in various directions. Often these complaints did not go unheeded, particularly at the beginning. One or two kings of the Árpád dynasty did their best to improve upon the powerful achievement of Stephen. As their strength declined, so too the lot of the landed peasants and domestic servants and labourers deteriorated. It is well known that possession of land gave the right to control the affairs of the country; therefore in those days of old the history of Hungary is the history of the great landlords or great estates and the squabbles among the chief nobility. We know virtually nothing of what a landed serf or slave ate and did, say, in the reign of St Ladislas.* Bishop Otto of Freisingen, who died in 1158, discovered the people of the Great Plain living in tents even in the middle of the twelfth century. Our historians generally content themselves with the explanation that these peasants and slaves were foreigners, thus gently implying that we need shed no tears over them. The conquering lords, on the other hand, acquired the right to own land and to rule with their blood at the Battle of Alpár.** As we have just seen, the opposite of all this is the truth. As their ingenious names show, the slaves were Hungarians. Not even the leaders of the Hungarians took land into their private possession; they did not recognise its value, since

* 1077–1095.
** Traditional scene of a fierce conflict between Árpád's forces and a Slav army during the occupation of Hungary.

only animals were regarded as assets. Péter Ágoston,* who certainly cannot be accused of national prejudice, also shows clearly and defends the view that the first private landowners and their successors too were almost without exception foreigners, chiefly Germans, who from their experience of the more advanced agriculture of the West already knew the value of land and how to acquire it. It was they who established the big domains and reduced the former freemen to the status of serfs, doubtless appealing even in those days to historical progress and the special situation of Hungary for their authority. There was a time when labour services in Austria were 12 days per year; in Hungary at the same time they were three days per week.

At the end of the fourteenth century serfdom was virtually abolished in England. Economic necessity demanded new methods of production throughout the world. Not long after this feudalism began to deteriorate in Hungary, defying as it did so historical progress and the interests of both the country and the people. The agricultural labourers, who hitherto had been strong and quite successful, even bold, in their own way, became enshrouded in such a black night of oppression that it became impossible to distinguish between farm servant, landed peasant and even impoverished noble. For centuries there was only a gleam or two of light, or else a great conflagration. The peculiar Hungarian globe began to revolve; in this respect, incidentally, Hungary differs only from developments in the West; exactly the same was happening in Poland and southern Russia, for example.

Máté Csák,** it will be recalled, to realise his dream of kingship, introduced on his estates feudal customs which were already known in the West and among the Czechs. This was a po-

* 1874–1925; author of a book on secular large estates in Hungary.
** c.1260–1321; he set himself up as virtual ruler of a vast area of northern Hungary, chiefly by seizing land.

litical gambit and may well have increased his popularity and the enthusiasm of his army. The rebel voivode Ladislas* in Transylvania restored the customs of the East, which were simpler and more humane. In the first place they were not defeated by force of arms, but by a cunning and temporary borrowing of their measures. Thus the peasants were still able to defend themselves with weighty arguments. How did it come about that a great number of the Hungarian lesser nobility began to be caught up in the ever more frequent peasant revolts? And the parish priests too? Who were these folk? History has steeped them in curses and ignominy.

There was land in plenty, but not of course for the agricultural labourers. 'Article 2 of the legal code of 1411 mentions small and large *portae*.** The large *porta* means a whole serf plot—for tax purposes a whole *porta;* the small *porta* was only a part of the serf plot, because all parts of the country were settled fully in accordance with the conditions of the time and there was no more land which could be cleared extensively; thus the whole serf plots began to be broken up into halves, quarters and eighths. Moreover at this time the landless serf, who had no agricultural land but at most a vineyard or just a house and dragged out an existence by performing certain services by the side of the landed serfs, began to come more and more into prominence... this type formed the lowest stratum of society in the countryside.' So writes Acsády of the ancestors of the farm servants.*** Unfortunately he only mentions them in passing and does not deal with them at length.

The landless serfs, then, had no land, and the farm servants even less. They lived on the pusztas and their voice was rarely heard. The employees on the large estates of Váralja and Solymos amongst other requests plead that in the depths of winter

* Died 1315: his career was similar to that of Csák.
** The basis of taxation. A fixed tax was paid for each 'gate' or *porta*.
*** See footnote on page 76.

they may be allowed to wash the wheat and clean pig-guts in their little houses at the bottom of the hill and not on the hilltop, since clambering up the icy road takes too much out of the women who carry their babies with them. It is a typical farm servant's request; even today the people of the pusztas might well stammer out similar ones if they dared to let their voices be heard at all... This request was made to the landlord at the beginning of 1514, through his officials; this is confirmed by one or other of the particularly bloodthirsty decrees enacted by the Diet held in October of the same year after the suppression of the revolt of Dózsa. Again and again there is mention in them of certain herdsmen, who are sentenced to have their right hand chopped off if guns, pikes or other weapons are found on them. Article 61 deals exclusively with these cowherds. The other articles speak generally of peasants and landed serfs; in addition to depriving them of all human rights or even a subhuman existence, they lay down precise instructions concerning their execution in given cases. This was the age when not the homeland, but the land was defended, the age of Werbőczy,* who likewise made no distinction between peasant and peasant. His plan, which won him both a reputation and a statue erected in our time, provided in articles 15–20 for every married peasant to pay 100 dinars every year in addition to the services he already performed, irrespective of whether he was a landed or a landless serf. And in addition two geese and a pig, then one chicken, monthly... They thought of everything. The *Tripartitum* brought about the most perfect equality between the peasants. 'Apart from the wages and rewards of his labour the peasant has no rights whatsoever on the lands of his master with respect to inheriting them; the ownership of the whole land is a matter for the landlord.' Which means that according to the law even the peasants had sunk to the level of farm servants.

* See also footnote on page 14.

And the farm servants themselves? In the Middle Ages the landlord kept servants to maintain order not so much on the land as among his serfs. But with the dawn of a new age, he could turn his produce into gold and everything that could be obtained for gold, so he went in for agriculture on a larger scale. He needed land and means of cultivating it. It is surprising how swiftly history can progress, whenever it can do so in an inhuman direction. Very soon we come across large estates run as big business and organised almost as efficiently as they are today. They were occupied chiefly with cattle-breeding.

There was much talk in the Diet which met in the autumn of 1572 of the large numbers of landlords who had seized their serfs' plots and given them instead 3–4 hold* of their own land at any rent they cared to choose or in return for a quarter of the produce. Later there was mention of the landless serfs also, of whom one county statute distinguishes three types: those who live in houses, those who are squatters and those who live in penury in other folks' houses, possessing nothing whatsoever in the village. The fields tended to get more and more into the hands of single individuals. And the large estates with their insatiable appetite swallowed up the lands not only of landed serfs and peasants but also of the lesser nobles. The estates of the defeated Rákóczi were dismembered by his former comrades-in-arms and enemies (who had become heroes only after the battle was over) in just the same way that Dózsa's roasted body had been pulled to pieces by the peasants. Or shall I speak of the various courses of the enormous feast swallowed by the 'neo-acquistica commissio', whose appetising scent penetrated as far as Spain? After years of battle the episcopal estate suddenly swallowed the town of Veszprém and all it possessed, while Count Schönborn, Bishop of Bamberg, took over Munkács and Szentmiklós. How much further need the unhappy chain of events be continued merely in order to prove that there

* 1 cadastral *hold* = 1.42 acres.

always have been folk whose lot was that of farm servants and landless serfs? We have almost reached the present age; only a few links remain to be mentioned.

After the census of Joseph II, the nobility refused to allow their lands to be measured. According to the statistics of 1787, 58 per cent of the land in western Hungary was in the hands of the higher nobility. How? 'The chief aim of the oligarchy,' as Pál Nagy wrote later in 1834, 'is to consolidate its holdings, which means more or less the destruction of the lesser nobility. So enthusiastically is it pursuing this end that in the neighbouring county of Moson alone, where at the beginning of the last century there lived more than 300 noble families, today there are barely three.' And Széchenyi writes in his *Hitel:* 'Some of us possess a five-hundredth part of Hungary, some own a hundredth part, and some are so rich that... they are lords of a thirtieth of our poor dear motherland!'

In every age the population on the pusztas and large estates was less than that of the villages with their landed serfs. According to the statistics of 1828, the number of landed peasants between 16 and 60 in Hungary at that time was 564,643.

The number of landless serfs and farm servants on the pusztas was 587,288.

It would be no exaggeration to conclude from this that the area cultivated by the farm servants and landless serfs and owned by a few aristocrats was at least twice the size of the land cultivated by the landed serfs and regarded as theirs, subject to the obligations then binding them.

Even in 1848 Táncsics* has bitter things to say in his paper of the 'estate farms'. 'The majority of them are stolen property... which the estates, ably assisted by the noble courts and the mag-

---

* A leading figure of the revolutionary movements that led to the 1848–49 War of Independence; editor of the *Workmen's Gazette*.

istrates, partly obtained by fraud, thus committing theft, and partly seized by force, thus committing robbery.' But enough of this carping article, which goes on to make other allegations too. Once again the essence of it all is that there has always been plenty of privately-owned land in Hungary, and therefore there have been plenty of people upon it too: drivers, shepherds, swineherds, and—in the mud hovels on the farms—hired labourers and farm servants. Their overseers, managers and bailiffs figure in the earliest Hungarian novels. But of those under their command, there is only an occasional glimpse of an antique grey-haired Hungarian, 'the living example of loyalty and honesty', usually he leans on his stick and desires to sacrifice his life for his master—all quite unaffectedly and naturally without any recompense. It is surprising, however, that the younger individuals of this type appear before us as hardened brigands, who lurk in the reeds and roll their eyes as they yield up their wretched souls after a gallant hero or two has shot them brilliantly with his pistol. We can also find pretty peasant women; at first they nurse their infants, but in the middle of the nineteenth century they suddenly develop a passion for singing, indeed the whole century through they are liable to burst into sentimental songs at the slightest pretext, cutting capers as if they were in some mad operetta. The country smiles its approval, but even now does not ask where these folk have sprung from. At most they regard them—in their thoughts—as nice domestic animals. Certainly they do not include them among the landed serfs, the folk who were liberated in 1848. The Diet then abolished feudal dues.

And very nice too, but it would have been even nicer if it had acted earlier. Then the nobility might have been called generous, but now that it has done so out of sheer necessity and terror, it cannot claim this title. The honourable nobles and orders, the most worthy magnates and goodness knows who else received the news that Sándor Petőfi had encamped on the field of Rákos, not by himself, but with 40,000 peasants, and this pleasant surprise urged them to such generosity that they immediately abolished the feudal dues... It is preposterous for them to boast of their generosity...

These words are not mine. The whole paragraph, word for word, was written by Petőfi; I have merely omitted the quotation-marks to rejuvenate the text. He is not boasting. Years later the members of the nobility who were there themselves admitted that apart from news of the revolutions in Paris and Vienna and the blood-thirsty peasant risings in Galicia, it was first and foremost the fearful rumours about Rákos field that carried them away. Later they did everything in their power to restore the status quo. The revolutionary parliament for months debated excitedly the problem of how much compensation the landlords should receive. Windischgrätz was at the gates of Pest, but they did not lose their heads. Schlick defeated Mészáros and the fall of Buda was a question of days, but in the crumbling fortress they were still haggling over the amount per plot: should it be 500 or 400 forints? On December 30th even the level-headed Deák lost his temper. 'We ought to be ashamed of ourselves in the eyes of the future,' he cried with a glowing face. 'Let us not besmirch the pages of history by raising at a time like this a matter which is of particular concern to members of the parliament.' (Of these members, not one was a peasant or landed serf, nor were there any farm servants among the electorate.) Not a soul thought of the complete and swift solution to the difficult problem, 'the abolition of villein services and tithes without compensation', which Táncsics had suggested long before. Yet the *Workmen's Gazette* here and there gives voice to the ideas of the peasantry. 'If all those landless serfs,' writes a correspondent from Veszprém who is himself obviously one of them, 'if those eight million landless serfs do not pick up the sword and fight the enemy, our country will perish... In our town the poor say: "Why should I give my 19-year-old son to the army, when I own nothing? What is there for my son to defend? The wheatfields of the titled no-

84

bility?"... Well, where is the land from which I, as a member of the body which supports the whole nation, can feed myself and the family which I have hitherto brought up in rags?' It is where it still remains today. Hungary did perish... The Hungarian nobility began with truly estimable self-sacrifice a bourgeois revolution which it could not win because it was not in itself bourgeois. A few excellent intellects who were well before their time were so bemused by the possibilities of the future that they renounced their privileges. The whole class, however, could not subscribe to this because the possibilities of the future—the factories and industrial enterprises which were to replace the big country-houses—were only dreams for the time being.

The problem of compensation was never solved by the revolutionary government. It was solved by the Austrian absolutist regime, mainly in an attempt to weaken the lesser nobility, an untrustworthy element in the eyes of the Monarchy. Although the landed peasants paid a certain amount for compensation into the fund set up for this purpose, the government in Vienna hardly allowed any of it out to the lesser nobility, thus proving that land-problems can be solved without immediate compensation. Only a few influential magnates got money from the fund. So for the first time in history the landed peasantry smiled wryly, though they did not laugh, for a short time at the two quarrelling parties from outside. And even this smile soon froze on their lips. It could not have been otherwise. Nobody had acquired freedom and land for the peasantry so far. The leaders of the great French Revolution were good revolutionaries but they agreed to the seizure of land by the peasants only when they could do nothing more to oppose it and not a day before.

The imperial patent of 1851 did not distribute land either. This decree, like the plan devised by Kossuth's committee, did nothing more than set its seal of approval upon developments. The landlords probably suffered even more than the peasants from the shackles of the villein services and tithes. When they were ordered to perform their due services, the serfs merely wasted time. Their work was not sufficient to cover the wages of the overseers and supervisors once the absolute power *(jus gladii)* of the landlords had been abolished. According to Ervin Szabó, who wrote a detailed survey of the party strife of 1848 (though he never came across the people of the pusztas), both bills merely set down on paper what had already been achieved in practice by the landed serfs.

The landed serfs, let me repeat. But of all the agricultural population of Hungary at that time, how many peasants had land? It is certain that the majority of the land still remained in the hands of the great landowners despite the imperial patent. The Emperor did not regard the magnates as untrustworthy, nor indeed were they, as is well known. When the common pastures were divided, they received the main share. An acre or two at the most fell to the landless serfs and they could not even hold on to that. True, the villages of landed serfs now blossomed into 'bourgeois' villages. But how many villages were there, for example, in the ocean of great estates in Transdanubia? At the end of the village a few noble houses would perhaps sulk and wait expectantly for Kossuth to come and bring them money, but out on the pusztas order was kept. The gales of these great times blew unnoticed above grandfather and his family.

In other parts of the country the 'barbarian good-for-nothings' also tried to acquire land. István Oláh, one of the inhabitants of Orosháza whose ancestors had come from Tolna, was a 'rhyming huckster'; in 1848 he cried not only his wares—soap, lace, and the works of Petőfi and Táncsics—but also ideas of how to acquire land. He must have been successful, otherwise he would not have been hanged that same autumn together with Ádám Frey, who had likewise had thoughts on the relationship of the landless to the land. 'Gyuri, my boy, give land to the peasants,' the irresponsible György Ágoston falsely proclaimed as the word of Kossuth among the landless peasants. And the peasants believed him rather than Kossuth, who in the end was compelled to put a stop to this nightmare of a movement by open letters and by summary courts. In some places the landless peasants had to be firmly instructed just how far their freedom extended.

They were serfs just as much after the revolution of 1848 as before it or during it. They were not inflamed by oratory. Where was the fire of the old popular risings, even of the kind roused by Hunyadi? The chronicles recorded that at Nándorfehérvár (Belgrade) Hunyadi's peasants bore down upon the serried ranks of Turkish soldiers with sticks and stones. True, they had something to defend and to fear for. In peace too Hunyadi knew how to deal with his men, and the peasants on his estates were better off than under the other oligarchs or on the Turkish side. The lesser nobles had a better time too. Some 40,000 of these poured out on the ice of the Danube to meet Matthias merely because he too was a Hunyadi. Now neither a Capistrano arose, nor even a Blind Bottyán, who likewise knew what makes the people's blood boil. Bem also knew. Some people angrily refuse to call the 1848 War of Independence a revolution. No doubt it was a revolution, but it had not reached the stage where it could have achieved significant and lasting results. That the peasants might have redeemed their lands from the landlords? Why, the majority of the agricultural population, the landless serfs and farm servants, had nothing to redeem. It is true that in Hungary not even revolutions dared to touch the lands on which they lived. That outstanding figure, Pál Királyi, in 1845 painted a glowing picture of what the happy future might bring, 'if the 175,000 Jews and especially the 43,000 gipsies were settled on the land, if we were to show them a plot for their houses and give them ploughs.' He fights doughtily against prejudice for 'it would be an enormous gain in status... to win the power hidden in the two muscular arms of these masses for Hungarian agriculture.' He demands the right of private ownership of land for them, but not for the farm servants. The naive blindness of the age is absolutely astonishing. The fashion journals deplore the lot of the Negroes, but they have still no eyes for the people of the pusztas and the landless serfs. So we should not be surprised that their fortunes did not improve with the great events of those years. Could they move freely? From the frying-pan into the fire. Were they beaten any longer? They were. If their fortunes changed at all, the change was quite independent of the great promises given in parliament and at the street-corner. It was caused by the buffeting of forces of which even all that went before were but symptoms.

Grandfather ascribed the change to the trains and he was quite right. Then to men's greed, the wild lust for money which gripped the great nobility from one day to the next. He was no lover of change; ever since he had been able to think, each change had only brought trouble. What had it been like before? Then the people of the pusztas had merely been shepherds, they had lain around in the sun or in the stables and had not broken their legs by hurrying. The estate had produced only as much corn as was needed for its inhabitants. 'When I was a child, scarcely any land round here was ploughed up. I knew a lot of folk who never held a hoe in their hands their whole life through.' Scythes? He himself had never held a scythe except perhaps to try the feel of it. 'There were sheep and cows. And there was so much dung that they didn't bother to take it all out to the fields, but used it for fuel. The whole estate was pasture-land.' The farm servants could keep as many animals as they were able to buy. Nobody ever asked, 'János, what's your cow been eating to make her so fat?' or 'What are your wife's ducks and hens eating?' There was food and in plenty. Had an ox gone lame? 'Slaughter it and divide it among the farm servants. Have it free, to my health!' For then even the gentry were real gentry. In other words they were not concerned about small details. One of the Counts

Zichy refused to give his bailiff a pension saying, 'He could have got enough money together for that by himself, I didn't stop him!' Every year grandmother sold 300 forints' worth of butter, chickens, eggs and lard in the market at Ozora. Sometimes she had driven as many as twenty-five sucking-pigs to market. Cattle-dealers visited the estates and first of all looked at the animals of the farm servants because they were always better than the estate animals. It is common knowledge, after all, that the estates learnt almost everything about intensive cattle-breeding from the farm servants. It was from them that they discovered how to fatten pigs, breed cows, keep bees and more recently sell eggs. People were better too. There wasn't so much bad language. Nor did they put on airs. One set of garments was sufficient for an adult man or woman all their lives. Only the sick slept inside. For then there was good health too. And then the trains came—'if only the fire had burnt them all up!'

It is certain that the first decades of the second half of the nineteenth century brought some temporary relief to the people of the pusztas, at any rate in Transdanubia, if not elsewhere. There were no more labour services on the big estates, and more manpower was demanded by methods of production which were all geared to profit. The shepherd was respected. The farm servants were no more demanding than they had been in the age of slavery; they lived in mud huts half dug into the earth, they made their own clothes and their spiritual needs were fully met by folk song and folk art. Thus even the smallest improvement was regarded as a blessing from heaven. The estates really took very little notice if one or two of their more astute farm servants began to spread their wings a little. All they needed were trustworthy and loyal employees to look after the animals, and none could have been more loyal than they. Even if grandfather and his companions regarded the property of the gentry (whose living standard was scarcely better than theirs) as a kind of common property, they did so only for their own benefit and jealously preserved it from the hands of strangers. They kept a sharp eye on the villagers and landless peasants, whose stature also grew somewhat.

But this happy age had to come to an end. The railway came, and now it was possible to convey not only live cattle but wheat also to where they would fetch good prices. There came the era of good corn prices—as yet free from overseas competition—and this meant production for even greater profit. The pasture-lands were ploughed up and machines arrived on the farms. Meanwhile even the peasants began to realise that liberation had dangerous consequences as free competition was sprung upon them. For years past they had done all the ploughing on the estates and all the reaping; they had done all the threshing in the huge threshing-barns right up to Christmas in most places. But now steam ploughs began to turn the earth. The peasant plots were divided into ever smaller strips, and more and more of their children were driven off the land to become farm servants or landless labourers. The farm servants grew in numbers and the greater they grew, the more the earth beneath them groaned and cracked like ice beneath the weight of a crowd. They tried to struggle, they even tried to save each other, sometimes with heroic persistence and self-sacrifice, but all in vain. History again betrayed them. They sank inevitably and soon reached the stage they had achieved after the *kuruc* wars. In the 1900s the total income of a family, with every possible item included, amounted to 200 forints. They recalled the good old days with a sigh and did not realise that they had been only a brief glimpse of the sun.

When the family gathering turned into a mild entertainment and everybody, in accordance with the ancient tradition, sang his own particular song, grandfather from Nebánd would shake his head gloomily when it came to his turn. They tried to get him to sing the song which might well have been composed for him, but it was no use; in it came the line 'I'm the Esterházys' most renowned shepherd, with my long cane and sheepskin coat'. 'That's all over now,' he said bitterly, but a little proudly too, for everybody must have known that he had kept his head above water. For a time I identified myself with him, or rather not with him personally, but with the more distinguished members of the family, who smiled at grandfather and looked down on him as if he were a jovial old family retainer or a piece of furniture. They now felt themselves to belong to a completely different region, and would certainly have protested in alarm if they had been reminded that they were children of the same stock, that unkempt, impoverished mass of two or three centuries before, whose fate I have outlined here fairly roughly, but perhaps not superfluously. If ever they read a novel about the Middle Ages, they shared the feelings of the knight or the love-lorn maiden in the castle. They applauded the institution of feudalism because 'in those days there was order' and because they arbitrarily imagined themselves in the role of the nobility in the past. When they heard of the age of slavery, they did not think about the fate of the slaves. When they passed judgement on the rebellion of Dózsa, they did not pause an instant to decide who was right, the starving crusaders or the followers of the pederast Zápolya. As for grandfather's antecedents, they were willing to overlook them and forgive them, since they could not deny their relationship to him. They regarded his life as something of a temporary aberration, like that of a prodigal son who fortunately abandons his doubtful environment and returns to the proper way. Were they mistaken in this? This was how they had been educated in school, in society and through their reading of newspapers or calendars. They had none of the self-confidence of grandfather who after all had made his way up in the world: he had given orders to a shepherd-lad or two and later to a few hired labourers. But he did not want to show that he was somebody by isolating himself and by standing high above the common folk; he did so among the shepherds and labourers. He had the manner of the gentry. Had a sheep gone lame? 'Eat it, to my health!'

he said generously to the hired labourers, forgetting that the sheep was not his, and that he would have to fib about it when called to account. He accepted his responsibility, and often did not wait for the sheep to go lame. He would send a young lamb to a wedding-feast and brush aside all thanks with the pride of the lord of the manor. He behaved like a true aristocrat in the way he imagined the aristocracy ought to behave. He would sit in the stables with his men who addressed him familiarly. Smoking his pipe and making wise pronouncements, he enjoyed the respect for which he had to struggle sentence by sentence. What was it that suddenly made me too discover real aristocracy in him? It was not his worldly wealth. I could not say now when it was that I stopped on the dangerous upward ladder and turned towards those who around the little island of the family and sometimes clinging on to it were desperately battling with the current, the current of poverty, squalor and depression which in my childhood had once more flooded the puszta as it had done so often in history.

CHAPTER SIX

How the puszta is governed. Shepherds, foremen and farm managers

Uncle Fekete was the foreman of the puszta, Uncle Mózes the foreman of the hired labourers and Ferenc the first waggon-driver... it was they who first appeared to my youthful consciousness after the members of the family. They were splendid figures, whose heads touched the sky. They bent over my cradle—for I still had a cradle, and what was more, it rocked automatically by means of a clever pedal-mechanism invented and constructed by my father. If I looked upwards to the sky, it was their tanned faces with their huge moustaches that bent over me; it was their enormous spade-like hands that descended upon my round head either with the warmth of a caress or with the threat of a box on the ears. They had the freedom of our house as had Uncle István Nagy, the foreman of the threshing-barn, and the steward and all the members of the large Tóth family from the lower farm, who were more or less related to us, since they too had shepherd-ancestors. These formed high society on the puszta.

All through the ravages of time they were in charge of the estate, and commanded it like a ship. They shouted without ceasing, they crawled into cellars and attics, night and day they kept watch over the machines and the tall watchmen's huts. The gentry might change, the bailiffs as often as the owners and tenants, but they went on for ever. They had been born there on the puszta.

Their job was handed down from father to son; the most inflexible caste-system prevails on the puszta. The steward's son would sooner or later become steward or someone of equal rank; the puszta foreman's son, even though he went through the stages of boy labourer, ordinary labourer and carter, would certainly become a foreman by the time he was an old man. But whoever was taken on as an ordinary labourer, he and all his children would keep this status until the end of the line unless they moved elsewhere, in other words, if the children too were employed on the puszta. Nor do I know of any case where an ox-driver was promoted to work with horses. It was most unusual if a carter became chief carter. The chief carter drives the first pair of oxen in the lengthy caravan of ox-carts... His yoke is the most gorgeously decorated, and he may put knobs on the horns of his oxen... It is he who chooses either the shortest or the longest route to their destination; the puddles or molehills which he avoids are likewise avoided by the whole caravan; if he raises his cap to someone on the road, all the rest do so in turn. His position is the greatest dream of the carters. Yet even he is one of them, for he may be dislodged from his high perch from one year to the next and take his place once more among the followers. It is impossible to imagine a cattle-foreman being down-graded; he would sooner leave. Nor could a carter be demoted to ordinary labourer without causing a tragedy. And as for putting a horse-driver among the ox-drivers, it would be like trying to make a Negro out of a white Yankee. Even the very rare marriages between their families are regarded as a mild form of race-degradation.

In these circumstances, where every tortuous detail of ancestry counted, I was a princeling. On both sides of the family, I had the most favourable forebears. I very soon came to realise what the word 'shepherd' meant. From the very first days the shepherds, whose occupation was lost in antiquity, were the most aristocratic members of the community of farm servants. The cowherds went round the puszta with haughty faces like primeval inhabitants faced with a rabble of newcomers, and the carters' daughters blushed with emotion if a horseherd caught them round the waist. But all these grew dumb whenever a shepherd raised his voice in their presence. 'What was the reason for this respect?' I asked my grandfather, from whom we had gained such glory. There were a thousand and one important reasons, but it will be enough just to mention the right of sitting down.

'After all the swineherd is a kind of shepherd too, but what sort of a shepherd is he?' He is more like a watchman, if not a mere day-labourer. He is forbidden to sit down. He must always be on the watch. He holds the whip in his left hand, for the real swine-herd can make it crack with his left hand too, and in his right hand he holds the short cane with which he hits the animals if they become quarrelsome. Well, he may stick this little cane under his seat if he ever grows very tired of standing up. 'There he stands, poor chap, like a statue,' with his full knapsack slung round his neck—he dare not put it down, because the pigs will immediately turn it inside out—and his little axe at his side. This pleasing little weapon he carries to defend himself if any of the boars turn aggressive, but it is most in evidence in processions and at Sunday dances.

The cowherds? Apparently they are allowed to sit down. 'If they happen to slip in a cowpat,' said grandfather haughtily, taking a grim pleasure in his words. He stood up for the common cause of the shepherds, but was not loath to turn scornful when it came to details. 'Cowherds, oxherds, hungry highwaymen,' he said with a good laugh. They can sit down if there are enough of them to encircle the whole herd. But even then, they may only sit so that their knees touch their chin. 'That's the rule for them,' said grandfather. 'Can it be regarded as a sitting posture?' Obviously not. But they lean on something too, hence their long sticks. 'True, they may lean forwards and some of them even sleep like this, they are so adept at leaning on their sticks. But what's the use of arguing. Do they

95

get a beast under them?' grandfather asked playing his last trump, carefully and delicately referring thus to the donkey, about which he had doubtless had to suffer a good many pointed remarks. 'Although the swineherd and the cowherd have just as far to walk as the shepherd.'

And a good deal further. This is the truth. 'And what about the horseherds, grandfather?' 'They draw water all day long,' he waved his hand and turned his head away—it was obvious that only politeness prevented him from spitting. 'Those folk?' and again he waved his hand. He must have had serious differences of opinion with them. We may as well pass over them too; their life is no bed of roses either.

In contrast let us consider the shepherds. Even when grandfather found it impossible to walk from the table to his bed without catching his breath, he would always raise himself up in his chair when he talked about them. Nor can I really mention them in this offhand way; out of respect alone I ought to write a separate volume about them. Sit? The shepherds could lie down just when, where and how they pleased. There was an unwritten, but complete code concerning their privileges, which grandfather and certainly his ancestors too defended in the same way as the towns defended their rights. Not to mention the donkey. One day grandfather was sunning himself as he lay on the hill at Pincehely. A carriage pulled up on the main road and from the box the driver began to shout: 'Hey there, you there, come here a minute!' Neither grandfather nor his dog moved a muscle. A gentleman got out of the carriage (the driver had to hold the reins) and clambered struggling up the hill. 'Are you deaf?' he asked, 'my driver has been shouting for half-an-hour. I am the chairman of the Board of Guardians at Szekszárd.' 'I've not heard anybody say anything,' replied grandfather. 'Where can I find water for the horses?', asked the gentleman, swallowing hard. 'Over here and over there,' replied grandfather, without a single word of greeting, because he himself had not been greeted. He gave his answers leaning

96

on one elbow, like a prince on a couch. 'I can see you're a shepherd,' said the chairman of the Board of Guardians.

He grazed his sheep wherever he liked. At noon he drove the flock near the puszta and dined at his own table. In the afternoon he wandered off towards the vine-clad hills of Ozora, where there was a little wine-cellar. But even there he was careful to choose whose jug he drank from, because he knew he was a cut above the peasants. Such was the esteem in which the shepherds were held.

My father was also on this same footing, though it was only in his demeanour and manner of speaking that he preserved the characteristics of a shepherd—and in his nature too. The excellent ewes' milk and paprika stew, the soft, sweet inviting earth all made these shepherds grow strong and tall. Among the wizened, shrivelled farm servants the male members of my father's family walked around like giants among dwarfs.

My father was not among the chief ranks of these lesser officials on the puszta. He had two or three men beneath him, directing them not so much by word of command as by preceding them at work. But from Nebánd a mysterious light shed its rays upon us. As they passed by our house, labourers and overseers would call to my mother in the kitchen and say something nice to her. When grandfather was visiting us, it was more like a reception at court.

The farm managers and their assistants lived in an aura of high mystery, though in the daytime they would gallop across the puszta on some business or other. They lived in one wing of the manor-house, which was empty for years at a time, and when they went in through the garden gate, they seemed to disappear among the clouds. There were different ranks among them too, of course. The assistants were scarcely better off than minor county officials. Today they receive a salary of 800–1,000 pengős per year and full board, with one room. They would remain as assistants for years until they could obtain a manager's post. The manager is far better off. He receives a salary of 100–300 pengős per month, then each year 12 quintals of wheat and 12 quintals of barley; he keeps three cows and two calves at the estate's expense, and in addition has four *hold* of land and a big, comfortable house, usually in the middle of a large garden. He may keep as many pigs and fowl as he wishes. The bailiffs receive about the same in kind, but their salary is less, amounting to 100–200 pengős per year. But however great were the differences between them, and however much they bickered among themselves, the mortals beneath did not observe anything of it; even the least of them stood on such an ethereal plane. There were some kindly and understanding folk among them, particularly when their perquisites began to be diminished and when the old legendary world of free acquisition came to an end for them too. Then they began to feel that they were mere employees. But most of them preserved their traditional firmness, which in any case was expected of them by the estate. Those I knew in my childhood tried to avoid contact with the ordinary folk, with whom they found it difficult to get on. They did not understand their language; mostly they merely thundered and lightened like gods. Their detailed instructions were handed down to the overseers and foremen. This middle stratum filtered and transformed the higher directives into something effective. The various overseers were not gentry; with one or two exceptions they were far worse—they were the slaves of the gentry.

There was Balog, for example, the cattle-foreman. The landlord himself could not have been more haughty. His very appearance—his legs set wide apart, chest thrown out, jaw running into his double chin, well-waxed moustache and his gaze—all proclaimed from afar the mean externals of his desire to be one of the gentry; he was imbued with this ambition.

He was dull-witted, but cunning. He beat his men, his wife, his children and his parents, but not his animals. He kept discipline, such was his boast. Whenever they heard the sound of his voice—a deep and glorious resounding baritone made even more resonant by the cavernous stables—the herdsmen, though reeling with weariness and lack of sleep, would jump to work like fleas. His father and his grandfather had also been cattle-foremen and, according to the old folk, had been just as hard-natured. This was their family inheritance. It was odd that he did not yield an inch of his pride when in the presence of the gentry. Even the toughest of the foremen became humble, if not mealy-mouthed, before the bailiff. Balog, however, even though he stood there politely with his hat in his hands, received his orders with an air of conceit and with knitted brow, as if to accuse the farm managers themselves of sharp practice and itching palms. 'My stables', he would say, and 'my animals'. If he had known him, he would certainly have regarded the count himself as an idler and a thief. For whom did he work then? For he certainly worked unstintingly and to the limit of his strength. For some obsession? For some intellectual ideal? Everybody detested him, the landlords included. Yet both gentry and labourers probably thought of him as the ideal farm servant in their imagination. He fulfilled with precision all the duties his lot imposed upon him.

We lived in close relationship to the other foremen and all the members of this odd 'middle stratum' of puszta society. In the realm of child education this meant that every adult on the puszta treated every child on the puszta as if he were his own. In the morning we would scramble up on to the carts beside the drivers. 'I'm taking the boy to the Island,' Uncle István or Mihály or whoever it was would shout to mother as they ambled past the house. 'Well, bring him back while it's still light,' mother would reply, and she would not worry any

99

more. Sometimes it was only when she looked for us that she discovered we had wandered off with somebody; she knew that we were in good hands. One summer my elder brother was seized with a passion for gopher-stew such as the swine-herds made, or perhaps it was just the joy of hunting gophers, and from dawn to dusk he roamed the fields, sometimes even staying out all night. When he turned up again he was thrashed, but in a somewhat desultory way; he had not been out of bounds. If we misbehaved, in the heat of the moment the carters would thrash us too and we took this as if it had come from our parents. When I had gained a clearer view of the social structure, I tried to protest against the ordinary labourers being allowed to lay hands on me when they felt like it. 'You deserve it,' said my father. In this realm equality was preserved.

Yet what was it that distinguished us from the farm servants? First of all, perhaps, it was that we began to wear top-boots in winter a week or two before they did, and in spring stopped wearing them a week or so later. In other words, we looked after ourselves. We had winter coats too, and gloves as well, or rather mittens, though we normally left them behind because we could not get used to them. And we, the third generation, had handkerchiefs also; sure, on the instructions of our parsimonious grandmother we used them only to wipe our noses properly after we had blown them in the good old-fashioned way. There came a time when all these distinctions tended to make me feel that we were indeed superior.

Apart from the democratic principles of my maternal grand-mother, who cared not a scrap for the social scale and looked only for signs of humanity and sobriety (and this she found more often in the unpretentious carters' wives than in the ambitious wives of the bailiffs), my father too gladly passed his time in the company of the least of the ordinary labourers, perhaps just to enjoy his superiority, or like his father, the sound of his own voice. When they were talking, he would go

100

and stand behind them, pretending to take no notice, as if he had just stopped there in the absence of anything else to do. But he waited eagerly for them to make an obviously stupid remark, so that he might deny it and take over the conversation, at first with an air of superiority, but gradually warming to his task until finally he was roaring with laughter with them. If they asked his opinion, he would go miles away to give it. Since he had nothing else to give, he gladly distributed his knowledge, his favours and his esteem; all were gratefully accepted by the people of the pusztas, who knew their value too. They would wake him up in the night to help with an ailing sucking-pig, and he would leap out of bed gladly, giving loud and almost churlish instructions on his bare feet. Perhaps the greatest event in his life and one which in old age he never ceased to relish, was when the enormous threshing-barn caught fire in two places at once and under his improvised fire-brigade was burnt down completely to the last straw.

Our popularity was increased by the sewing-machine. We had one of these, the only one on the puszta, and mother was an expert at sewing and cutting-out. Through grandmother's foresight, she had perfected her knowledge in Simontornya and Pálfa, and later on in life she certainly made good use of it. She ran up skirts and blouses for the girls and women on the puszta. They repaid her not in money, but in work. Typical of her was the agreement that while she did the sewing, the customer would hoe the garden or the land she shared, or husk maize, or feed the animals; in other words, the customer did her normal work for her. Grandmother, who was better versed in the ways of the world, protested against this simple exchange of work. 'And who pays for the work the machine does, Ida? The machine cost money too, remember.' 'Czabuk, my god-father, gave it to me free.' (And moreover it was a wedding-present.) 'And if it gets broken?' 'János would be only too glad to mend it.' My father was indeed happy to mend it, he had it in pieces at least once a week on the average. 'And what about your skill?' 'I've got that anyway.' She refused to see the point; she was stubborn. Or was she ashamed to take money? On the puszta a peculiar form of morality made all money appear to be suspect and humiliating. It was too rarely seen for it also to be considered dangerous. It was still easier to sew than to ridge potatoes or draw water, and my mother regarded the difference between the two forms of work as a justifiable gain. Yet grandmother might well have mentioned what the customers ate at our house as well. For mother entertained the ladies of fashion as they arrived with their hoes and spades. Apart from all this, however, the argument was obviously theoretical—my mother would not have got any money even if she had asked for it. The wives of the hired men had absolutely no money. Whenever a little small change jingled in their pockets, they held on to it jealously. The women would even send their letters by the puszta postman to the post-office at Simontornya accompanied by a couple of eggs or a crock of beans. And if they needed a bigger coin for some superstitious ceremony or to put on the eyes of a dying relative, they would go the rounds of their neighbours to find it.

The result of my mother's theory of values was that the women from the drivers' and carters' dwellings would often use their sewing as a pretext or an introductory manoeuvre. Little barefooted, shiny-nosed girls would push their way past the piece of drugget covering the kitchen door, carrying two grimy pieces of rag and a highly suspicious bowl. 'Mother says would you please sew these together along here and could you lend her a little lard?' The little girls would put in an appearance when their mothers shrank from coming after many unfulfilled promises of 'I'll let you have it back after the next payment in kind.' And this was the better of two evils; there was no need to listen to the stream of gossip which the wives of the labourers, misinterpreting my mother's bitter silence, poured out in an endless flood.

The more uneasy my mother felt, the longer she would remain silent, both when she was in company and in her ordinary life. From her mother she had inherited her sharp wits, though without grandmother's magnificent claws, and from her father his softspokenness and dignified bearing, but without his inner calm. She did not retreat from her surroundings, nor did she feel herself to be superior; she merely wanted to be somewhere else. She was born and brought up on a puszta, and was at home in its very lowest depths, yet she longed with all her being to get away, to be free of it all. Where would she go? She herself did not know. She grew more silent. When we were children, I remember, she would sing from morning to night and did not care if half the puszta gathered beneath the window when she sang the arias from *János Vitéz** as a special number. These she had learnt from the wife of the teacher at Pálfa. Later something seemed to snap like a tendon and put an end to her happiness. Her soul became numbed. I never found out why. About this time, as about everything that pained her, she would not say a word to me, and she carried her secret to the grave.

On the puszta, however, it was her silence that they liked. Everybody could be quite certain that no gossip was ever spread further from our house, so all the more flooded to its doors. My mother's heart became the place where all the complaints, insults and worries of the puszta were unloaded; perhaps this is why she felt stifled in these surroundings. The women grimly stripped each other of their good reputation.

Strangely enough, the women were not so much at loggerheads with each other as the men. Elsewhere the women are the real guardians of the caste-spirit. These puszta women would slip nimbly under or over the dividing walls for a fight or an embrace. The wife of the cattle-foreman sobbed on the breast of the swineherd's wife when her husband had beaten her. This

* Petőfi's folk epic, set to music by Pongrác Kacsóh.

was no less than if the princess had gossiped and exchanged embraces with the wife of a porter. Yes, here the families of the cattle-foreman and the swine-herd were together all day long. The foremen lived in the farm servants' dwellings, normally at one end of them; the main distinction was that they had a separate room and sometimes a separate kitchen. They lived in better style, but everybody on the puszta used this to be able to hoard a little. The foremen lived hardly any better than the farm servants. One did not begin by dressing better, but by trying to get a foothold in a village. The Mózes family already had a house in Szokoly when they were still living like gipsies. They lived like emigrants who will undertake any work in the distant parts of the world because it is only at home that they count themselves to be real people.

Thus there was direct contact between the overseers and the hired labourers. After all, they grew up together and had the same schooling; they knew all the secrets of each other's lives. As a rule they were on familiar terms too. The foremen had to struggle for their position every day. Most of them went around with set faces. The knowledge that they had unbounded authority over the others, which of necessity depresses the spirit, drained their features, like some physical illness. Even those who were still able to drop their mask could rarely do so, for they spent all their time, day and night, under the gaze of the farm servants. They displayed their arrogance and were churlish even when they were being kind, when they were 'helping' the labourers to get something and when they were turning a blind eye.

There were some, however, who really wore this mask to hide something. Or perhaps their hearts had remained noble and were out of place behind the animal faces, the stultified brains and nerves. This was the case of Uncle István Nagy, the foreman of the threshing-barn, at least so it seemed to me.

Such a welter of filthy language bubbled forth from him, even when he prayed, that even the menfolk would try to check him. From the threshing-barn up on the hill his fearful curses floated over the puszta like those of a demented prophet. He went around with a wooden axe and a huge stick, which he was always waving threateningly... And in the meantime he 'acquired' for the farm servants everything he could lay his hands on. If the news of the 'opportunity' did not reach the needy person in time, he would himself shoulder the half-sack of potatoes or maize and take it to him. This too he did with flashing eyes. He would hurl the sack into a corner and instead of saying 'Here you are, eat them up!' which is perhaps what he wanted to say, he would utter a rhythmical stream of obscene curses.

There were several such folk—my father's father had a similar nature. Such was the estate swineherd too, who made good use of the estate pigswill according to his own discretion. Incidentally he was Uncle István Nagy's best friend, and resembled him not only in heart, but in mouth and speech also. It was one of the favourite amusements of the farm servants to impersonate for themselves how they conversed, how the two old men would treat each other to the most appalling curses if they ran into each other of a morning.

They were intimate friends of our family. They often dropped in, particularly Uncle István Nagy, who had the freer range of the puszta. Then he would try to muzzle his mouth; my mother would smile to hear the struggles of the would-be gallant old man, who finally burst into a stream of curses because he could not stop himself from swearing. Our house, like grandmother's, had the reputation of being a place where only pure speech was heard. I am not certain that this may not have been the real basis of our prestige.

The foremen who usually growled like bears became tame as lambs as they poked their heads through our door. In the evenings, my father would stand outside the house and the circle around him kept their conversation as refined as in a gentle-

105

men's club; every word could be heard inside the room, and if anybody accidentally let himself go, he would look terrified over his shoulder. But as the darkness deepened, the mood grew less restrained. My mother would shut the window and order us into the kitchen. At last the men would move off in the direction of the manor-house. And we would be released and follow them; until supper we could play outside once more. In our presence they did not restrain themselves. Barefooted and deliberately staying a few steps behind them, I snatched up the words they let fall and bit by bit learnt the speech of men, which contains the true spirit of my own folk in its broad, heavy content, full of meaning in its slightest vibration. They would still be talking and complaining about their work.

They gathered together to receive their orders, the last but most direct link in the chain of command on the puszta. Those who were responsible for maintaining order met in groups outside the office. Some of them dashed off to the well for a quick wash and ran a gap-toothed comb through their hair. Inside an oil lamp was placed on the table and the assistants scribbled there, whiling away the time, while the farm manager and bailiff studied the farm diary in which was noted every day the state of every field, and the duties of all the various labourers on the puszta.

The foremen entered the office one by one, stiffened to attention in front of the table and gave an account of the work done that day by the team under their command, together with the health of the animals and the behaviour of the men. Then they received orders for the following day. 'You will go here and here, with six yoke of oxen, three carter's mates and five day-labourers, etc. etc.' The foremen nodded, then almost saluted them. They then hurried back to pass on the message to their men, so that these in turn could tell their wives that evening which part of the estate to bring their lunch to next day.

CHAPTER SEVEN

Weekdays and Sundays

High up on the hill in front of the ox-stables, a big rusty plough-share hung on a piece of wire from the tall gleditsia tree, whose trunk had been worn smooth by the animals that had rubbed up against it. A few minutes before three o'clock in the morning the night-watchman emerged from the stables and with an iron rod or yoke-pin beat on this ploughshare which to judge from the sound, was cracked. It produced an infernal noise which could be heard for miles; it left in the air a long-drawn-out vibration like the squeal of a pencil on a slate or the squeak of a knife-edge on a plate. The puszta came to life with a mild shock.

Wells creaked. The carters sucked water out of the bucket, then spat it on to their hands and rubbed them over their faces, chiefly round their eyes. They dressed like lightning. Shouts could already be heard. Just as life begins in a Moslem village with the muezzin's call to prayer, here it began with a resounding rosary of curses, and first of all in the ox-stables.

In accordance with the usual timetable of work in Hungary, the animals in the cowsheds, ox-stables and draught-horse stables are fed at precisely three o'clock. Thus at three o'clock in the morning the herdsmen, ox-drivers and horseherds are already busy with their forks. They throw fodder into the mangers, sweep the manure into heaps and then carry it out on hurdles. By four o'clock, when the foremen appear on the scene the animals are being rubbed down, curried and combed. At five o'clock they receive a second feed, then they are driven out to water. While the oxen are lapping water from the long troughs and bellowing their morning yawns to the skies, inside the drivers quickly spread new hay to replace the manure and sweep out the stables. Then they too may eat; they pause for breakfast from half-past-five to six. This is when they take a five-minute nap to tide them across from sleep to perfect wakefulness; they also give themselves a good scratch and put a twist in their moustaches. At six o'clock precisely the gentle angelus chimes from the belfry, and by this time all of them must be sitting on their carts. Meanwhile the swineherds also emerge to the sound of lively tooting.

In the coach-horse stables and piggeries the rising-hour is four o'clock. The horseherds also get up at four—hay-spreading takes them less time. The shepherds rise at five...

The reapers, on the other hand, have to get up at two, the day-labourers when it begins to get light, and the women when the cowherds and swineherds drive out their animals. By the time that the twilight has given place to light and shade, the puszta has already got over the initial impulse of work.

The carts now creak in the distance. In one of the fields, the threshing-machine pants rhythmically among the stooks, while in another the overseer does likewise behind the day-labourers. It is remarkable to see how every portion of the huge concern is in lively activity, as if it knows why it is alive. The farm servants work.

The ordinary labourers dig the potatoes out of the clamps, clean them, sort them, throw some away, turn them once or twice, then pick them up and pack them into the clamps once more. With big wooden shovels they turn the wheat, they dress the seed, weed the crops, bend down in front of the sifter and turn the wheel of the maize-shelling machine. The drivers plough and harrow, gather up and carry the threshed corn to the railway station, then they take out the manure or liquid

108

manure, the last in big water-carts. The horse-drivers do the same work. On the narrow-gauge estate horse-tramway, the waggons set out with the milk which has already been collected, strained, cooled and poured into cans by the cowmen in the excellently-equipped dairy. The foremen rush hither and thither shouting. The farm officials despairingly wipe their brows and wave their arms, then shaking their heads get into the carriages which bowl them from one field to another. From the blacksmith's shop can be heard an incessant clanging, for the smiths bounce their hammers on the anvil even when there is no hot iron for them to strike. The wheelwright works away at his wood, the bricklayer plasters a wall and the barrels are scrubbed in the wine-cellar. What do the gentry do? To this there is no answer; the gentry are not on the puszta.

The whistle of the threshing-machine signals the noon break, or in winter the ploughshare already mentioned. Between St George's day and Michaelmas, that is between April 24th and September 29th, it lasts for an hour and a half, and is used chiefly to add to the night's sleep. Round about eleven o'clock the procession of wives carrying lunch still leaves the puszta, though not so cheerfully as it did in grandfather's time. The women, all dressed up, still carry on their heads the old large wooden bowls, but at best only a little soup splashes about in the bottom of them. This procession resembles a weird, medieval religious ceremony which has now become devoid of its meaning, but is nevertheless carried on day after day by the guardians of tradition, who perform all its detailed rites with tortuous care. It would be quite easy for two or three women to carry such food as is now taken to the fields; why then does every single labourer's wife sally forth? Not one would stay at home. Each of them prepares her bowl separately and as carefully as if she were taking a present of food to someone. The cloth is carefully folded over the top of the mug even when it contains not even a few drops of soup, but a piece of bread and a wizened gherkin. They also put kerchiefs on their heads as if

109

they were off to mass. They wait for each other, then start out in dignified procession; they are the priestesses of sustenance and fulfil their duties. They separate when they have reached their goal. The day-labourers eat together out of a common bowl, but the drivers do not. They are their own masters, and have households. The women draw their husbands aside and set out the meal well away from each other at the foot of a tree or in the shade of the rick. Why do they part thus? 'They're very cunning,' a bailiff once said to me concerning the modern reason for this, which one of our best preachers recalled as an excellent proof of the spiritual power of our people. Several of the drivers plied their spoons as if they had meat in them instead of absolutely nothing. 'Some of them even wipe their mouths after it!' Did they mislead me too? As far as I can remember, everybody ate at Rácegres, little though it might have been. If there was nothing else, there was at least bread. There were families who for weeks in autumn had nothing else but bean soup. In winter, it is true, things might become difficult... My own favourite food was boiled corn-on-the-cob, eaten cold, with a little salt. But what was it like to those who day after day, at breakfast and indeed often for lunch too, ate it salted to death so that after they had eaten it they might have a good drink of water? They rarely ate meat; some families were unable to slaughter a pig for years on end. They kept the smaller fowls for summer-time, when there was hard work to do. They liked noodles, particularly those made with potato-flour, and could have eaten them every day, as indeed they did as long as the flour they received as part of their payment in kind lasted. When it ran out, the wives tried to make something tasty out of mangold-wurzels, not very successfully. They were not very good cooks, as our social historians quite rightly remark.

In winter the lunch-break is shorter; it lasts only as long as the meal itself. There is less work also. In summer the animals must be fed three times, but in winter only twice, morning and evening, or rather when night falls. These two feeds, however, are large ones, because the oxen, for example, must be built up in winter for their heavy summer work.

After lunch the work continues in the same monotonous way; despite the continual goading, it goes as slowly as in the morning, in fact, all through one's life. Only in summer is there a break of half an hour in the afternoon, and then, of course, only for those who are working on the land—the carts, for example, do not halt on the road. Then darkness begins to fall. The various herds of animals wind their way homewards, the sheep naturally arriving first. Feeding, watering and bedding-down the animals in the cowsheds, ox- and horse-stables take place around six or seven o'clock. For the foals it is at five, and for the sheep in winter at seven, in the spring and autumn at three or four. 'Well, that's one more job done,' say the men when the last load of hay has been forked and they gather in front of the stables or inside under the ancient stable-lantern with its equally ancient cobwebs. There they wait for the foreman with his orders for the next day. This is when they have a good wash, which is only natural. What would be the point of cleaning themselves up in the morning, when a moment later they will be coated in sticky filth from dust, chaff and manure? Now they take their places among the womenfolk and get a plate in front of them, for in the evening they all have a hot meal. The evening angelus tolls. I can almost see my grandmother far away in Nebánd cross herself as she lets in the hens; trying to ignore the screams of the women or children down in the labourers' dwellings as some husband returns, she begins to pray quietly.

For about an hour and a half, the time it took for the labourers to stroll home after receiving their orders, the puszta on weekdays lived a somewhat more human kind of life. As they waited for their supper, the men would gather into groups outside the doors. Even today I find it difficult to recall these evenings without emotion; each one was like a mysterious journey

111

with the promise of a thousand surprises. I prowled here and there in the darkness. From the kitchens a yellowish light was thrown on to the eaves, illuminating one side of the group of men. They looked as if they had been modelled in relief out of the darkness itself. I looked in through the windows. I was reminded of the world of the sea-bed lit by searchlights as I caught glimpses of the life within. I knew the dwellings and the people who moved inside; by day I roamed around among them. But seen from outside by night they riveted my attention as something strange and unusual. I knew how they lived—after all a stranger glancing through our kitchen window would not have noticed any great differences between their life and ours. All the same, had I not stood in front of the enclosure at the zoo labelled 'Dog', behind which there indeed lay a common or garden dog? 'So those are the Szabós' or 'the Egyeds', and I try to fill in the details. The Szabós and the Egyeds were farm servants, without anything else to distinguish them. Women walked on the clay floor in their bare feet, a man stood there stretching himself or, putting the spout of the water-can to his lips, swallowed a mouthful of water. All this was interesting and mysterious. In those days at Rácegres there were still numerous rooms where more than one family lived. This was not obvious from the furnishings; the room was not crowded. In each corner there stood a high bed and beside it a chest of drawers or simply a chest, while in the centre there was still plenty of space. Tables were rarely to be seen. Only in one corner would there be a lighted lamp. The members of the various families seemed to use previously determined routes; they bustled around, but never got in each other's way... A girl slipped out of her bodice, but nobody took the slightest notice. The children had been put to bed, which meant that supper was ready. Everybody took supper in the kitchen, with the bowl or plate between their knees. They had soup for supper; in the evening practically all of them would have a bowlful, and with it a slice of bread, a savoury scone or even *prósza*, which was

112

the name given to a small meal-cake made of maize-flour. The farm servants of Rácegres were known far and wide for their high living. 'Rácegres!' said the people of the neighbouring pusztas enviously, 'that's where there's still some solidarity.' And this was true, the farm servants there did not change as much as they had on other estates. Among the lowest stratum of hired labourers there were fewer traitors than elsewhere. Was the result of all this that they somehow acquired a little more for themselves? The farm officials who arrived there stumbled up against obstacles of obscure origin, which were the last remains of the primeval constitution of the puszta.

I might wander around until I could hear my mother's voice from the house calling us by our Christian names in that endearing, flattering tone that she also used to the chickens. We had our supper too, but at table. 'You live like the Count,' grumbled grandfather from Nebánd when he was eating at our house, yet there was commendation in his voice too. He would flutter the table-cloth as if to question its usefulness and try at least to slice the bread with his own knife. In our house everybody had not only a spoon of their own, but also a knife and fork and even a glass as well.

After supper there was still a little breathing-space, a few intense, electrically-charged moments before we went to bed. Now, right at the end of the day, folk seemed to have discovered something worth living for; the sensation of wellbeing given by a stomach satisfied with hot food seemed to raise them to a level of freedom above the stifling atmosphere of the ordinary week-days. The foremen shut themselves in. The mastiffs were let loose in the courtyard of the manor-house—with the exception of the groom, they attacked all the inhabitants of the house. The puszta watchman and the foreman of the threshing-barn had not yet begun their nightly rounds, but the doors of the shared kitchens were already shut. The tramp of boots could be heard between the houses, and here and there a lamp bobbed in the darkness; the drivers slowly made their way out

113

to the stables. There was a sudden peal of laughter; above our house on the hill, where a long line of acacia shrubs stretched as far as the cemetery, there could be heard the thud of running feet and a cheerful shout. I peered excitedly into the blackness beyond the window and if it was possible escaped outside the house, putting up with the unpleasantness of having to wash my feet a second time, for we had to wash our feet every evening before we got into bed; in the daytime we went around barefooted. The last speck of dust settled and through the open doors of the cowsheds the warm scent of cows percolated through the puszta. From the threshing-floor a whimsical flood of smells poured down the valley—mouldy hay, vetch or lucerne, it was possible to distinguish them all. Sometimes we waited up for father and then we might run off to the boundary of the puszta. Or we might have supper at grandmother's. Although I knew the ground between the two houses so well, in the darkness I trod along it as if I were stumbling through a morass in some distant part of the world. I listened hard, my heart beating fast. Rarely did I succeed in catching something of the mystery. Somewhere a mother called her daughter, 'Kati-i!', and in the long drawn-out cry something of the mystic charm drifted along under the vertiginously high stars. There was no answering cry. Only the pigs grunted once or twice and the hens flapped their wings in the coops. Or sometimes there would be a crash as a window was broken. In its wake a wild screaming and quarrelling poured forth as if the window had been pushed out by the uproar like a cork by fermenting liquid. In one of the common dwellings conversation before sleep had broken into a quarrel. The wives had already learnt how such scuffles might degenerate into something more serious, and as soon as the knife or the axe was brought into play they quickly smashed a window. This was a sign of danger to the outside world and also a means of stopping further trouble inside. The damage shocked the fighters and stopped them—a broken window cost more than a broken head and had more serious

114

consequences. If only because of such family rows, the men did not like sleeping at home.

Later this died away too. Sometimes a fox would step on to the trap and rashly let out a cry at the sudden pain. The men would rush there with lamps and axes and expertly kill it.

After this belated carts would return home from some lengthy trip. In the darkness the squeaking of their wheels as they slowly drew near always filled me with apprehension, as if they always brought with them a load of misfortune. When I was very young indeed eight carts in such a caravan had brought home eight wounded men and one dead.

The eight carts, with their drivers and a foreman, had taken wheat to the station at Simontornya. After loading had been completed, the men had been given a tip by the merchant. All of them, as usual, had wanted to buy tobacco with the money, and one of them was entrusted with the purchase. On their way back from the village to the puszta they stopped for each to take his share. How did the quarrel start? The real reason was never disclosed. It was alleged that the shopkeeper had given back three kreutzers too much in change. Were they unable to divide this fairly? They all remembered a little about how the fight started. The driver who had bought the tobacco struck his younger brother in the face, whereupon the latter drew his knife on him. His uncle tried to restrain him with a yoke-pin. What happened after that nobody knew for certain; the spectators became involved in the quarrel, as did the foreman, who could not say very much about it because he had immediately been kicked so hard in the groin that he fainted.

How long did the fight last? When it was all over, those who could still move loaded those who could not on to the empty carts. But by the time that the caravan arrived at the puszta, only the driver of the first cart was still able to sit up—the only damage he had suffered was that someone had taken a bite out of his hand. The rest were all lying in the bottom of the carts; all of them, understandably, wanted to appear victims of the

115

fight when they arrived at the puszta. I remember the blood, the damp red patches on the straw which gleamed saffron-yellow in the light of the lamps.

The day came to an end, and almost as soon as it had ended the next began with the sound of the cracked ploughshare. The days and nights passed by; time went on, alternating with fearsome rapidity between light and darkness, which ran into each other like a line of print pulled suddenly away from before one's eyes. Even the most startling events melted into it, losing their true significance.

On Sundays life was a little more cheerful. The puszta awoke even then at the usual time. But towards two o'clock in the afternoon, a more festive spirit descended on the farm servants' houses. The horse and ox-drivers did their chores which could not be neglected for a single day, not even if a divine miracle occurred. They put down new straw and swept the stables and sheds. The cowmen milked the cows; the grooms combed the horses and fetched water. They dashed out to their plots of land, did a little hoeing and tore out a few weeds. The women smartened up the children and swept them out in front of the houses with the dust and dirt. The midday meal took the shortest possible time. Afterwards razor-strops began to slap—they were hung from the latch or the window or from the big toe, if the owner were sitting down—and the blades glinted dangerously in the light as they flashed up and down. Little round pocket-mirrors were brought out, or they took down from the chest of drawers the adjustable mirror fixed on the little toilet-box; then the men, bending down and hissing, would scrape from their bony cheeks the week's growth of beard which they softened with sticky household soap. Those who possessed them took out of the box a pair of new boots, while those who did not blacked those they were wearing, spitting plentifully into the little wooden box of polish. The girls dressed themselves up

116

too. They wore a variety of colours, but not the old folk-costumes; they went for the new ones which could be bought ready-made at the shops. Over the incalculable number of lace-fringed underskirts, they put on skirts of startling blues, greens and reds. When they went out of the door, they held in their clasped hands a coloured velvet kerchief folded into a rhomboid shape exactly as Catherine de Medici had ordered for her ladies-in-waiting when she entered Paris. The women put on their ceremonial black clothes, which they had inherited or collected piece by piece with considerable difficulty, only when they were called away from the puszta by some family event, a funeral or a wedding. The young men put flowers in their hats; with many of them this was the only sign that they were dressed up. When the noonday feeding was over, it was as if the sun had appeared suddenly after a long period of grey skies. The puszta relaxed, the sounds of laughter and of the zither could be heard. Folk greeted each other from afar with smiles that seemed to reflect the light of some secret star.

The older ox-drivers sat on the doorstep of the stables. Try as they would, they could not tear themselves away from here. Squashed close together they squatted on the long doorstep like hens on a roost and chatted. The night before they had had a good wash. They had clean shirts and clean underwear and had combed their hair. Their thoughts and words were clearer. From the hill where the stables stood, the old men had a wide view. The puszta lay spread before them and they found plenty to talk about. Sometimes almost all of them gathered round the same threshold, and they fetched out the fodder-boxes and milking-stools. One of them would talk about his army experiences or about his distant relatives whom nobody here knew. Best of all, however, they liked to tell tales. These old men with white moustaches and bent backs amused themselves with children's fairy-tales. With sparkling eyes they listened to the adventures of Johnny Son-of-a-Horse with the gryphon, laughing, shouting their approval and slapping their thighs they would interrupt the story like the audience at a suburban cinema in Paris. There was hardly ever mention of material things.

Sometimes such a sudden peal of laughter would burst from them that heads were turned in their direction from the distant parts of the puszta. The old folks were having a good time. They told each other anecdotes. The stories were either concocted or contained a germ of truth, and in other circumstances would not have raised the ghost of a smile on the faces of the audience, but here they caused laughter that rang like a peal of victory. What kind of things made the people of the pusztas laugh? The straightforward tales always ended with 'He gave him what for.' The hero was 'the man in the tale' or some farm servant of old whom they themselves referred to as 'uncle' and who usually gave the landlord what for. A certain Ferenc Kasza, who long before my time had once been a donkey-driver at Csillagpuszta, became an almost mythical figure in my imagination. His donkey kept straying into the wheatfields belonging to the count next door. Once the count himself caught the old man there. 'If I see that donkey here ever again,' said the count, 'I'll carry her off!' 'I shall have a fine son-in-law then,' replied Uncle Kasza. A tenant took over the puszta where Uncle Kasza was employed. He had been deceived, because the land had been so exploited that even thistles found it hard to grow there. The tenant, looking out over a hummocky field asked Uncle Kasza, 'What can I turn in here?' 'Somersaults,' came the swift answer. On another occasion he was put in charge of building a haystack. 'That stack is going to fall!' shouted the bailiff to him. 'Nothing lasts for ever,' retorted Uncle Kasza. I never laughed so much in my life as I did at the clever tricks of the late Uncle Kasza. It was tales like these that amused the old men on the hill.

The young men gambled. They drew a long line on the ground and threw kreutzers at it from five or six paces away. The one who got nearest to the mark collected the money, threw it into the air and won according to the rules of heads or tails. The game was forbidden—because it was a game of chance. Some managed to win 10–15 kreutzers in an afternoon. The men always gathered round the lower entrance to the manor-house on Sundays; when the farm officials or gendarmes approached (they were liable to appear on the puszta on Sundays), they scrubbed out the line with their boots and, hands in pockets, withstood the gaze of the authorities, to whom the crime was obvious, but it could not be pinned on to anybody.

We children also roamed around the garden of the manor-house at this time. We jumped over the slimy green puddle of a ditch and climbed up the fence of willow saplings carefully, so that we should not be seen from inside. In the garden the white tennis-balls and the skirts of the nimble young ladies swished to and fro on the red gravel of the tennis-court. We got a lot fo excitement out of gazing at the gentry even if they were only sitting in basket chairs and talking or having tea. Sometimes they brought out the gramophone and played music. One day a guest of the Strasser family who rented the estate lifted me over the fence, stuck my head into the big loudspeaker and then allowed me to wind up the machine. It was one of the greatest events of my life.

Down among the ordinary labourers' dwellings the mouthorgan moaned and wailed, breaking into the sound of the zither, then the girls and after them the young men began to sing some droning melody. They never sang cheerful songs. On the other hand, their dances, if ever they reached that stage, were always of the wildest kind. But such occasions were very rare. The girls sat beside each other on a wooden log and seemed to be swayed to and fro by the melody like crops in the wind. The young men in a separate group propped up the wall of the house a little distance away and beat out the rhythm with their boots, muttering the words. Very occasionally one or other of them would sing out loud, and then the girls would grow silent.

'Oh I'm a hired driver,
    Six forints is my pay;
The New Year's come: the cart is here
    To carry me away.'

This was the 'new song' then. The melody was long drawn-
out and full of pain, like the whining of a dog. It was the song
of the homeless, a true hired labourer's song.

'I'm sad to leave my oxen,
    My iron yoke-pin here.
I'll miss my beautiful carved goad;
    I'll miss my little dear.'

The driver may well miss his yoke-pin and his goad; there is
nothing else to bid farewell to. The song was a moan, and was
sung haltingly, in broken phrases, as if they were carrying a
sack as they sang it. But the third stanza suddenly changed
its mood and turned saucily away from the theme of the other
two; even the rhymes sounded quite different. The lads sang
it crisply and defiantly, their heads turned towards the sky:

'My horses in the meadow,
    My cows are in the grass;
My gallant steed is at the door
    And I am with my lass!'

'Gallant steed?' The drivers never sit on horseback their
whole lives through—they shuffle after the oxen. And the
proud possessive—*my* horses, *my* cows! For a long time
I could not understand this bragging, indeed this obvious lie,
which followed the two matter-of-fact stanzas. Now I understand it. It was a revolt, a deliberate turning away from reality,
from which they could only free themselves if they cocked a

120

snook at it. The lads put their hands on their thighs and swayed to and fro, their hats thrust well back on their heads.

At five o'clock paradise came to an end. A long call sounded on a cow's horn brought it crashing into ruins. Watering began. The old men leant on their hands as they struggled up from the stable doorstep, with their old bones cracking like rifle-fire as they did so. With a sigh they turned into the stable. The gamblers swiftly and angrily played a last round and then made a dash for the animals. The plaintive lowing of the oxen took the place of the mouth-organ. From the big troughs they tossed their heads restlessly into the strange silence, shaking a long curtain of water from their mouths. Dusk fell and with it came the discordant squeaks of the sucking-pigs, for feeding-time had also arrived. Then it was time to go to bed. The day for which it was worth while dragging through the week, through life, was over. Some indeed slept undisturbed right through it. Sadly I set off home, kicking at cockchafers or at flowers or at the bricks frozen to the earth, according to the season. I was bitter, not with resignation but with annoyance as if I had been robbed of something. Without a word I mixed and carried the pig food out to the sty in the old slop-buckets from which the swill kept running out on to my heel. I cut hay and fed the calves which had been taken from their cows. With a load of hay or maize-leaves in my arms I went up to the cows who lavished their love on me instead of on their separated offspring; they licked my face and neck from both sides, however hard I tried to protect myself.

When I came out of the cowshed, it was already dark. Light filtered through the windows of one or two of the farm servants' dwellings. It began to snow or rain.

CHAPTER EIGHT

Discipline and its enforcement. Division and speed of work.
The indifference of the farm servants and the reasons for it

Up to the age of thirty to thirty-five, the people of the pusztas are generally struck on the face. After this they usually receive blows on the back of the head or the neck and then just one blow as a rule. If, however, it is necessary in certain circumstances to deliver a blow from in front, the experts say that it should be swift and disarming, decisive and conclusive, like the full stop at the end of the sentence, so that by the time the victim has recovered from it he should have got over it and feel that there is no point in appealing against his punishment. With old folk such direct disciplinary methods are used sparingly. Over the age of sixty most of them will begin to cry at the mere sight of a hand raised to threaten them—not because they are afraid, but because of the humiliation. By that time they have gained some idea of human dignity. The use of canes, sticks and riding-whips on those over twenty is to be avoided as far as possible. For while they usually take direct punishment administered by one living body to another with resignation or even with a smile, seeing in it some kind of human contact, punishment inflicted with the aid of some external appliance arouses in them incalculable reactions. Similar observations have been noted by researchers into animal psychology. Their behaviour is not determined by the magnitude of the pain they feel. Here I am reminded of a young married labourer in my youth. 'Don't hit me with a stick, sir!' he cried, his face suddenly turning scarlet, when the steward, who had already given him a fairly lengthy beating with his bare right hand, slashed at him with the thin cane he held in his left hand as if to finish off the affair. Children may be punished in any way with any available weapon.

The farm servant who is still a minor comes under the domestic discipline of his master until he is eighteen, in accordance with the final paragraph of section 3 of Law XLV of 1907. A description of this discipline is to be found in a later section, 46/b, where it appears to be almost a slip of the tongue. This states that the contract between the farm servant and his master may be terminated immediately if 'the master, a member of his family, or any agent of his empowered to act on his behalf or entrusted with supervisory duties assaults a farm servant who is not under his domestic discipline, or otherwise endangers the life and health of the servant or the servant's family by his treatment of them.' In other words, up to the age of eighteen the servant may be assaulted by his master within the meaning of the act—indeed, in accordance with its instructions. It is only after that age that his life and health may not be endangered. Obviously this is a long-established tradition. 'It can be affirmed that in none of the countries so far discovered on our planet are folk beaten so thoroughly and so *con amore* as in the land of the Magyars,' writes Ellrich, the German traveller, in his book *Die Ungarn wie Sie sind*, published in 1843. Just as long before St Gerard had been unable to sleep because of a woman singing, so Ellrich found it impossible to keep his eyes closed in the endless peace of the pusztas, owing to the screams of people who had been beaten.

Naturally these customs vary slightly from district to district. In Upper Somogy it is inadvisable to lay hands on the young folk; they are difficult to break in. In the region of O., it is best not to touch the people of the pusztas from Saturday evening until midnight on Sunday. However mild they are on

123

weekdays, they become touchy and cantankerous on Sundays and certain holidays, as for example on St Peter and St Paul and on St Stephen's day; it would be interesting to discover why. Almost everywhere they bear their punishment in silence. There is a proverb which runs 'The servant should not utter a sound until his soul leaves him.' Only the district of P. is notorious because there even the men howl 'as if they are being killed'; thus on the pusztas they are mentioned with a certain disgust and scorn, even by the other farm servants. The Calvinists are generally less amenable to discipline than the Catholics and are therefore less readily employed. They are alleged to have spread the spirit of resistance, for after the First World War there were some cases of servants striking back. Naturally they were dismissed on the spot. For a brief time after the war it was also the fashion for the injured servants to complain to the magistrates or to the gendarmerie in the nearest village. This did not last for long. The gendarmes are quite frequent guests on the puszta, but it is not the farm servants who invite them. The estate welcomes them and in many places reserves for them a permanent room which can be turned into a rest room or anything else at a moment's notice. The farm servants call it the 'confessional room'.

The people of the pusztas do not trust the representatives of the civil administration. They find it difficult to make their way to the higher courts. Apart from the obvious reasons for this, there is one which is peculiar to the pusztas. Very many large estates are at the same time administrative bodies; each forms a so-called 'theoretical commune', which is independent. Its magistrate is normally one of the farm managers. Obviously the estates were made into these 'theoretical communes' in order to relieve them of the expense of maintaining schools, of paying parish taxes and other burdens levied on the basis of income by the villages upon their inhabitants. The theoretical commune exists only on paper, hence its name, but it is independent, which means that it pays taxes to itself in accordance

124

with the ideas of the independent members of its body of representatives, who are also drawn from the farm managers. It is they who listen to the complicated affairs of the farm servants and try objectively to administer justice even when, for example, the servants have a complaint against the estate or against the magistrates themselves.

Certainly the people of the pusztas cannot be made to understand unless one speaks to them in a loud voice. The stranger has the impression that the air there is of a different density and is not subject to the ordinary laws of acoustics. Everybody seems to be a little deaf. Thoughts and feelings are communicated in shouts and repeated two or three times, chiefly from above downwards. The labourers listen to the shrill commands with impassive, stony expressions and move around as if they were coming out of a dream, like Adam when he was still half-formed of clay.

A farm servant once told me that long before, in his childhood, the lines of beaters at a hunt were set in motion by someone giving the two outermost men a hearty cuff. 'This was what made the whole lot of them understand what was wanted,' he said laughing, and produced a shout of laughter from his audience too. This was also the usual method of starting work or of speeding up the pace. The work is carried on under strict discipline. Behind every little band of three or four folk hoeing there stands an overseer with his stick; his only job is to spur them on. His work is not easy, nor is it very successful. I would not go so far as to say that he would sometimes get better results by himself if he were to turn into direct labour all the strength he squanders on perpetual encouragement, bickering and quarrelling. This excessive supervision has at least one result—the moment they realise that they are out of range of an overseer, the folk immediately stop working. The officials on the puszta allege that they have developed a sixth sense for this.

It is common knowledge that it is no use speaking to a farm servant to wake him up, nor is it the usual method. It is no accident that everybody who talks of them compares them with animals, nor is it deliberately offensive. A farm servant may spend his whole life trudging behind oxen which move at snail's pace, and the quickest way to get oxen up off the ground is with a pitchfork. He may sit from dawn to dusk on a cart drawn by buffaloes, which, as is well known, will stop and lie down in the nearest puddle unless they hear behind them the swish and crack of the whip and the driver's shouts. Such folk sooner or later take over the tempo of these animals, particularly if there is nobody else to talk to for weeks on end. The ox moves only when it is shouted at once or twice and the driver, who for his part is just as much in harness as a draught-animal, unconsciously begins to resemble the animals, whose behaviour is not entirely devoid of wisdom or of some reasonable conception of life. It is an instinctive defence, and like protective colouration it has its reasons and uses.

It is not only their allotted tasks that the farm servants perform with such tortoise-like deliberation; every movement in their private life is similar—their tone of voice, their facial expression and their mode of thought. It takes half an hour for a driver to blow his nose. The people of the pusztas are certainly lazy or rather slow to move. But even this measured slowness has an almost spectral quality. Anyone accustomed to the normal speed of work feels after watching them for a time that he must be viewing madmen, or weird machines, or a slow-motion film.

Once I was sitting on the driver's seat with old Uncle Róka. For more than two hours the oxen had been shuffling along the road out to a distant farm. I could have done the whole journey on foot in half an hour. For more than two hours we had sat silent. Suddenly the old man let out a long sigh, then after a pause he laid down his whip behind him like a clumsy conjurer performing a trick. Then he carefully felt the inner pocket of his coat as if the slightest movement of his arm caused him intense pain. It was as if he were feeling a bad heart or the scab of a wound. His pipe was not there. At this he gazed ahead for some time, wondering whether some hidden clue might give him the whereabouts of the pipe. Finally, like someone who has no choice but to take his medicine, he put his hand into the outer pocket of his coat, felt inside, and once again gaped in astonishment, leaving his hand there. Out came the pipe, and Uncle Róka nodded his head, staring at it as if he had never seen it before. Very warily he opened the lid of the bowl. It took him longer to produce the pipe-cleaner than the pipe. At last he finished cleaning it and took the pouch in his hand. All he had to do now was fill it, but the old man happened to glance up into sky. Should he wait until that cloud had passed? He handled the matches as if the matchstick in his hand were the last possible means of making fire and the fate of all mankind depended on it, all the other fires on earth having died out. The pipe kept going out because the old man would forget to pull at it. He had been a driver for forty years.

This explains everything. Daily work which begins at two or three in the morning and finishes at nine or ten in the evening is too much to endure for four years, never mind forty. It is work which never ceases, uninterrupted by a single day off or holiday, because the animals, after all, need tending at all times. Such working hours would be too much even if they were spent only in watching or guarding the crops or in some occupation where one may lean on a stick. It would drive a man gently mad if all he had to do were to sit in the same place, say, in the middle of a meadow full of flowers. But the work of the farm servants is no joke. Drawing water, carting manure, loading carts and spreading hay for ten to twelve hours a day without any consolation, excitement, joy or visible results—just try to imagine it if you have never tried it. It should be added that no rest-period is a genuine one, because one may be called out at

127

any time. The estates realise that nobody can carry on the work of a cowman for more than three or four years. Those who are not finished off by the work which goes on night and day are laid low by the air in the cowsheds, acrid with the stench of dung; from this the 'decent' cowman can get away only for a few moments at a time. Or by the time he is coughing out his lungs he may have the decency to spit blood outside the door. As I say, the estates know this well, but this does not mean that anything is done about it unless the farm manager acts on his own responsibility.

The legal relationship between master and farm servant was last clarified in Law XLV of 1907, from which I have already quoted. I shall quote further.

In order to obtain a clear picture, a distinct profile of the characters in this book—for they are so often misrepresented—let me begin with the definition of the farm servant at the beginning of this law:

'The agricultural (external) farm servant is one who undertakes by contract to fulfil personal and continuous services for at least one month on an estate for wages.

'Those who enter into a contract to perform agricultural work for a daily wage or for a fixed wage (e.g. day-labourers, jobbers, sharecroppers, etc.) are not to be regarded as agricultural farm servants.'

From the prohibitive clauses in the law (in other words, from what was prohibited in 1907), we may deduce the customs which existed before the law was enacted or which still exist where it is evaded.

It was forbidden, for example, to engage a minor under the age of twelve as a farm servant. Also forbidden was 'the type of contract whereby members of the farm servant's family are compelled to perform certain work or services without previously determined proportionate and separate payment (the so-called *robot*, villein services, usufruct, tithe, free labour,

128

etc.).' These are, of course, typical of the age of serfdom. There are also provisions for free movement.

But 'a farm servant under contract, during his agreed period of service, may not be granted a passport before he receives his certificate of termination of contract, without the agreement of his master.' This is obviously aimed against emigration. As for his place of work, 'if at the appointed time without legal cause or justification or with deliberate intent, the farm servant does not commence his service despite any action taken by his superior authorities, the master may lodge a complaint within eight days and the court of first instance must compel the servant to go to his place of service by using force.' If a clerk or a factory-worker does not turn up at work, that is that; with the hired labourer force is used. Supposing even then he refuses to work or does it negligently? 'He must be compelled to reimburse the master for the expense and damage he has caused.' The servant cannot withdraw from any agreement either by a 'unilateral restitution' of the advance payment which he may have been given when the contract was signed. On the other hand, if he does not fulfil his duties, the court not only punishes him, but compels him to carry out those duties and pay both damages in full to the master and the costs of the proceedings. In general he is responsible for everything. 'If the servant fails in his duties, the master may punish him as a member of his domestic staff; but he is not empowered to threaten the servant with fines or deduction of wages.' (In a subsequent part, however, the law stipulates threatening with deduction of wages, for it says that 'the master may, up to the value of the damage caused by the servant, withhold the wages and other allowances due to him—except for board and lodging, and fuel—if the servant has failed to discharge his liabilities or give assurance that his debts will be paid.') On the other hand, if the servant refuses to fulfil his duties or incites his fellow-servants either singly or together to do so before the termination of their contract of service, the master may dismiss him immediately without notice.

Despite all these regulations, the master must 'take care that the servant shall not be burdened with work which exceeds his strength or endangers his health and that the servant shall have sufficient time for rest at night in accordance with the general agricultural custom of the district and appropriate to the season.'

Finally the law concerns itself with working hours. Here too the well-known 'custom of the district' prevails, as does 'agricultural discipline'; in conformity with these, 'the servant is obliged to fulfil, according to the instructions of the master or his representative, all the work he has contracted to do, faithfully, exactly and to the best of his ability.' No closer definition is given.

Much more is to be found about free days and Sundays and festivals which are to be kept on pain of mortal sin.

This states that 'the master must see to it that on Sundays and on great festival days there shall be a rest-day for the farm servants. The master must arrange for the servant to be able to take part from time to time in the morning worship of his own denomination without neglect of his duties.'

Thus the servant may celebrate the Lord's day 'from time to time' if not every week, for after all 'the master may not normally demand of the servant any work on rest-days except the usual care of the animals and of their quarters—feeding, cleaning and preparation of their daily provender; and in addition the home farm must be kept in order. If, however, certain work can not be postponed because of the damage that would ensue and is so urgent that failure to perform it would involve the master in serious material loss, exceptionally the master may require the servant to fulfil such work on rest-days also, in return for separate and immediate payment in accordance with the customary daily rates in the district, and the servant is obliged to perform such work.'

But unfortunately 'the regulations in paragraph 1 do not apply to the drivers of carriages needed for personal transport, nor to those servants who have contracted to perform household duties also, nor, finally, to those who have contracted to perform such duties whose interruption is rendered impossible by the nature of the estate or by the purpose of their employment (i.e. watchmen, milkers, game-wardens, shepherds, etc.).' In other words, to put it briefly and without beating about the bush, the beneficent regulations apply to hardly anyone. 'In this regard, if there is no more favourable clause in the contract the master is obliged to arrange for a system of reliefs, so that the servant has at least one whole day's rest per month or half a day's rest per fortnight.' This is the essential point. Looking back now, I am astonished that while church sermons in my childhood dealt frequently and often very passionately with those who absented themselves from church on Sundays, I cannot remember a single occasion when the farm servants were mentioned. The pastors of the various churches obviously realised that if the estates in principle could work out such a rota-system (for after all a servant can be relieved by some means or other for half a day every fortnight), they were unable to do without them for more than half a day per fortnight.

The 'type of estate' and freedom from work on Sundays 'without neglect of duty' are described even more exactly in the so-called domestic regulations. These can be found on the back page of the contract. What the law leaves in obscurity is illuminated here. For example, it is stated:

'The servant must perform not only the work which is detailed to be performed each day, but also, without regard to Sundays or festivals, he must tend and clean the animals entrusted to his care; he must in particular clean the stables, remove the dung and spread it properly on the dunghill. These duties he must perform with his fellows every day so that they are completed by the time that the animals are put to work.'

131

'During the summer grazing season, drivers are required to guard the oxen by turns, both by day and by night, and are responsible for any damage caused by them during this time.'

'If night-watchmen are required by the estate, the servants are obliged to take their turn in this duty.'

'The servant may not leave his place of work without permission on Sundays or on festival days, and still less on working days.'

This is supplemented by the statutory law which states that 'the servant has no right to receive into his dwelling, even temporarily, any person who does not belong to his own family, if the master forbids it.'

And this is supplemented by the domestic regulations... in any way they wish. Under the printed text there is an empty space with dotted lines, awaiting the legislative inspiration of a farm manager or bailiff.

All these details I have copied out of a contract and a service-book in front of me. For the servants, on pain of punishment, must be in possession of a service-book; without this, they may not be employed, again on pain of punishment.

This service-book is a little, cloth-bound affair of 16mo size, made out in the name of one Sándor Tóth. How did it come to be among my family's rubbish? I do not know. I try hard to recall its owner, but in vain. Uncle Tóth? Uncle Sándor?— There is no echo from the past. Uncle Tóth, like so many of his fellows, has vanished without a trace. Like the flag on a sunken ship, now only this little book flutters on the surface. The most moving thing about it is its emptiness.

In the middle of the first page is written in thick letters: Servant's Service-Book. Above it are the Hungarian arms between two angels, and a 30 fillér revenue stamp. Above these is the serial number A 325628, and above this in the top left-hand corner: 80/1908. On the right, set in three lines partly printed and

132

partly handwritten, Local Authority: Veszprém. District: Enying. Parish: Szilasbalhás. Issued August 25th, 1908, by the parish council. Signed Lelkes, assistant clerk, Dániel Erdély, village mayor. Between the signatures is the seal of Szilasbalhás, dated 1817.

According to the personal description, the 'agricultural servant' Sándor Tóth was born in 1857. Religion: Roman Catholic. State: Married. Permanent residence: Szilasbalhás, Tóthi puszta. Build: Medium. Face: Oval. Eyes: Yellow-brown. Eyebrows: Brown. Nose: Regular. Mouth: Regular. Hair: Chestnut-brown, greying. Teeth: Gap-toothed. Beard: None, clean-shaven. Moustache: Brown, greying. Particular marks of recognition: None. Signature: + + +.

This description of him does not bring Uncle Tóth to my mind either. But the details—the missing teeth, the oval face which really implies a square Tartar face of mere skin and bone, the medium build which also means that he is bent, the clean-shaven beard, by which is implied a stubbly growth, and the greying moustache which droops into his mouth—all these taken separately are so spectrally familiar, that in my imagination they suddenly fuse together into a huge, supernatural form. Uncle Tóth stands before me as a gigantic sample of his type. I see his yellowish-brown eyes, which by the way are characteristic of my family also. I see the special marks of recognition which escaped the attention of the clerk—his bear-like gait, his fingers knotted and bent, for nothing can ever straighten them, a little quiver of the mouth or of the eyelid that inevitably appeared whenever Uncle Tóth was shouted at; there must be scars on his head, his two hands and feet and he stands and sits with difficulty because his back hurts him. I can see his life too, in equal detail, from the time of his birth; despite all his illnesses, curses and beatings he finally managed to stand on his own feet, one of a huge family. At that moment he began working. He guarded the crops, did some day-labouring, or acted as a beater at hunts, as the opportunity arose. When at his command the first ox stopped or started, he was engaged as a farm-boy. This was when his adult life began, at the age of eleven or twelve, when he made himself independent of his father's and mother's commands, for after all he was now bringing home his earnings, even if they were only half-pay. Was he a soldier? Yes. After that, or perhaps even before he did his military service, some girl told him that she was going to bear his child. They acquired a bed—this was the beginning of their family life—and he got full wages. The child arrived and others followed, almost every year. By the time the last one was born, those of his first children who had not died of disease had become farm-boys and answered him back. Then they were scattered in all directions. He himself grew too old to serve any more. Then he died. If he did not die, thus becoming an exception to the rule, he became an indoor servant, spreading hay and sweeping out the stables. When the brush fell from his hands as the whip had done before, then with a great many others he too should have died. And if he did not die even now? Then they made him a watchman in the cornfields, but once again on half-pay, as if to warn him not to expect too much, for by now even his children had died. Once again for a time he guarded the crop. Then one All Saints' Day, at the hirings, his name was called out. 'Well, Tóth, have you anywhere to go?' asked the bailiff. 'No, sir, I haven't.' 'All right, you may still sleep in the stables.' Where the vagabonds sleep. Now he got no pay, but the wives of the farm servants would offer him a bowl of soup or so. Then all of a sudden he went off after the other vagabonds, if he did not die in the meantime. His service-book remained behind in the office; he was ashamed to ask for it.

On page 4 of the service-book is the complete text of the law I have mentioned. On page 21 can be found Law XVI of 1900, concerning 'financial aid for agricultural workers and servants,' then on page 33 the supplementary law, XIV of 1902, which gives exact details of the scheme; this never came into force. Then follow the spaces for the places and dates of service, and the names of the masters served. Not one of them is filled in. Sándor Tóth served in one place all his life.

Now we may imagine more or less what the circumstances of his service were. Only more or less, because just as the law concerning financial aid for sick servants never came into force, so only one or two of the other laws were able to survive the journey from the statute-book to reality, from the fine words of the lawgivers to the point where the steward commands work to be speeded up without lifting his hand. And to the point where Sándor Tóth does not regard what is cast up in front of him during the day's carting as the special providence of God.

They say that all this cannot be changed. It cannot be changed owing to the peculiar climate of Hungary and its even more peculiar agricultural methods. And perhaps because of the position of the stars. For it can be done, for example, in Denmark, in France, in Italy, in the Scandinavian Peninsula and indeed in Austria too, not to list practically every country in Europe.

This, however, the people of the pusztas do not know. They know only their own situation and try to adapt themselves to it. Even here they are dependent upon their own traditions and inventiveness. They are led by their discretion to believe that they must spare their strength if they want to live. And they do want to live.

It happens occasionally that a bankrupt village smallholder enters service as a farm servant. Scarcely any of them stay in one place; they cannot bear their new job. At first they work at the same pace as they did at home. Two or three months later they prod their back and chest in horror. They try to fit into the work-rhythm of the puszta, but only about one in ten succeeds. And sooner or later they are carried off the puszta either by illness or by the farm servants themselves.

135

True, they carry their thrift to excess, and their inventive capacity is exhaustless. It is certain that with better division of labour and different treatment things would go better not only for the landowning class, whose interests are not primarily the concern of the author, for they exceed his knowledge and the limits of this book, but also for national productivity, which would undoubtedly show better results. It is very probable that the farm servants would be more diligent if they worked on their own land or for themselves in some way or other.

No, it cannot be stated that the landlord's happiness fills them with enthusiasm. They are well aware that they are at least behaving as if they knew what they have been trained to do, and heaven forbid that they should lift a finger to do anything more. Uncle Sutka, the Alsómajor driver, was dismissed for the following episode; I happened to witness the final scene.

A butcher in one of the neighbouring villages bought from the estate a magnificent fat pig. The enormous animal was too fat to move, and so Uncle Sutka was commissioned to cart it to the village. In due course he arrived with it at the butcher's yard. There it transpired that the pig had died on the way; it was so fat that it had been stifled by the shaking of the cart. Of course the butcher refused delivery. It was a big loss and the estate manager could not choke back his anger. 'Why ever didn't you stick it with your knife?' he screamed at Uncle Sutka. 'Why didn't you let its blood when you saw that it was stifled? Hadn't you got a knife with you?' 'Yes, I had a knife,' faltered Uncle Sutka at length. The estate manager swallowed hard. 'Well, if the pig had been yours, would you have let it die like that? Would you?' 'No, I'd have killed it,' he admitted after a long pause. 'Well then...' shouted the manager, but could not find any words to say. He turned purple and dashed into the inner room; there he burst out, obviously to heaven, 'He's filched eighty pengős from his lordship's pocket!' Only then did he return, puffing and panting as if he had forgotten something in his haste, and kicked Uncle Sutka in the rump. I watched the stiff, unemotional face of the driver. It was devoid of expression and showed no understanding whatever of the simple problem; it was so lacking in interest or endeavour that he might have been standing in front of a blackboard full of mathematical symbols at the university. It was obvious that faced with the same situation again, he would act in the same way. It never crossed his mind that he might have some inkling of the problem. It simply had nothing to do with him. In the depths of his soul he was in revolt—unconscious revolt, but just because of this all the more stubborn and determined.

It is difficult to defend oneself against their indifference and 'couldn't care less' attitude, all the more so since they display rare ingenuity and cunning in slowing the pace of work. 'Only their eyes move, not their hands,' their betters are wont to say of them, and they are right. They search for any little hole through which they may creep to avoid work. They have eagle eyes—of which use was made during the war. A member of my family who had been an officer told me that there was no need to explain to them how to find cover; they would hide behind a molehill, and went on patrol with the invisibility of ghosts. For three days they sat motionless in a crater. They were wide awake all the time and bore it patiently. 'That's what they had been doing all their lives.'

The unexpected also helps them. Or is it that they unconsciously help on the unexpected? Who would imagine, for example—and even if he did, who could prove that it happened by deliberate human intent—that of the carts full of corn lumbering to the distant railway station it was most often the first or second that broke its axle and never the last? Did it happen on purpose? It did not; the drivers never did deliberate damage. It was not they, but the unexpected, perhaps the will of God, that put the faulty waggon at the head of the procession, and now it would lie idle there in the mud for half a day. For though the drivers slither off the carts and scratch their heads, spending hours in deliberating what to do and where to send for help, they can never think out any sensible plan themselves. They stand and wait, and this is the best they can do, for if they unload the sacks of corn from the cart, they are quite certain to dump them in the mud.

There is no malice aforethought. Nor is there on the part of the farm manager who starts shouting from a distance as he arrives somewhere, pouring out curses and gesticulating to the point of apoplexy.

CHAPTER NINE

The people of the puszta among themselves. Their colloquial language. Brawls. Presents. Opportunities for enjoyment

Abuse is borne by the farm servants with Asiatic indifference. 'I'd only like to know who there is for that poor ox to curse,' said a driver to me one day, shaking his head in a moment of sudden emotion after a tremendous dressing-down. For even abuse has its own well-defined hierarchy. The landlord abuses the estate manager, he abuses his assistants, they abuse the bailiff, he abuses the overseer, and the overseer the servants. After them there are only the children and oxen left. 'Perhaps he curses the cart,' added the driver, 'and the cart curses the wood. And that curses the Lord God Almighty who created this...' and without noticing it he slipped back into the usual rut after his momentary weakness.

When villagers meet one another, the demands of etiquette are as rigid and complicated as in any royal court. Emotions which are hard to express or embarrassing things to say— whether a guest is welcome, for example, or whether a lad can pin his hopes on the girl he admires—are communicated not in words but with slight movements, which may vary not only from village to village but even in different parts of the same village. To make it more difficult, they change almost every year. Who takes the visitor's hat, the master of the house, his wife or his daughter? And where is it put, on the chest, on the bed? The visitor learns more in a moment than he could be told in six months by mere words. In this maze, of course, a stranger cannot find his way in a lifetime. I spent one of my school holidays at B., and often visited the family next door to my relatives there. On my way out I usually shook hands in turn with them all, and on one occasion with the unmarried daughter of the house also. She was somewhat reluctant to take my hand and later I seemed to remember that she had blushed as she did so. That night I heard that her father had given her a merciless beating the moment I left.

If a girl offers her hand to a boy it means that she admits they have an affair and is not ashamed to admit it either. Or rather it has this implication only when they shake hands in front of relations. And it only has this meaning at the top end of the village, and never at the bottom end. There it obviously has some other connotation.

There is no such formality among the people of the pusztas. They live side by side all day and all night too, and are in such close contact with each other that they hardly bother about saying 'Good day'. If they do greet each other, they do not express a wish but make some direct objective statement. 'It's fresh,' they say early in the morning, to which the reply is 'Yes, it is.' To someone approaching with a hoe, they say 'Is it all done?' or 'Is there any left to do?' or 'Is there much still to do?'. And the reply, in the case of a man, is 'yes, there's some left,' to which is added any swear-word he cares to use.

Greetings are used only when one enters or leaves a house. On the way in one says 'Good day' and the reply is 'Good day.' On the way out they say 'God bless you' and the reply is the same. They do not really know any other forms of greeting. Once I parted from Aunt Szabó saying, 'Well, Aunt Szabó, see you again soon!' Aunt Szabó blinked in confusion. 'And to you too, my dear,' she said, blushing.

Social contacts are all the more intimate because in the little community of the puszta naturally almost everybody is related.

To the young folk every old man is at the very least 'God-father'. I had something like twenty-five of them, for this was

140

the way I addressed not only my parents' godfathers, but those of my brothers, sisters and cousins too. This was also the way to address one's sponsor at confirmation; he was even closer than a real godfather, because as one's spiritual guardian he had to be invited later to perform all the duties of a best man.

This permanent and intimate contact with each other and with their sufferings makes them all the more irritable. They find it difficult to put up with each other—it is as if they are for ever seeing a reflection of themselves. The young people live peacefully with each other; the older ones quarrel. They grumble, grow envious and snipe at each other; they themselves would be the first to register astonishment if someone could make them realise that despite all this they stick together closely. They live together like a pack of wolves, they squabble from time to time, and when they are in dire need or see a chance of booty they grab at each other's throats, but for all that they will not leave each other in the lurch.

The stranger is astonished at the tone of the puszta folk in their casual conversation. In the depths of their being, these peaceful and servile folk use coarse swear-words even to express flattery and good wishes. They have a scale of curses to communicate all the delicate shades of meaning which the peasants express with their complicated customs. How rich and varied is this scale! 'May the thunderbolt strike not you, but only a yard away from you!' This, for example, is indeed a curse, but not an offensive one. By an odd twist of meaning, 'The devil take the bride at your wedding-party!' counts as something of a compliment to a young girl. Or the phrase to incite someone to work: 'Don't hang your head like a sunflower!' verge on the familiar. Warnings which are emphasised by using similes are frequently phrased in this way because the simile sounds good, such as 'Don't be missing, like a good tip!' This has the effect of a friendly pat and causes amusement. Unfortunately there are far better, more ingenious and tougher expressions than

141

this. In this sphere the people of the pusztas display rare inventiveness.

We might well expect folk to be able to express their emotions most exactly when they reach the depths of emotion and are seized by an almost lyrical passion. Strange to say, this is not so. The tongue of the exuberant lover begins to falter and the purer his passion, the more certain he is to stutter out the one well-worn cliché that has been used by humankind since the first couple on earth. In most languages one finds just one or two dull set phrases to express anger and annoyance. The vocabulary of certain nations in this respect is simply deplorable. The most varied causes of wrath produce the same three or four words quite automatically from folk of the most diverse education. This is not true of the people of the pusztas. Must this too be ascribed to an inherent lyrical sense in them?

It was such curses as these which in my childhood first gripped my so-called artistic imagination and perhaps instructed it too. I marvelled at the apt observations and bold similes and at that truly artistic attribute which is termed imagery in poetical theory. I was well prepared in advance for a philosophical dissertation on the psychology of swearing.

The rich piling-up of adjectives and their sudden release and the rhythm of their complex sentences suggest the existence of a regular method of construction and rhythmical scheme. Their improvisation, which undoubtedly demands an exceptional richness of thought and inherited inspiration which is ready at all times, calls to mind the poetry of our linguistic relatives, the Voguls. The chief characteristic of their verse is improvisation, the singer takes his own feelings or an adventure, a journey or a bear-hunt and turns it directly into song, keeping the general rules of parallelism and refrain-construction. The sometimes equally lengthy but never monotonous curses of the puszta folk may be compared with the artistic expression of the Voguls and can certainly be taken as a spiritual proof of their relationship.

I find it difficult to bear the cursing of educated folk, because I feel it to be arrogant and a mark of their incompetence. I have often been brought up with a start by that of the puszta folk. I have even discovered humour in it. There is no doubt that here exceptional artistic ability has overflowed its proper channel and stagnated in the slough of obscenity, this is one of the forms of folk-poetry. Or is it the bastard remnant of some primeval religious sentiment? Is it part of the faith of a despairing people, nurturing nothing but anger against heaven? They all find it difficult to pray, but can swear by every saint in the church's calendar on the spur of the moment.

What fearful stifled emotion opens its floodgates in these curses? What tension is there in the spirit which can give voice only in extremity, using endearments of Asiatic sweetness and magical expressions of Asiatic ferocity? Lovers will talk of violas, pearls and doves and then go on to describe ways of destruction which it is impossible to write down. What mixture is this, the perfume of flowers and the stench of rotting corpses? They drink it in with their mothers' milk.

For a long time I consoled myself with the thought that all this showed the decay of the language and not of the soul, that they simply used different words to express ideas. When the servant's wife, instead of saying a quiet and appropriate 'Now, now!' to a child, shrieked 'Damn your eyes!' or 'The devil eat your inside out!', I thought this was merely a different way of saying it. But the flush of anger which rushes to the woman's face and the blow she aims at the child prove that the curses have deep roots and come from the heart. And what conclusion am I to reach when I recollect that every word and every sentence is mixed with swearing; every thought is preceded by a curse spat out by the brain like a special invocation, and when the mind pauses for a moment, the gap left in their speech is automatically filled with swear-words? In the presence of their superiors, they observe a limit of sorts. When they feel at home with each other, they show it with a pithy phrase or two. With their first free breath they hurl a curse into the world. What suicidal instinct is it that makes them call down on each others' heads —and so on their own too—the most varied kinds of painful death from morning till evening, shouting at the tops of their voices, their faces flushed, and quivering with emotion? They are like souls possessed. Sometimes I try to imagine the God who must dwell in their souls at such moments, the Being whose face might be depicted in the words addressed to Him. It is not the gentle face of the Nazarene, but that of some Chinese idol, twisted into a terrifying grin.

It is not only curses received from above that are handed on down the line, but also blows. There are exact regulations concerning beatings too. Up to a certain age parents beat their children, then there is a brief pause. When this is over, the situation is reversed and the children beat their parents. This also is an ancient tradition. There was a famous anecdote about Uncle Pálinkás, an old acquaintance of our family. His son used to drag him by the hair through the common room and kitchen, and when they reached the doorway of the servants' quarters, Uncle Pálinkás would shout, 'Let me go here, son, this is as far as I dragged my father!'

In the depths of their being, the people of the pusztas are peace-loving, indeed gentle. If some exceptional external event —a tragic death, a new fur hat, a good drink of wine—made them forget their lot and raised them to a human level, they would go up to each other with smiles and chat happily. They consoled, encouraged and heaped heartfelt good wishes upon each other; they stammered awkwardly, tears filled their eyes, and they embraced one another. Occasionally they played ribald practical jokes on each other, but even here so much goodness of heart and disguised affection lay hidden that in the end

144

both joker and victim would be wiping their eyes, not from emotion, but from the atmosphere which, like a tear-bomb, the original good deed had created. But when could they become human?

As far as I can recall, it was not laughter like this, but imprecations and squabbles which caused a stir in the ordinary mood of the puszta. At Rácegres it seemed as if the whole year were one long quarrel. There was a lot of bickering in the neighbouring district too. But perhaps this is due to the partiality of the memory, which has a peculiar instinct for preserving the bad side of things. I know of districts where for months on end the servants do not lay hands on each other. Tolna and Somogy, however, are proverbially notorious for their quarrelling as if the folk there were driven mad by some secret, sirocco-like wind... This is not the cause. In Tolna the German villages built next to the Hungarian ones are strikingly different, not only because they are neat and comparatively affluent, but also because there is peace and quiet there. It is the poor, in other words the Hungarians, who usually squabble. For on the pusztas almost everywhere I found pure Hungarians, even in those parts of Transdanubia where national minorities predominate. Did they quarrel very much? It all depended. Serious quarrels were relatively rare, hardly more frequent than in a slum tenement. But there were any number of minor squabbles, which they themselves did not regard as fights or brawls. Nor did they regard the daily, that is permanent, disciplinary actions as such.

The women would caress and fondle their children, then suddenly strike them such a blow with whatever they happened to seize in their hand that one thought, 'Well, that child isn't going to move for some time.' Often they did not move. Then the mother would burst into loud wailing and snatch up the child, running to and fro with it in despair. Sometimes she would dash straight to the village to have the bone set. The children knew how quick their parents could be with their hands and at the first movement would take to their heels. But anger, once roused, is just as thirsty for fulfilment as love. One of the frequent sights and delights of the puszta was that of an angry-faced mother cursing and chasing her agile offspring as he circled around, turning from time to time like Hector to reply to the stream of curses. The people of the pusztas, who were no more mercifully inclined towards their own children, would always take the side of the pursued on these occasions. 'Take it easy, Rozi,' they would say, grasping the wildly panting woman, 'after all, he's only a child.' From the group trying to calm her down, the mother would shake her fist at the fugitive. 'Just you stop, you'll come back when you're hungry!' He did too, but by that time the danger and the memory of the crime had usually faded away with the anger itself. No mother ever gave her child a deliberate beating to correct him.

On the contrary she would defend him blindly, whatever the circumstances. Wrangling among the women generally arose from children's quarrels. The mother of an infant thrashed while playing would set out with sharpened claws to gain retribution, even if it was obviously her child who had been in the wrong. This surprised me. If we ever fell foul of anybody, we could be quite certain of getting into trouble at home as well. The husbands usually hit their wives with a strap, and for the wives self-defence was forbidden by propriety. Later they used the leg of a top-boot, following the fashion set by a driver from Somogy. It hurts, produces a suitable noise, but does not break any bones.

The men, the farm servants, lifted their hands to strike each other only when they were by themselves and never in the presence of the gentry.

What made them attack each other? Mere trifles, as is usual wherever there is tension. Insults from above could not be repaid by a sound or a single flutter of the eyelid, but they made them peppery and liable to explode without warning. They would pocket the most shameful abuse from one another and smile at it, then suddenly at the most innocent allusion a blow would send someone's hat skimming off his head, knives would flash, and shaky-legged old men would run to the cart-shed for a yoke-pin. Quarrels spread like wildfire in a second. Perhaps this is why they came to an end so quickly, losing their heat in a second too. A swine-herd in the pigsties saw red and let out a shout, and the next moment battle was joined in the ox-stables, a wild ululation rose from the women in the servants' dwellings, and perhaps even the drivers out in the fields exchanged a swift couple of blows. But by the time the overseers had run out, order was restored; the only evidence of what had taken place was a body or two writhing on the ground and on them a wound spouting blood. Naturally nobody ever owned up to the deed. By then unity prevailed once more, more firmly than before.

When the women came to blows, the men looked on smiling. They rarely intervened and if they did, it was merely to maintain discipline. Each man dealt with his own wife either by words or with his hands, as the occasion demanded. They never defended them.

The women on the other hand defended their husbands like tigresses. They hurled themselves resolutely among the fighters. They were not allowed to strike, but they parried the blows. If an unmarried girl went to anybody's defence, it was an open admission that they were having an affair.

The most complicated emotions were resolved in an instant at the flash of knives. The wife of one of the Karikás boys was seduced by a cowman from Döbrönte and he wanted to marry her. The husband did not have much to say against it and even entertained the seducer when he came to fetch his wife. They had supper together. The cowman had brought wine and so they drank as if to set the seal upon the affair. The wife had already packed her belongings when the two men suddenly came to blows, perhaps not over her at all. With grim fury Helena rose to defend her husband and though she was caught by the first real blow, she held on and seized the seducer's arm while her husband succeeded in giving him a good thrashing. They

147

both hurled the dazed lover through the doorway. 'It was then I realised the one I loved,' said the woman later to the farm servants who were making fun of the affair.

Only rarely did they report each other or make complaints. There was no point in searching for 'justice', for who could have delivered justice in their complicated affairs? Once the inhabitants of two farm servants' blocks fought each other all afternoon—and all because of a cat, or its kittens, or rather because its dead kittens had been scattered around—nobody knew exactly why. On another occasion a woman had her head broken, not by the person she was fighting, but by a third woman who had nothing to do with the quarrel; she happened to pass that way and kicked the victim who was already on the ground in the head.

Two women came to blows outside Mrs Hajas's kitchen. Mrs Hajas dashed out and threw a pail of water over them. She said it was to calm them down, but later events proved that it was merely to give her the right to interfere.

Another squabble took place in one of the common dwellings, where two women started to fight. The third occupant, young Mrs Beszédes, grabbed some saucepan-lids and banged them together to encourage the fighters until they hit her on the nose.

They used the threat of a complaint to scare each other. They called it 'standing someone on the floor', an expression whose origin was that the only floor the servants could stand on was in the manager's office. But it was very rare for anybody to take a complaint as high as the farm officials, for even if he did, he would usually make a muddle of what he wanted to say and at the end of the case, which could never be thoroughly investigated, he would receive just as much of a dressing-down as the accused. 'You might just as well live in peace; haven't you enough trouble as it is?' Such was the standard formula delivered from above which this time declared the full truth. Even the most sympathetic official had to say this sooner or later.

148

For if he displayed the slightest indulgence, and if he bothered himself about the private affairs of the servants, he opened the floodgates of complaint and suffering day and night. He never had a moment to himself from then on. Either a new world had to be built or he had to get used to the existing one. The world continued as it was.

The servants would quarrel and then suddenly forget all about it. They knew none of the blood feuds of the southern countries, but neither did they know the tearful reconciliation scenes of the northern Slavs. One Sunday the younger Tóth boy hit one of the Szabó boys on the head so hard that he had to be led home by the hand. A week later the bailiff saw both of them in the same band of gamblers. 'Aren't you still angry with one another, then?' he asked in astonishment. 'Not now,' said Tóth. 'It's all over now,' said young Szabó, pointing at his head.

There were close contacts between different pusztas too. The farm servants shied away from the peasants, but like members of the same animal-family scented their relationship from some distance away and decided with infallible certainty how each person should be addressed. Visitors from one puszta to another were rare; as a rule they only arrived when there was some carting to be done. The old folk for years on end saw each other only at the market, if they had anything to drive there. The young folk met at church festivals. And they brawled.

Gereben Vas, a popular nineteenth-century novelist, for example, who grew up at Fürged, one of the neighbouring pusztas, observes of the national festivals at Ozora that in his childhood they were the traditional celebrations of bloodshed. The youths who had made enemies during the year either in person or through gossip made this the date of reckoning. After making their way there through the night they went to mass, met together and after introducing themselves briefly, beat each other to death. This custom was still flourishing in my childhood, with the difference that then the fighting began after the litany and continued in a series of scenes, so to speak.

While the drivers were killing each other, the shepherds leaned on their sticks in front of the inn and waited their turn. They were calm and looked around as if they knew they could not escape their fate. They gave the appearance of wanting not to fight, but just to receive a blow, bleed to death and die. A recruit from K. happened to be there on leave, and intoxicated by the extraterritorial rights imparted by his uniform and side-arms, threw his bayonet on to the floor of the bar, saying that he would shoot anybody who dared to touch it. He shot four lads one after the other before he was struck down from behind with a soda siphon. The gendarmes usually intervene in such fights only at the end, when the participants have worn each other out. If they appeared any earlier, the combatants would come to terms in a flash and indeed league themselves against the new enemy. One Easter Saturday in Ozora the drunken landless peasants and farm servants crucified a gendarme on the door of the inn, wreaking on him all the cruelty they had just heard mentioned in the sermon on the death of Christ. Later half the village gave evidence at the inquiry. Half the village had watched the terrible scene.

There may yet be some fashionable psychological explanation of all this. But who can solve the mystery of the death of young Szappanos? He was ploughing with his companions in the fields at Konda one day when there happened to be a shoot. One of the guns, a friendly townsman out on his own, got into conversation with them and then showed them his Winchester shotgun, as they were interested in its new design. He even explained how it worked and put it into the hands of a young labourer called Pál Rátki. 'Is it loaded, sir?' he asked with a grateful smile, then raised it to his cheek and still smiling happily took aim at the younger Szappanos, his best friend (the ensuing investigation confirmed that he was indeed his best friend); then cheerfully, as if all he wanted to do was to bring him into the game as well, he shot his head to pieces from three paces away, the gun being loaded with grapeshot.

Poor folk everywhere like to give presents to their masters, and the farm servants, naturally, are no exception. They jealously guarded their belongings from each other and hung grimly on to articles which they themselves could not possibly use. To their betters they would gladly offer their dearest family relics. For years I pestered my grandfather's younger brother for a wonderful wooden money-box inlaid with lead, which he himself had once made. It was, I thought, a suitable repository for my mineral collection. He would not give it to me. He gave it at the first hint to the estate manager. He cleaned it out, repaired it and himself took it up to the manor-house. He had tears in his eyes when he returned; the only thing that upset him slightly was that the estate manager had asked how much he owed him for it. He owed him nothing. Uncle István, like every farm servant, like every poor man, liked to give free presents to the rich. Was it in the hope of some distant recompense, perhaps, or to strengthen his own position, to win favour?... The estate manager did not live on the puszta; he was on a short stay there. The poor are unselfish in their giving; the more important the person they can surprise, the more gladly they do it. When a pig was killed, the richest and tastiest morsels always went up to the manor-house. They did not expect thanks for them, indeed they shrank from it. Perhaps it fulfilled a spiritual need, like a sacrifice offered to the gods. Or was it one form of the secret revolt of the conscience? Did they want to show that they were just as much human beings as the gentry? With three years of hard work the swineherd at Ike braided a wonderful, thick watch-chain out of black and white horsehair; it was about a yard long, and he was determined by hook or by crook to present it to the king. The mere mechanics of the procedure —the writing of the accompanying letter—cost him five forints.

But they also gave each other a great deal of pleasure, without being conscious of it. What was fine and humane in their contacts, and even more, what was sometimes touchingly unselfish, had almost without exception been made so by some

151

old tradition, but what tradition? From the fragments that still existed, one might have assumed that it belonged to a long-disappeared, happy paradise, when men still loved each other. Not only when pigs were killed were dishes covered with cloths sent hither and thither. It was proper to send something to women in confinement also. It was not generosity or consideration, but propriety—this is the correct word—that made them do it, for on such occasions even hostile families would send gifts to one another. They even pressed them on women who were well looked-after and had no need of their help; here quite frequently the food would simply go bad.

My little sister would send me with some such present of food almost every week, or when she was baking plain cake or fried dough, to one or other of her girl-friends. This method of swearing eternal friendship was by then restricted to girls, but the name of the custom and the poem I had to gabble before I fluttered the cloth aside prove that it was once common among men or even families. The crowning of the Whitsun Queen was another custom which survived only among the children—it was still performed at Rácegres. Four older girls held a sheet over a younger one as they went singing from house to house. At the end of their song, the four girls ran to the middle, snatched up the little girl in the sheet and then they ate whatever they were given.

Even entertainments had their own prescribed customs. Most of the amusing scenes were sparked off by long-forgotten religious practice, though they appeared to be thought up on the spur of the moment. As they wearily plodded homeward, the drivers would begin to tease each other and shove, just when the onlooker might have expected the first blow to fall, they would suddenly burst out laughing, join in quick repartee and fire off catch-questions. These too followed a regular pattern, as the experienced listener might have discovered.

Laughter, as well as mourning and bloodshed, had its own traditional festivals. On the first spring day everybody had to smile and whistle. Everybody was prepared for this day, and on the first sunny morning whistling and singing echoed everywhere, as if by magic. There were days when half the puszta dressed up as animals or devils, with fur caps and cloaks turned inside out, just for a good laugh. At other times they dressed up as ghosts, with sheets and candles stuck in scooped-out pumpkins, to frighten folk. We laughed and trembled as ancestral custom demanded.

The lads and youths and sometimes even the older folk also turned their occasional big feasts into a kind of mass entertainment, by improvising verse, dancing and cutting capers, like the Attic Greeks at their goat-festivals. They would act whole scenes which made no kind of sense whatsoever; why did the puszta roar with laughter as if they were having an outing? Where there was a pig-killing, the family would put in the window a beautifully carved 'fork'; it was a small branch stripped of its bark, with the new twigs on each side cut down to form spikes. On these they would spear pieces of bacon, sausage and crackling. When there was a wedding-breakfast, the 'outsiders'—the youths who had not been invited in— would likewise gather outside the window, from there they would ask for and get something good to eat if their witty remarks deserved the critical appreciation of the bridal party, which was ready for the scene and had its ripostes prepared in advance. When the children performed the traditional scenes on St Lucy's Day and Twelfth Night, they had to adapt themselves to different situations and demands in every kitchen, according to the audience there; such were the rules of the puszta *commedia dell'arte*. On Christmas Eve the whip-lashers ushered in the feast with a positive barrage of crackling fire, and from noon onwards the puszta re-echoed to the noise like a battlefield.

In May the maypole was danced out. It was a strong, slender poplar, with all the branches stripped from its long trunk except for a little foliage left at the very top, about the size of

153

an umbrella. Once they used to set up a maypole outside each house where there was an unmarried girl; later one had to do for the whole puszta. Originally this was set up outside the farm manager's house, but after the wife of one of them had forbidden this owing to the appalling noise, another place was found for it. They rammed it into the ground outside the ox-stables, this being the next place of honour. Custom demanded that it should be set up during the night of the first of May.

For weeks the maypole stood in all its glory in front of the stables. It was brought down on Whit Saturday, when its real decoration began. Now every unmarried girl had to tie a ribbon to it. It was also the duty of every craftsman on the puszta to put something on it. The cooper made a little wooden tub about the size of one's hand, the smith a horse-shoe decorated with brass, the vinedresser a raffia garland, the shepherds each gave a piece of cheese. The farm officials would contribute a bottle of wine or two, if they happened to be in a good mood. Then the tree was set up again. We were burning with excitement. After lunch on Whit Monday the festival began. Those who possessed zithers and mouth-organs formed themselves into a band. They played just one overture, the latest hit-tune, and they had to play it really well. Then came the tree-climbing. Everybody except the children had the right to climb to the top of the tree and bring down whatever he wanted, but only one article, of course. It was a noble trial of strength for the young men, or rather for those who had a pair of top-boots, for these were compulsory. What an entertainment that was! The audience grew noisy. 'Try harder, Sanyi!' they shouted, 'Get down to it!' Here I quote only those cries of encouragement which can be quoted. Sanyi got half way up and slipped down again. 'Poor old chap,' they said, and their enthusiasm turned to mockery and then to witty improvisation, for this was also a contest of wit. In the end somebody reached the top of the tree and flopped down again with the bottle of wine—if it really was wine in the bottle, for in one or two of them the yellowish liquid resembled wine only in colour. This was the kind of trick played by the folk in the manor-house to increase the general amusement. Nor was it without effect. The farm servants, fleeing from the victim who tried to spray them with its contents, had a good laugh at the expense of their comrades. When all the objects had been brought down from the tree, the dance began. It lasted until they began to fight each other.

CHAPTER TEN

Subsistence on the pusztas. Income. Payment in kind.
A farm servant's tenement

Poverty flooded over to us from Fejér county, in persistent and irresistible waves. Long ago, my maternal grandmother had undertaken to bring up the daughter of a distant relative of hers in addition to her own family. The arrangement had been made before the girl was born, and even the christening was my grandmother's concern. This girl, my Aunt Malvi, following her own desires, fell in love with a fine figure of a corporal, a regular soldier by the name of Dániel Szerentsés, and married him. The good-looking corporal had turned up on the puszta with some official commission which was buying up horses for the army, and in the heat of his passion threw up his military career to please my aunt. Aunt Malvi woke to reality when he was stripped of his magnificent uniform; in civilian life her husband was simply a driver.

She stuck to him heroically. With head erect and the pride of a martyr, she plunged smiling into the appalling world of the Szerentséses. After the first impact she identified herself completely with it, as if she had bathed in some fairy-tale magic pool. All the members of my mother's family spoke softly; after one month, Aunt Malvi shouted, put her hands on her hips and swore like a trooper, threatening to throw everything out of the house. Her children were all twins. In three or four instalments she brought six children into the world, of whom one died regularly every year, so that only two of them ever reached the age of ten. At the end of the fourth year of their married life, the good-looking driver also died, of tuberculosis. Even up to this time, Malvi had shared board and lodging with her father-in-law and his family—he was also a driver. Now she stayed on there, living on their kindness, a fact which they never let her forget.

These Szerentséses streamed into the world from the estate of L., near Vajda. There were hordes of them, and they enthusiastically maintained relations not only with us, but with my father's family too, obstinately withstanding the indifference and icy glances they received there. After tramping the whole night, ancient ladies of a hundred or so would shuffle into our house and foist themselves on us for two or three days, the Lord alone knew why. It was not for food, because they hardly ate a thing. 'A little whey will do me nicely, my dear,' they would whine in a soft, unassuming voice—like that of a decrepit bird, if it could speak. It was no use for my mother to offer them food, getting redder with annoyance all the time, they would dip bread into the whey and suck at it, for at home this was the usual food for old women. Not for the world would they ever sleep in our room. 'What? Make this beautiful room stink?' (A home-made rag-carpet held the place of honour in it.) 'What, me, in this lovely home?' one of them said once; I remember it because my father afterwards told the story often, punctuating it with laughter. It was one of his favourite tales when they settled down to tell stories after the evening meal. He saw in it some inner refinement. 'Well, as far as that goes, Aunt Teca was right, because she was quite smelly.' This was the point of the story. But he never annoyed the old women; perhaps he even rather liked them. My father usually slept in the kitchen, so we made up a bed for the old ladies in the loft or in the porch. In the daytime they just sat and listened, with a slightly offended look as if they expected to be asked something. They had to be offered everything in the house from the baking-shovel to the cock until it came

157

out what they really wanted. 'Well then, I'll just take this little pair of boots for our Imre, if you're going to throw them out anyway.' Aunt Teca, or Rozi or Kati would sigh. Then seizing the basket which had been waiting in the corner or on the peg, its mouth wide open, she would arrange in it the pair of boots or shirt or pastry-board and be gone in a moment. Sometimes the men would make the journey of forty kilometres or so, all for a forint. Some of them would come out with their request only on their third visit. These we succeeded in persuading to sleep in the stables, for they were just as self-effacing. Such were the Szerentséses, 'the famous booters', said my father in amusement; for once he happened to catch sight of one of them with his boots slung over his shoulders (this being the usual custom in Hungary) walking barefoot through the fields in our direction; it was only at the end of the puszta, by the ox-stables, that he put them on.

A constant stream of them, men, women and children alike, made its way to us, some in boots, some barefoot, some in shoes, some in carpet-slippers. Aunt Malvi was the channel through which they might break away from the stifling, seething atmosphere of poverty. First of all, naturally, they besieged grandmother. She nobly held the breach, but not even she could stem the flood. She did not withhold her pelican-like affection from Aunt Malvi, whose strange transformation she regarded as an illness which unfortunately could not be cured. In any case she always paid most attention to the member of her family who was in the greatest trouble, and perhaps also lavished most love upon her. With the eagle-eyes of a referee, she determined the scale of trials and troubles that beset her children in all their rich variety. Unfortunately she could do nothing to help Aunt Malvi, whose own troubles were mixed with those of the Szerentsés family, and these not even God himself could have cured. Without a moment's rest, Aunt Malvi would take to her bed, have children and bury them. Week after week the messengers came from Ürgepuszta and, sighing, took back fat, flour and particularly honey which, according to the evil tongues in the family, was gobbled up on the way back, for we knew that Aunt Malvi, for example, could not bear honey. 'Now she'd just love some of that,' whimpered the messenger, well knowing that if she were asked, grandmother would even take the shed roof to pieces for them. We invited her again and again, but it was no use; Aunt Malvi never returned among us. She accepted the fate of the Szerentsés family even after the death of her husband and children. She took their side and praised them; I think she slowly came to detest us. 'It's easy enough,' she once said, 'for those who have a hot meal every day.' Sometimes grandmother would put on her head the big bowl and, with a basket in each hand, set out to strangle the hydra in its own den. I liked to go with her, because at Dorog we crossed the railway, and grandmother would sit there with me for hours so that I could see a train. All of a sudden a gentle humming could be heard in the distance. The train appeared suddenly in the fresh green valley at the foot of the tree-clad hills. We stood up on the side of the bank, uncertain whether to stay or to run away until in the end we went back a step or two, holding each other's hand tightly. I planted my feet firmly apart. Grandmother pulled her headscarf down over her nose but I held up my head and enjoyed every minute of the hellish rumbling, the wild magic of the rushing wind, the dense, stifling smoke, and the quaking that shook earth and sky. My face was licked by scalding steam that cooled immediately—the tongue of the devil. I shut my eyes and drank in a deep draught of the sulphurous smoke. By now the train was whistling far away in the distance; I could just see its tail as it was sucked in between the next two hills like a worm disappearing into a duck's bill. It was such a tremendous experience that my memory hardly dares to recall it now. If Leviathan were suddenly to appear to me in the heavens as it did to John, I should merely wave it away; it would have no effect on me now.

Háromürge puszta was situated in a delightful place on the top of a hill surrounded by woods. I often went that way—I wonder why it is that now, as I try to recall it, I see it in its autumn colours. We went down into a valley, where gossamer gleamed in the warm sun like a fairy lake. On both sides in the woods giant oaks reached the sky and rustled their rust-coloured crowns. The tall grass had withered and on the tip of each blade the melting frost glinted dazzlingly. Rabbits poked up their heads everywhere and coveys of partridges flew up with a loud *hrrsh*. We even saw deer. The whole district was bathed in a primeval, virgin happiness. On the far side of the valley the hill was covered with pines and a road curved through them in a regular S. Above this enchanting landscape lay the puszta with its teeming inhabitants, like an army of ants swarming on the corpse of a bird.

Apart from the stables, sheds and barns, there were three long farm servants' houses and that was all. There was no manor-house and no farm managers' quarters; no church and no school. Háromürge was merely a subsidiary puszta, belonging to an estate which lay far away, somewhere beyond the idyllic forests and hills. In this part a farm foreman ruled the roost. There was not even a well; water was brought up from the valley in a water-cart for the stables and in cans by the farm servants for their own use.

The Szerentséses lived 'under one roof' with another driver and his family—this meant in the same room. When we stepped in... but in the meantime I must add that whenever we went there some extraordinary event, apart from Aunt Malvi's peculiar troubles, invariably greeted us. Once it was a watchman who had fallen into the lime-pit, on another occasion a barn was on fire. There was always something happening at Ürge-puszta. The bull would get loose from time to time and trample on someone. The moment we caught sight of the puszta above the blue haze in the distance, we were seized by a fit of depression. Sometimes they would be preparing for a wedding and a

160

funeral at the same time, and in the midst of it the swineherd would be chasing his daughter with an axe through the assembling multitudes. The folk of Ürgepuszta lived their regular life.

When the revolution or extraordinary event of that particular day had run its course, and we finally entered the Szerentséses' lodging, having made our way through the dead puszta worn out with excitement, we were greeted by a veritable kindergarten—a rebellious kindergarten based on Rousseauesque principles. On the bed, the earth floor, the chests, the window-ledge there lay or sat children, most of them naked and grabbing at each other's hair. On the lower and upper seats round the stove there were lines of children too, squashed up against each other as in an altar by some over-enthusiastic baroque master. They whimpered and starved.

The Szerentséses starved in unison and—here at home—quite unashamedly. The family that lived with them also starved. The whole puszta in general could have done with something to eat. Their eyes did not rattle in their sockets from hunger, nor did they clasp their stomachs and howl: they starved quietly and regularly, but they were obviously starving. They gathered mushrooms in the woods and ate them. When there were no mushrooms, they would go out into the estate sugar-beet fields to steal beet-leaves and eat those. For they ate something every day, but it was so little that probably it did not restore the strength they expended on chewing it. 'I'd be glad to give you something to eat,' said Aunt Rozi when she finally appeared and swept a horde of children off the table, offering us seats there, 'but we only have a few vegetables left, if these infants haven't eaten them all up by now.' They had. A minute later they had also eaten what we had brought with us. They ate Aunt Malvi's portion too; she was either expecting or in mourning, and refused the food with a sniff. She was the only one on the puszta who was not hungry.

I was always amazed at beggars, but at first I frankly despised these stick-in-the-mud, regular starvelings and other destitutes. Thus later, as if to do penance for my previous attitude, my feelings for them were all the more sympathetic. We did not starve. If I now had to relive the kind of life I had in my childhood, I should perhaps regard it as penury, but at the time I did not do so. We did not live very well, but we ate regularly. At the most it was not what we would have liked, and sometimes we were very reluctant—'spinach again!' or cabbage, or fried noodles, or potato by itself, that is, without meat. In general, there was quite a lot that we never tasted and thus if we suffered, we did not know that we were suffering because we never had certain food. And if in winter we were cold (and we often were), we attributed it to the cold weather and not to our primitive lodgings. Our frequent illnesses occurred because 'we didn't look after ourselves.' As an exceptional occurrence, I well remember how we once ate chestnuts, which we had got as a present from some distant relative. I also remember the celebration one evening when my father returned from a nearby market with a tin of sardines; enthusiastically and happily—as always when he had an opportunity to hold forth—he described to us their origin and the way to enjoy them. At my first communion I received three oranges and when weeks later I had grown tired of smelling them and began on the first one, slices went to neighbours far and wide; we ate the skin and pips too. I first sampled ice-cream at the age of 13. One of my school friends persuaded me to buy one during the terminal examinations and in my greed I almost squandered not only the price I got for the school-books I sold so hurriedly, but also the money I had received for my fare home. The terrible row it caused—and it could hardly have been avoided—fixed it firmly in my memory. Ice-cream—it was useless for me to try to explain at home the sheer delight that had caused my downfall. At home we ate only what was necessary. All the same, we ate in the morning and in the evening, and sometimes at tea-time too, a slice of bread. Why then did the Szerentséses live in privation; indeed, why did not only the whole of Ürgepuszta, but

162

almost all the farm servants on the pusztas generally starve like them? For theirs was the usual life on a puszta. In the very middle of the enormous fields of corn, bread was kept under lock and key in the servants' quarters; in vain did the children try to open the bin, in vain did they kick at it, in vain did they howl for an hour after their unnourishing lunch. Why had even the adult workers to tighten their belts? I can give precise details here.

The payment of the people of the pusztas can be checked in every detail. The contract of service or service-book gives a precise list of their dues, which may be divided into 'cash, payment in kind and land to work on.' All these together make up the so-called 'convention' *(konvenció)*. The conditions of the 'convention', or 'commention' as the servants call it, cause their lips to twist in a bitter grimace, accompanied as it is with so much servile whimpering and weeping of women; they grow worse from year to year. Even before the First World War they were severe and appalling to any educated person. In the very place where the landowners cite scientific works to support the necessity and direct profit of good feeding and provisioning, these contracts allow the servants just as much food as will keep them alive. On the pusztas one can see magnificent studs of horses, groomed so that they shine like mirrors as they step proudly along. There are trumpeting bulls, coal-black and huge as railway engines. I cannot recall a single fat or even well-built farm servant, working driver, reaper or herdsman. The very idea that they should be fat is unimaginable, and I find it quite out of place and even humorous. The people of the pusztas are not inclined to stoutness. They are a gaunt, bony race. They are sunburnt and therefore appear to be muscular and tough even when they are really at death's door. One of our learned anthropologists has likened them to the Dinaric type of skin-and-bone Dalmatian. I am afraid I must refute his argument. The overseers and supervisors who are drawn from their ranks are almost without exception inclined to grow stout.

The explanation of their typical characteristics, in my opinion, is to be sought in the 'convention'. I am certain that the basis of the usual modern contract was laid in the days when it was indeed only a basis, and the servants could still obtain various additional acquisitions. In the old days the 'convention' must have been merely provisions for the winter; in addition there was still a free field and—with the virtual agreement of the landlords—a free threshing-floor too. At the end of the last century even the very poorest servants, as I know from my own family-history, were able to carry on a little independent farming, almost without exception. They could sell the produce from the land they were allotted, and could feed their own animals on the produce of the estate. But with the rationalisation of agriculture this gradually came to an end. Only the contract was left, if indeed it could be called that. Economists of the nineties mention payments in cash of 100 and 60 forints, two pairs of boots per year, free clogs, cloaks and sheepskin jackets. And today?

It should be noted that there are three types of contract. The first concerns regular farmhands working with oxen or horses, the second is for ordinary labourers who do not work with animals and normally perform the same work as day-labourers, and the third is for the children working as boy labourers. There are few differences in income between the first two types, while the child labourers receive half the amount given to the other two. There is also a quarter-portion, or beggar's portion, which is granted as a favour, very rarely, to some faithful old servant who can no longer perform regular work and is suitable only for the duties of a watchman.

The cash payment to a servant on full contract varies from twelve to forty pengős.* If it is forty pengős per year—then at the very most this is 11 fillérs a day.

---

* The pengő, consisting of 100 fillérs, was worth about 9d.

Let us suppose that the family consists of five individuals, husband, wife and three children. This will work out at two fillérs per head per day. If the father of the family receives twelve pengős per year, then the amount per day for the whole family is 3 fillérs, and per head 0.6 fillér. There are some places where the farm servant receives nothing whatsoever in cash.

They receive about 1,600 kilos of grain, the amount produced on one *hold* of a 3–4,000 *hold* estate. Of the 1,600 kg, 600 are wheat, 500 rye and 500 barley. The first two can be made into about 500 kg of bread per year and some 180–200 kg of flour-paste. That is 0.27 kg of bread per person per day and, again calculating on the liberal side, 0.11 kg of flour-paste.

For cooking and heating they get 5–6 cubic metres of logs every year. They supplement this with straw and dead branches picked up on the roadside. And they make up for the lack of heating in the winter by the natural heat given off by human bodies packed into one room.

Apart from this, they have for their own use about 1,100 square metres of garden and 5,800 square metres of land for maize or potatoes, which is ploughed by the estate. Sowing, hoeing and looking after this ground in general is the task of the women, who can perform this work only to the detriment of their health or of the work itself, because they are so fully occupied with other duties.

The maize or potatoes grown on their land may be used to feed either their animals or their family. The new regulations do not strictly permit the produce to be sold. The usual practice is to eat it all, and mostly before it is fully ripe.

The law mentions that the land for the farm servants' own use must be allotted from land deemed 'moderately good', while their corn dues must come from the best quality corn destined for sale. Several estates allot as 'convention'-land that which has been drained of all its goodness under the rotation-system, and the corn dues are distributed from such bad, chaff-laden corn that the farm servants are frequently compelled to refuse it.

The farm servant may also keep animals. He may keep one (or very rarely two) sows in farrow, but the piglets must be sold as soon as they are taken from their mother. He may also keep 20 to 30 hens. In my childhood, five eggs per hen and five chicks per broody had to be sent up to the ladies of the manor-house. One or two ducks may be kept too. On the puszta of X., where my father served the last years of his life, one out of every two ducks reared and looked after by the farm servants at their own expense had to be delivered to the lady of the manor-house.

In the old days they also kept cows. But as the pastures were ploughed up, this practice ceased in most places and instead the farm servants received one litre of milk per family. Later this too was discontinued in a great many cases.

A great deal was discontinued. I would hazard a guess that the custom whereby the farm servants' wives had to perform unpaid labour in the manor-house for a certain number of days every year was not ended by the law promulgated at the beginning of the century. When I was young it was still customary, despite the law.

At one time they also got salt and bacon, some 20 to 30 kg per year. In our area this too was discontinued.

Exact calculations have been made by excellent economists concerning the monetary value of all the possible dues of an ordinary farm servant on full contract.

We shall disregard the value of the labour expended by the servants (or most frequently their wives) on working the bits of land or rearing the animals allowed by the 'convention'. The total income of a farm servant under all possible heads—that is, including not only the wheat, rye, barley and firewood but also the lodging given by the estate—is about 350–400 pengős. If they wished to sell it, this is what they would get. Thus in the nineteen-thirties each of a family of five received an average of

25 fillérs per day. This is what they have to provide not only food, heat and light, but also clothing for themselves; out of it they must also satisfy their mental and spiritual needs and pay for travel.

These figures refer to the recent past and the present, to normal circumstances of peace. There are no complaints. But the young children scream, shaking and kicking at the locked bread bin.

This was the income of the Szerentséses and indeed that of almost every puszta-dweller except for the overseers, who had the right to keep rather more animals. This was our income too, with the difference that my father was able to graze four cows. It was these four cows that later pushed us painfully out of the quagmire of puszta life. It is because of them that I am here today... And before them there were those six piglets, which under my grandmother's supervision grew fat with astonishing rapidity and were exchanged at the market for their thin successors. I have no need to say that we sunned ourselves only in spirit, so to speak, in the wealth of my paternal grandfather. Of his famous fortune we never saw a farthing, nor did we make any claim upon it. 'You must water a tree when it is planted in new earth,' said my father understandingly, and he too was happy if from time to time he might sit in the shade of these trees. 'Now my young brother Imre,' he would say to the puszta folk, and to him it was worth while losing a house to be able to add, 'the one who is a cooper in Gyönk and lives in his very own house...' More than once we scraped the edge of the life led by the Szerentséses and by the people of the puszta in general. Nevertheless it was a life which I really got to know only at the Szerentséses.

Unable as she was to rescue Aunt Malvi now, grandmother wanted at least to save her children. She would keep inviting them to her house, or rather to ours, because she had too little room for them.

The trouble was that they would only leave their family with the utmost difficulty. The Szerentséses suddenly hung on to them as if they were their only source of happiness. No, never! They could not possibly live without these particular children. In the end, when they let them come, it was only in accordance with the strictest reciprocity—we had to go and stay with them for some time too. My elder brother was the first to go to Ürgepuszta, and he brought back fantastic tales. I spent months with them also, but now not at Ürgepuszta, because in the meantime old Szerentsés had been transferred elsewhere, either on loan or as a replacement, and had taken Aunt Malvi with him. I followed them to Hegyempuszta, to the estate of a famous banking family. This too was the world of the Szerentséses.

We were for ever eating soup made of turnip-tops. I remember this because from the very first day to the end of my stay, though I was not finicky, I always felt mildly sick when I dipped my spoon into it, and closed my eyes as I raised it to my lips. There was really nothing much else to eat. It was a red-letter day when Aunt Malvi cooked some vegetables too—a few potatoes or beans. The Szerentséses clearly did not bother very much about this. In general they did not give much thought to eating: it was an incidental business, they thought, a kind of necessary evil. Thus they did not lay the table for lunch. When the food was ready, Aunt Malvi pushed a bowl and spoon into our hands on the doorstep, and everybody had his meal where he liked, under the eaves, on the chopping-block, or on the bank of the ditch. The drivers usually ate on their carts. This must have been a tradition with them, because they asked for their food there even when no horses were harnessed. The ox-drivers on the other hand —again in accordance with some obscure tradition—had theirs under the waggons, or if they happened to be on the puszta, squatting on the threshold of the ox-stables. After the soup, we ate blackberries, wild strawberries, the sticky sweet stuff on the edge of the gleditsia flower, we ate Jerusalem artichokes and sorrel, whatever the season of the year had to offer. We ate the tiny, honey-filled stem of the acacia flower, and for hawthorns we would wander three fields away. Some of them would peel young green maize stems, chop them into slices and suck them; they were sweet but rather sickly.

In winter the Szerentséses lived chiefly on baked pumpkin, fresh and hot at lunch, warmed up in the evening and cold for breakfast. As for milk, they received a litre of it, but since this could be sold, they did so. Only after Christmas did they begin to use potatoes from the clamp; up to then they did not touch them. This was what they ate during the spring.

True, as far as the Szerentséses were concerned there was a basis for the charge so frequently made by the intelligentsia of the puszta—that the farm servants do not know how to manage things. The Szerentséses had little idea of how to divide what they had. The estate gives out the dues of the farm servants every quarter, deducting from them any advances that have been wangled in the meantime. On quarter-day, when this took place, they cooked and baked night and day. How the fat crackled and spat! The Szerentséses were mad on pancakes, so for almost a week we ate nothing but pancakes, hot, cold, with and without jam. This was how the other families lived too. On the enormous hearth wet branches crackled all day long and smoke billowed around in clouds, making both eyes and nose smart. And instead of the usual fighting, folk offered each other food, and called each other 'my dear' or 'my darling'. Where had the usual kitchen smell of cold soot disappeared? All day long we thronged around the sizzling frying-pans.

Four rooms opened into the kitchen. In the middle of it stood the enormous mountain of a hearth, made of clay. Everybody laid their own fire on the top of it. From the wide chimney, between whose soot-caked, glistening walls the rain would beat down, there hung chains to which they hooked the big iron pots over the open fire. Saucepans were placed on two bricks and the fire laid between them. Everybody whitewashed the part of the kitchen wall nearest their own door and, dipping their brush into the soot, created some very pleasing designs on it. Nobody kept any pots or food in the kitchen, these, even in their own room, were kept locked in a separate chest.

Here several families lived in each room. In that belonging to the Szerentséses, as far as I can calculate from memory, only nine people slept, the couple who had been assigned to them were still young, and the wife was nursing her second child at the time. She was called Viktor, and was such a mild, frightened little creature that we did not notice her. Usually she did not even sleep in the room, but fed her babies to sleep and then went out to her husband in the stable.

The other three rooms were all the more crowded. The one next to ours, separated from it only by a wall, was inhabited by three families, all cowherds and great music-lovers. They even woke up to the sound of the zither. The chief musician among them was old Uncle András, who would even dash home during the noon break to 'strike up a little tune'. When he got back in the evening, he would pick up his instrument—which was the size of a tub—and whether happy or sad, would thump out tunes on it until they went to bed. From the sound which accompanied him, we were able to tell which of the cowherds had arrived home. They played beautifully; have you ever heard the sound produced by this kind of zither? It can sound soft and delicate, gentle as the chirping of a cricket. The women accompanied it with a nasal droning. Sometimes it happened that in the middle of the night the metallic, but exquisite sounds would be heard in their room, one of the cowherds had been struck by a thought and could not go off to sleep until he had given it expression.

170

Opposite us, behind the door on the other side of the kitchen, lived Uncle Szabó with his own large family plus those of one of his sons and one of his sons-in-law. Here too there were crowds of children; the women more or less competed with each other in producing them, and old Aunt Szabó was not to be outdone in the race. Once she and her daughter had children on the very same day. The women went out every day to work and took it in turns to feed the babies, who were uncles and nephews to each other. Old Aunt Szabó would hold her own baby in one arm and her grandchild in the other, and proudly carry on a brisk exchange with the farm servants' wives; these in turn spread all kinds of immoral gossip about this family which flourished exceedingly in an Old Testament framework. The Szabós, it was said, did not confuse only the children. Certainly, on occasions when they had a family quarrel, the women screamed not the most edifying tales of their family life for the whole puszta to hear. As soon as the squabbling began, the menfolk quietly filed out of the room. It was usually Aunt Malvi who created order among the three women as they fought with rolling-pins and kitchen utensils. She liked them and defended them, and they loved her too. We were on terms of 'exchanging' children with them, which meant that if all the adults in the Szabó family were out of the house, their children were all herded into our room, while we were sent over to theirs if we had to go sparingly with the fuel for heating.

In the fourth room there lived two horseherds and their families; their name was *Csikós* (Horseherd) too. They never fraternized with anybody, not even with us, although one of their wives was born a Szerentsés and was a distant relative. But they were well off. Their children were in their teens and the two families had two half-plots of land in addition to the whole plots of the men. They walked through the kitchen with their noses in the air and did not respond if one greeted them. If any of us children got in their way, they simply thrust us aside. Sometimes they drank. One of them slung half a sack-ful of fodder over his shoulder and made his way with it to the village by night. He brought back some wine and by dawn the family had settled down to hard drinking. They drank silently and secretly. Their faces were even more severe than usual; only by the glint in their eyes could one see that they had been carousing.

There were three sets of common lodgings like this in the house, in other words twelve rooms in all. At the end there was a separate dwelling for the estate bricklayer. His wife was always beautifully dressed and wore shoes even on week-days. They had one child, a little girl, who was also elegantly dressed. We saw her very rarely. Once I came upon her in the farm servants' gardens. I happily went towards her and, as far as I remember, immediately wanted to tell her some tale. 'Mother has forbidden me to talk to you,' she said, and moved away rather affectedly. The words died on my lips. She was obviously quite glad to obey her parents' orders. I gazed after her uncomprehendingly.

CHAPTER ELEVEN

The children: how they are brought up and enlightened.
How they make friends. Love

As for us, the children... the children in the puszta live as
unhindered as the animals which wander everywhere in the
fields and among the houses without any supervision. It is not
the example or rules of existing society which accustom them
to the laws of the world or train them to control the ever-
increasing signs of life in their bodies, but rather the foals,
cows and bulls which gallop around them, biting and sniffing
each other. As the children dash in and out of the common
dwellings, rolling in the dust of the roads and in the puddles
round the drinking-troughs, they grow accustomed to each
other with the openness and boldness of virgin innocence and
examine each other, body and soul, like the last of a litter of
puppies. The puszta stretches to infinity; there is no need to
watch over the children, for they cannot wander away from it
or get lost. Beyond the enormous granaries, stables and sheds,
big as railway terminals, there are acacia groves, thickets,
woods and endless pastures, cornfields, bushes and impenetrable willow-copses along the river, which every spring pours
a sea of water over the flat hayfields.

I am not merely telling my own story here, but that which
might well have happened to me, because it happened to my
companions; in my memory the events in which I played an
active part and those I merely observed tend to run together
and become confused. So the words I use in the first person

173

extend, if they extend at all, to become the testimony of long-forgotten, different lives. In the room where I spent my child-hood years only the five members of our little family lived, but I spent so much time in those rooms inhabited by several families, where often twenty people had to be accommodated somehow, and my friends and playmates, who without exception crept out of such slums each morning, so often exhaled the atmosphere and morals of these dwellings, that in my memory I can almost smell again the stale air of their nights and hear the mixture of bumps, sighs and groans emanating from them. Sometimes it seems as if I really spent my own childhood in these rooms, in which everything from birth, or rather from conception, to death takes place in the hearing of others.

How many wedding-feasts I shared, and how many wild carousals in the estate barns, or in fine weather under the acacias at the end of the puszta, from which towards midnight the young couple would return to these common dwellings...
The wedding-feasts were always prodigally extravagant. On the long bean-shelling tables borrowed from the estate there were vast quantities of wine and dripping, and in the pots which had been collected from three pusztas there were rows of fried chickens and ducks, while the skinny-necked labourers crammed themselves with stuffed cabbages the size of a child's head and topped them off with milk-loaf. They were making up for a whole year of starvation, and gobbled up the year's provisions for the families of the bride and bridegroom. But even this unbridled gorging belonged to the ceremony. It was as indispensable a part of the wedding as the priest's blessing. Indeed, it was even more important, for while there were plenty of couples who got married without the blessing of the Church, there was not a single instance of a marriage in church before they had found some way of holding a 'proper' wedding-feast. They would never have lived down the shame of a 'barefoot wedding'. We all knew that our neighbour's

daughter was in love with a boy from Alsómajor, nor was her love unrequited, which meant that there was something between them; yet she did not marry him, but a local lad who, she rightly suspected even before the wedding, would beat her more than usual all her life through. She did not marry her real lover solely because they could not agree about the wedding-feast. Nor was it the two families that could not come to terms; the girl fell out with her future mother-in-law about who was to bake what and who should be invited. In that district either the gipsies were invited to play at the wedding for 15 koronas, or they called for the brass band, which for 30 koronas created a din fit to blast the walls of Jericho and could really be heard seven villages away. It was only the brass band that came to the puszta, from the German village of Nagyszékely. The daughter of one of our best friends among the puszta families, the most beautiful farm servant's daughter I ever remember, postponed her wedding for eighteen months while they collected enough money for the brass band, for the Germans demanded payment in advance from the people of the puszta. At Kölesd a lad hanged himself for a similar reason. 'He wore himself away because he could not marry the girl he loved,' said the farm servants sympathetically. In another family which was more or less related to ours, my mother tried hard to persuade the women to give the young couple some furniture or a couple of sucking-pigs instead of wasting their money on a wedding-feast. The result of her advice was that we were not invited to the wedding and remained in their bad books for years. In this desert of poverty and punctilious starvation the wedding-feast had to be something to remember. It was not an excuse, but rather a revenge for the long years of hunger. It was no entertainment, nor was it to be enjoyed; it was more like a barbarous, self-mutilating human sacrifice.

The worker in the city slum can drink himself silly every Saturday. The people of the puszta do not see alcohol for months on end—there is no public house there, nor is there any money for it; moreover the estate does not allow drunkenness among its farm servants who are under perpetual supervision. On the rare occasions when they got hold of liquor they threw themselves with the greed and fever of folk dying of thirst into the brief freedom, exaltation and forgetfulness offered by alcohol. How fine they were at these feasts in the stupor produced by wine and happiness, how angelically innocent and childlike after the first glass, in the first hours of their human consciousness thus artificially induced!

How triumphant and ceremonious was the procession of guests as it made its way on foot to the church in one of the nearby villages, ankle-deep in the autumn dust or winter mud! They sang the whole way. The lads, even if they could not prance around on horseback like the sons of village farmers, danced around on their own feet, kicking up the dust and leaping over ditches and bushes, even whinnying in their merriment. And on the way back there was the traditional salute outside the manor-house or that of the bailiff. Tradition—perhaps the recollection of the *jus primae noctis*—demanded that it should be distant, silent and grim, like a funeral ceremony, but even this was attended by happy smiles. After introductions had been made, the bridegroom went inside for his present, which was usually a steel-bladed penknife, and the bride received a couple of caresses; as they emerged they were greeted with loud cheers by the waiting crowd, whose bubbling good humour would have sent the whole county into peals of laughter. They stopped everybody who happened to be passing through the puszta, stuffed them with cakes and begged them to have a drink, pressing a bottle into their hands if they happened to have had their fill of wine. But the liquor they tasted so rarely quickly went to their heads.

According to custom, it is not proper for the bride to eat or drink at the wedding-feast. She just pecks at the food, merely to give her strength for the wild whirling of the bridal dance which lasts for hours. In this all the guests who have brought presents—a salt-cellar, an enamelled jug, a pair of slippers, or a fork with the monogram of some aristocrat or restaurant roughly scored out—dance her dizzy and shout themselves hoarse, crying 'The bride is mine!' But the bridegroom, happy man, can eat and drink, and so he does, for propriety bids him feast as never before in his life and most probably never again. He is stuffed like a goose. Meanwhile the bride has partnered all those who have obtained the right to her by paying money instead of giving presents; usually it was ten fillérs, but on special and memorable occasions it was one pengő. By the time it is the bridegroom's turn to dance the last dance, the so-called 'bridegroom's whirl', with her and then lead her away for a while, the poor fellow staggers to his feet from the place of honour in the centre of the long form. After one or two turns he stumbles hiccuping to their new home. Those guests who are still able to walk throng after them cheering and shouting rude remarks in verse at them; they rattle the income from the bridal-dance and watch to see whether the bride will notice the broom laid on the threshold, and whether she will pick it up or not—in other words, whether she will be a worker or an idler. The common kitchen also becomes a Scylla and Charybdis of superstitious tricks and prophecies. Finally the newly-weds reach their room. What happened after that was recounted next day with grinning and sparkling faces by my five and six-year-old friends, who had been chased off to bed even earlier than usual because of the wedding; their bed was either the common pile of rags or, if the inhabitants of the room were at daggers drawn, a corner of the room protected by the place where the adults slept.

What they described so exactly, not missing a single detail, or any of the accessories, was nothing new at that age either to them or to me. The puszta child, as soon as he has a brain of his own, is 'enlightened', and the very first matter he learns about is love. As I probe my memory, I wonder whether any harm is done to mind or body by this complete acquisition of knowl-

177

edge which cannot be described as early, because it occurs at the same time as their interest in it. Is it damaging, this introduction, step by step, to secrets through which one gets all the pain and joy that anyway must be accepted from life, whether one likes it or not, in varying degrees? And it is a gradual initiation, without all the adolescent upheavals so feared today. It is not my task to pronounce judgement, but merely to give information.

The emotional life of the puszta child is adjusted to the laws of the puszta before it has left its cradle. As soon as the babies begin to walk, all of them who are the same age, whether from the common dwellings or from the common houses, are put together, and even where the estate does not employ a regular 'children's shepherd', as their guardian is called, they are entrusted to the supervision of some very old woman who is fit only for this job; after all, on the puszta mothers must do more than merely be mothers. The children educate each other. And when they leave the warmth of this paradise, they look out on the world with eyes as full of curiosity as Adam's after his expulsion from Paradise. Who told them that it would be easier to suffer warfare and defeat if they chose a mate for themselves as soon as possible?

I well recall a certain little girl. My first memory of her is that one afternoon when my mother was cutting bread for our snack she came into the kitchen saying that she was my girl friend and wanted a slice of bread too. I must have been four or five; I know I had not started school. Ten years later when the scene was repeated with the same girl, I nearly sank through the floor in shame, but then I merely nodded agreement and everybody around me thought the direct admission right and proper. My mother smiled as she fulfilled her request, though it was more of a demand or the filing of a claim; she caressed and kissed the little girl. From then onwards she was a permanent guest and I could not shake her off. She arrived at the puszta school a year after I did. There too she introduced herself as

178

she had done in the kitchen and thus tried to secure her place and prestige among the children, whose society is far more strictly organised than that of adults. She laid claim to me, defended and directed me, organising unpleasant scenes with me and the others too. There is no doubt that if I had stayed in the social position in which she first got to know me and—goodness knows why—claimed me for herself, sooner or later I should have had to marry her, as most of my childhood friends also married their playmates. For many years, and even when I was away from home, she stubbornly stood by me. With ever-growing alarm she observed both inward and outward changes in me. Whenever I arrived home in the summer, she would stare at me with the look of a calf during whose browsing in the meadow a new gate has been set up at home. With the terror of an animal she detected in my voice the *hauteur* and pride I gathered year by year. Despairingly she sniffed at this strange development, and being unable to make any sense of it all, she slowly drew away from me in shame and confusion. Then she fled from me when I wanted to approach her at a time when I really began to grow fond of her, despite all my bragging and bombast. I should explain that I really had nothing in common with her at all. I cannot recall her among the gang of children with whom for years I roamed the fields and made all the trials of physical and mental strength that awaited us there.

I was forbidden by my mother to go near the main road, but apart from this only water was out of bounds—the river and the animals' drinking-ponds which were as wide as a mine-shaft. And she added the estate herd of pigs after they had gobbled up a five-year-old child. Everything else was unrestricted. I was even sent out of the house, and with good reason. When I was very young, I was a solitary, rather stupid child. If I was told to stay in front of the house, I would sit on the door-step for half the day. 'Now go for a little walk,' I can hear my mother say even now. I would wander off to the bottom of the garden and a minute later reappear in the kitchen with a query on my face: 'I've been for a walk; now what shall I do?' When I was about four, I had bad attacks of hysteria for a time. The first occurred at bath-time one Saturday night, when I was determined by hook or by crook to get into the bath-tub with my boots on. After they had dragged me away for the third time, my face turned blue and I collapsed senseless on the floor. From then onwards, whenever I was upset or annoyed, I did not burst into tears or grouse; instead I was seized by regular fits of shivering, then turned blue, and finally fainted away, despite all attempts to caress and fondle me. I was the last and smallest child, and they always jeered at me as a stay-at-home, my mother quite rightly feared that I should suffer the worst disability that can afflict a puszta-dweller—that I should never be able to make my way in the world. They poured lead,* they smeared me with a mixture of charcoal and water, but even the doctor himself could only say that this malady would pass in due course. And so it did, indeed I soon went to the opposite extreme, thanks to my grandmother, who instinctively handed me over to the other children to effect a cure. She enticed them to our house and gladly sent me out when they asked me to go roaming around with them. With serious face, I followed them round in all kinds of exploits. All day long I would squat in the little reed-thickets, in the depths of the caves we made in the hay piled in the lofts, or in the tents we built out of boughs. We dug ourselves up to the neck in the heaps of threshed grain, and trod on the soft clouds of wool spread out to dry, or buried each other in them. We lived like aborigines in the wilds. In their company I soon ceased to be a sickly child; I was one of them, but in the meantime every phase of our life in common became engraved in my memory. I observed everything closely as if I already knew that sometime I should have to account for it all.

* The molten lead, thrown into a bowl of water, was believed to show by its shape who or what was harming the child, and whether he would live or die.

The first gang of children consisted of those who could not be harnessed for child-labour on the estate, who had not yet completed the first four classes of the elementary school; they were still free... I was rather younger than they were, because I well remember being left behind with one or two others in the wild rush down to the river bank. I arrived panting, by which time the gang had finished its first dip and was sitting in a wide circle in a sandy clearing among the reeds, all competing with each other in self-gratification, as naked as the day they were born, and brown as a pack of monkeys. I settled down among them, but I did not yet know the rules and tried in vain. I merely gazed in admiration at the rest who knew the secret, and imagined that this could be understood only by those who went to school. That was where children received this kind of instruction. My suspicions were quite correct. But I was initiated even before I went to school by a little girl who was even younger than I was.

Every morning after we had been liberated from the wash-tub, or it may have been at dawn, for after all the whole family was up by five o'clock—mother had to work in the fields and it is possible to hoe properly only when the dew is still lying—this little girl appeared at the door and led me off by the hand. We trotted behind the pigsties on the side of the hill. Here there began a forest of nettles through which we stumbled to a pit overgrown with acacias, where once a farm servant's cellar had stood before it caved in. This was our house under the branches. I shivered in the cold dawn as she undressed me. I was rather reluctant too; I did not really know what she wanted of me, and I well remember that I was very offhand in my behaviour. But even so, why did I put up again and again with the shivering cold and the nettle-stings? To her great disappointment she herself did not know exactly what she wanted. She had heard something, and perhaps even seen what went on in the common room or in the common bed as she lay there curled up at the

181

foot of the wide bed. She still had a lisp as she talked of what she had observed, adding new details every day.

There we sat opposite each other, a couple of innocent babes trying to examine and find out the secret of each other's existence with that serious concentration given by wild animals to a ticking clock, or by children to a new toy as they probe it and pull it to pieces. We had escaped from the disciplined world and with a thrill of horror felt that we had found our tortuous way through nettles and acacia-thorns to the real, secret life of the future, and to a state of primeval freedom where we might find out for ourselves what it meant to exist. And there we sat, not quite knowing what to do, in the delicious Eden of opportunity; here there was, there must be some happiness about us, for we felt it weighing heavily in our breasts. Yet somehow we could not get to the bottom of it, we could not achieve liberation; we were still enslaved and it was all the more bitter because our prison was invisible. We knew everything we could know, yet we were still surrounded by some secret wall, and the key refused to turn in the lock. My little girl friend began to prance with rage in her helplessness, and burst into tears, but however stupid she was, she never complained at home or asked her mother what to do. In the meantime, of course, there was plenty of time for other games—it was from her that I learnt how to skim stones. But every day she began the examination again; she dragged me out and rolled me in the dust at the bottom of the pit like a fish in flour before frying, and I did the same to her. After a long period of trial some small result was achieved and I may well have realised what potentialities I had. I was not surprised, as might have been expected; I regarded it as quite natural, and recall instead her little winking eyes smiling at me. In any case, this was the last time we were alone together. She dropped me like a stone and never came for me again. She went off with somebody else and it never occurred to me to go and look for her. Later I turned over a new leaf.

The young folk in the villages live a life of perpetual observation. Who is really going to suit them, both in nature and in material ambitions? They frequently exchange their friends, girls and boys alike, without rousing much anger. This is also the method adopted by the landless peasants at the bottom of the village, the penniless who perform casual labour and harvesting, when they choose their mates. They do not consider the land, for they have none, but health, strength and ability to work; in these lies the fortune which pays interest. From the seasonal labourers who came out to the puszta I learnt that the youth who does harvesting in the summer takes on as his helper and gleaner the girl who has won his heart during the winter and is to be his wife in due course. For all the frolicking and laughter during the winter, pleasant and comforting as it is in the midst of poverty, does not count for much; summer brings the real test. How does the girl pick up the swathes after the scythe, how does she bend from dawn to dusk, and how does she stand the work? These are the decisive factors in the making of the marriage. The young man looks at his future mate with expert eye, as if he were at the market making a purchase to last a lifetime. And this too is how the girl watches the young man in front of her, as he battles with the scythe in the fierce heat. The others turn critical eyes on them both to see whether they will make a good match. For by working together as a pair they invite opinion and comment, and have made it plain to the whole world that they will remain together till death if they are suited to each other. This is their method, and it cannot receive enough praise. If they are suited to each other at work, the remaining tests will soon follow, those of the heart, soul and body.

Betrothal on the puszta is quite different. They are like the offspring of royalty, like the Hindus; usually they are betrothed if not in the cradle, at least when they leave school. The only difference is that it is not the parents who arrange the betrothal, indeed these are the last people to bother themselves about

183

such matters. Nor does it matter who marries whom. No girl brings any greater dowry to the new home than any other, and none of the boys inherits more than his comrades. They are not even interested in each other's health. Is this due to ignorance? Yes, but in any case if husband or wife dies, they can easily find a substitute—what is easier to replace than a human being?

So the children, without the slightest restriction or consciousness of guilt, make every trial suggested by a dim and slowly-awakening instinct, out of attraction, affection or love towards another person of like or different sex. And by the time that they are aware of the distant rule of social conduct that eventually reaches the puszta with a century's delay, according to which every human being must have lawful private property in love, if in nothing else, almost everyone knows the person with whom he will live out his life. The choice is not great, for on the average only twenty or thirty families live on each puszta, but they do not ask for much either. Those who do not find a suitable mate in this little world (and this applies only to the lads), or for some reason have lost the girl of their choice, or have not arrived on the puszta until adulthood, all seek for a wife in an area of six or eight miles around at the most. Naturally they confine their search to the pusztas, because the belief is still current, and quite correctly, that it is no good bringing a village girl to the puszta even if she would come. But she would not come. At least I know of no such case.

Thus attachments are formed in childhood and, in the view of the puszta, couples are faithful to each other from the time when the first real intercourse takes place between them. They do not hide their devotion under a bushel; this small society would be very surprised and laugh at anyone who tried to keep it secret. 'These folk have no modesty,' a bailiff once said to me, his face wearing the traditional grim mask of indignation. That day at dawn he had discovered a sixteen-year-old girl where the farm lad ordered to guard the piles of peas had made his bed. They were fast asleep and when he stirred them up with his stick the girl was not in the least embarrassed. There in his presence she calmly tidied herself up, 'just like a princess getting dressed in the presence of her maid.' What ideas there are here on the puszta of the vocation of a woman! And if I could only see what went on in the stables! Later I did catch an accidental glimpse of something going on... A lad and a girl were milking. They were so seated by their cows that their backs almost touched. Their heads were thrown back, and while their hands did not pause for an instant, their lips were locked in an endless, unbroken kiss. And all this in a tortured, neck-twisting position which drives the blood to the head, and in the midst of hard work which demands more muscular strength than almost anything else! Tears started from my eyes and I turned round. When I glanced back into the dim shed from the doorway, they were still firmly clinging to each other's lips.

The ideas of the puszta... Of these, virginity is regarded only as one of the many perquisites of private property. This is certainly my experience. Fidelity means more than mere physical faithfulness; it is more comprehensive and, I might almost say, on a higher level. The girl-friend or wife of the conscript in most cases awaits his return with patience and restraint, but even if she does not, no special complications arise. If they do arise, it is not because the woman has deceived her distant lover, but depends on the man with whom she has kept company. Once I was having a conversation on quite a different subject with one of the labourers, who happened to mention in passing that his girl had not remained faithful to him while he was away for eighteen months in Slovakia with the animals. In reply to my questioning glance he said, 'Deli was a good friend of mine, and when I got back, we went on the spree together.' Nor did he complain about the girl since she had 'stood by him, despite it all.' Is infidelity then really rare, or is it merely rare to hear it mentioned? It is very seldom indeed that the farm servants go to law with each other on this account And only does it reach such a stage when matters become serious as, for example, if the husband takes a few things from the house to his lover—a little lard or bacon, or a basket of corn; or if he 'acquires' things for her at work, or is planning to leave his family in the lurch for her. Incidentally, they generally settle such affairs among themselves, like so much else.

On the pusztas women are respected. This is not contradicted by the fact that they are sometimes beaten. Everywhere in the world, as we know, there are more women than men, except in some particularly barren regions where the opposite is true; here they are like a plant which requires a better soil and climate. Is this why there are fewer women than men, on the pusztas than in Tibet? This is true of almost every puszta. Even according to the census of 1930 there were only 125 women in Rácegres for every 140 men. Is it because male labour is the prime requisite on the pusztas? Or because society offers an easier way of escape to the girls by way of domestic service in the towns? There were quite enough, indeed too many, old women; it was the young ones who were missing. They had to be protected and this the men did, by trying to get on well with them in their own way. They did not demand more from them than was necessary. They did not usually come to blows over a woman, but how indeed could they have taken the possession of affection seriously, when for centuries past and up to the present day even this is decided primarily by that one-sided agreement that operates in the case of other possessions, and with which it is unwise for them to interfere? The gentry, from the landlord to the agricultural trainee, had absolute rights over the farm servants, not merely over the work of their hands, but also over their bodies. Against this there could be no appeal, nor does such an appeal exist. There are places where the farm officials, including even those overseers who have grown up in the labourers' dwellings,

186

can order any girl they wish to come to them. This phenomenon is an old one; it is common knowledge, part of the undisturbed order of things, traditional and almost idyllic by now. So it appears to me too. It was only by accident that it occurred to me to write about this subject also.

CHAPTER TWELVE

The defencelessness of the girls. The morals of the puszta.
The conquerors

The daughter of one of our nearby neighbours committed suicide. Male farm servants who are weary of life normally put an end to it by hanging themselves, the women and girls by jumping into a well. No other methods were usual. Even here they strictly preserved some tradition of propriety. The girl had 'gone up' to the manor-house; this is why she killed herself.

The cowherds pulled her out when they watered the cattle at dawn. By the time we arrived there on our way to school, she was lying on the thin ice formed by the water which had been spilt from the well. Under this covering the black clods of earth, the pieces of straw and dung glinted and sparkled like rare jewels under glass. There she lay with open eyes in which, like the small objects under the ice, was frozen the broken terror of a startled glance. Her mouth was open, her nose rather haughtily tilted, and on her forehead and beautiful cheeks there were huge scratches which had either occurred during her fall, or been made by the cowherds as they let down the bucket before they caught sight of her amongst the ice-patches in the dark winter dawn. She was barefooted, she had left her boots in the assistant farm manager's room, by the bed from which she had suddenly leapt and dashed straight as an arrow to the well.

The labourers who gathered there from the stables and granaries stood in front of her for a moment silently and with a shrug of their shoulders, until the farm official from whose arms the girl had fled to her death chased them off to work, irritably tapping his boot with his cane and shouting even more truculently than usual, which was obviously a result of his irritation. And this the farm servants respected too, for rather surprisingly they obeyed at the first command and even if they did steal a glance or two behind as they moved off, their eyes showed sympathy and understanding. The official —and I cannot help it if all this sounds rather like a medieval horror-story filtered through the imagination of Eötvös*— circled round and round the dead body, white as a sheet and utterly unable to do anything. He kept looking around, his face twitching, and kept everybody at bay, quite unnecessarily, like a dog with its bone. He was a squat, fairly stout figure, it was plain that he would not get over his annoyance, for he must have felt himself horribly deceived. The girl had transgressed custom and the usual order of things, for surely nobody could have been shocked that this was the girl he had commanded to come to him the day before. (The gossips said later that he had been drunk and wanted to pacify his more primitive desires.) Was it not the duty of the farm servants to obey in all circumstances? Neither he nor they could comprehend this rebellious act. She ought not to have sunk to this action for such a reason as that! Yet the girl by dying suddenly developed a personality and stood apart from the community. Her impenetrable silence provoked the anger of her own father against her. In amazement and indignation the old man stood there bareheaded, raising and lowering his arms as though excusing himself in front of the farm official. Later in my imagination this girl became the angel of defiance and revolt for me, with her pale, dead face and the raw flesh showing

* József Eötvös, statesman and writer (1813–1871).

through it. I envisaged her character, the powerful spirit in the 'simple peasant girl'; the spirit which revealed itself in the fire of suffering to me was like that of Joan of Arc... But at the time I certainly could not imagine what had made her escape from the world in such dire haste.

It was, after all, from her usual world where, in the cynical village proverb, 'only bread is not shared.' Had she a fiancé? Both she and her fiancé were born into a world where the reader, even having read thus far, would find it difficult to find his feet, where faithfulness can exist without physical fidelity. Both of them must have known that, like the bites of gnats and lice, there exist other kinds of bites and stings against which there is virtually no defence, but which can have as little effect upon one's honour or one's spirit as the former. The people of the pusztas are realists. After all even I, a child, knew this view of the world and regarded it as natural. I both saw and heard many expressions of it which only now, in retrospect, give me cause for reflection. 'Oh the old swine!' said the farm servants not long before this episode, of the old steward when the news got around that—in the strict sense of the word—he had been abusing the 12–14-year-old girls as they bent over the low troughs in the granaries where the wheat was washed... 'Is that right for such an old lame creature?' All their head-shaking and indignation was directed at him; nobody gave a thought to the girls. Not even the estate which in such cases, as in every other sphere, took action only if it thought its interests were endangered. On another occasion it became clear that one of the overseers of the day-labourers, whenever he was ordered to supervise the machines or maize-hoeing or thinning out the root-crops, always selected the same three girls for his gang and always made them fetch water, which was the lightest work. True, they were not yet of age. When it became known that he had 'made use of them', it was only the woeful pleadings of his wife and five children re-echoing through the puszta that prevented his dismissal. And not for moral reasons, but for his lapse of discipline. The puszta followed his family's fate with sympathy and anxiety.

Yet the relaxation of discipline for such reasons as this was truly rare. The people of the puszta did not abuse favours. Nor could the assistant farm manager who 'made use of' the girl destined to die complain on this account; he had used her not as a human being, but as one might use a drinking-mug or a shoehorn. The girl's family had not established any rights to undue familiarity or to any other claim. No, her funeral brought them no closer; in any case the assistant did not turn up at it. The girl was dead and her death was filed away in people's memory as if she had been snatched up by a machine or trampled on by a bull. Old Sövegjártó the coroner, who according to local legend decided the cause of death from the bitterness of the relatives' weeping, signed the certificate and we sang the girl away and cleared up after her. Perhaps I was the only one on the puszta who years later still attributed a romantic atmosphere of death and fate to the farm official, and almost expected him to shine in this role. He did not play this part. He could swear abominably (doubtless he tried to compensate thus for his youth and upstart origins) and he expressed his mental struggles and perhaps even his mourning by becoming even more churlish and irascible than usual for a long time afterwards. We understood this too.

I might also have expected the farm officials to defend and spare their peasant girl-friends, an attitude obviously based on stories of the rich count and the orphaned peasant girl. They did not defend them. The girls themselves did not flaunt such relationships, particularly in the presence of their illustrious lovers. It was certainly experience that taught them this. The gentry could not abide familiarity in public. I remember years later working as a day-labourer on a nearby puszta, tying up vines, I suddenly jerked up my head in surprise when I heard a farm official who had been sent out to supervise us attacking one of the girls who was falling behind. 'Do you imagine,'

191

he roared, 'that you can lounge about all day long because last night...' and here he used a word for intimacy which even the farm servants employ only to show their contempt.

The blood rushed to the cheeks of the girl concerned. This public disgrace seemed to strike sparks from her. She bowed her head and hurried on with her work, but when the official bowled off in his trap, she turned round, forced an unforgettable smile on her flaming cheeks and shouted after him a remark which I had never heard before from the lips of a farm girl.

At first I did not like this girl, not because I thought her depraved, but perhaps because she had been able to gain entry and insight into a world from which I was excluded. Moreover at this time the childish *hauteur* of folk who are debarred from something was beginning to turn me against it. However well I knew its inhabitants, the manor-house was still a feudal castle and a witches' den, and in its unpretentious way it did indeed swallow up young maidens. Did I envy the girl? Possibly. I thought her stupid to wander blindly in that bewitching world; none of its secrets surrounded her—she was not magically transformed into a fairy princess or into a cat. Every morning the poor creature appeared among us, sleepily yawning and rubbing her eyes. I turned away from her. But gradually my curiosity overcame this peculiar sulkiness. If we happened to be working side by side I began to ask her questions impersonally. What happened that night and how did it happen? My inquiries soon became mixed with other elements; I was beginning to reach adolescence. 'Tell me about everything in detail, from the moment you opened the door...' She glanced at me in astonishment over the leafy vines. 'Whatever is there to say about that?' 'What did they say, how did you know what was expected of you? How did they invite you there in the first place?' At lunch-time I settled down beside her. The more stubbornly she remained silent, the more I hung on to her and the more colourful became my imagination. 'I was given a pencil,' she said. I sidled after her everywhere and on occasion, with the coarse superiority of gawkishness, even wanted to make advances to her myself. 'Isn't it all the same to you?' I asked flippantly, but with face aflame. She hit me in the chest. It was of no account that she had gone up to the manor-house; that would not have upset her, nor shaken her sense of virginity, for it seemed to have happened in a dream. Around her too, perhaps because of her very silence, I seemed to sense an aura of death. I should not have been surprised if she had jumped down a well. She did not; she became a 'happy mother' of four children in one of the dark dens of the drivers' dwellings.

What I so much wanted to know in detail I found out much later when, far removed from my old superstitious prejudices, I walked in utter, real and unfeigned boredom through the musty rooms of those famous manor-houses, the last refuge of antlers, antique furniture, embroidery and chromo-lithographs of appalling tastelessness. Now I had to feign appreciation and delight. The inhabitants of these gloomy rooms could have been my friends; it depended on me how far they would take me to their hearts. I listened to the conversations with a fixed smile and nodded at the most scandalous stories and opinions, like an ambassador who has no right to interfere in the affairs of a foreign country. I was the writer who had travelled round the world. To those who had even been as far as Budapest I was the editor-in-chief, though none of them, fortunately, had ever read a single line of mine. I asked polite questions and restrained my astonishment at the ignorance shown by even the older generation about their immediate surroundings. I was astounded at the stubborn defence of the spirit evidenced by the young folk who were blind to the filth and squalor seething and bubbling all around them; if they were girls, they preserved their angelic innocence, and if boys, their idealistic patriotism. It is certain that they were able to remain pure; the infamy that welled up beneath them did not reach even the heels of their

193

boots. They simply took no notice of it, just like the refined young countess who smiles in accordance with the strictest etiquette as she gallops beside her beau over the spring meadows and utterly disregards the horse beneath her as it frequently relieves itself. Often after dinner, when the company had been suitably reduced as the wine went round, and the men who had stood the test were thrown together in affectionate companionship, I would use the warm intimacy of this all-male fraternity to ask how we stood with the farm girls. It was a welcome question, which brought out happy recollections, good stories and tales of masculine triumph everywhere. The ribald conquests of old turned into gallant escapades. 'Oh, in my time...' they began and their eyes grew tender at the sweet savour of the past. 'Last year on the puszta here...' they continued, naming the very girls I knew or to whom they would introduce me the next day, and they would vie with each other in telling me all the details. Homeric gusts of laughter swirled through the dense clouds of cigarette smoke. 'That one demands another drink!' I joined in their laughter and, in the brief interval after a round of drinks or the swaggering demand that we drain our glasses, my glance rose from the glistening red faces to rest on the ceiling and I was astonished to realise how little it needed for me to mingle with this society and how close my laughter was to being really sincere. Was this perhaps real life—this unconscious acceptance of sadism—and my pangs of conscience a sign of disease? Fortunately there was always somebody who overstepped the mark. They would grasp me by the arm and with the slobbering familiarity awarded by the half-educated to a writer (for a writer understands everything, and as a Bohemian must be a connoisseur of filth), they would tell stories, veiling their indecency in guffaws, and answer my questions in such detail that my taste, if nothing else, reminded me of the task in hand. 'You can make a jolly good little tale out of that!' I could scarcely bear to listen. 'Do you mind if I take some notes?' I interjected. The story-teller winked at me:

'Naturally without mentioning names, old chap...' 'Naturally,' I replied.

My old curiosity was rekindled. The tales were more or less the same everywhere and most of them went into details about the physique of the girls. What interested me almost to bursting-point was how the girls behaved. How did they know what they had to do and when?

'Tell me everything in detail,' I said to these casual acquaint-ances, barely concealing my excitement, 'from the moment she comes through the door and you call her inside. How do you let her know that she can come in, or rather that she must come in?'

All this went much more easily than I had imagined. 'Well, you just send a message to so-and-so to come that evening,' said a young, friendly-looking steward as he embraced me, 'to mend your clothes. I've only had girls come up to me to do mending. That's how they knew me. When they were with the machines or out hoeing, old chap, and I asked one of them if she could sew, she would look down at the ground and know perfectly well what she had to do. And there was one girl whose father brought her along. True, the old man had a reason for laying it on thick, because we were all ready to rap his knuckles for something he'd been up to.'

'So there are some who don't come readily, then?'

'Just a few, old chap, just a few, but all the same they all know what's wanted. At most they make a little scene when they're inside—that is, the cheeky ones. But all the lot of them will come—you know, it's a kind of honour for them, a sort of distinction... They envy those who have the "right of access", because they can tell stories afterwards. One of them scratched me horribly, a one-eyed girl; for three whole weeks I was dead keen on her, perhaps just because she was one-eyed, confound her. Another brought her elder brother with her, she had to have a chaperon. All right. Both of them had terribly severe faces. We sat down and started talking and soon became good friends. Round about ten o'clock the lad said, "Well, sir, shall I leave the girl here?" "Yes, leave her here, my boy," I said.'

Private conversation with the girls, of course, is hard to get going, but there is a remedy for this too. 'Drink, old chap, drink; without drink it's a complicated business, especially with those who are legally under age (not yet 16); once upon a time I took a great fancy to them. I was mad on them, my friend; I'd read some idiotic book and was crazy about them and them only—the unbroken girls, as they say round here—a whole stream of them one after the other... I was mad. Anyway, you want a bottle of wine; without that they're tongue-tied, and the whole game just isn't worth the candle unless you can talk a bit. Of course they don't even want to drink, they're dreadfully bashful. But if they won't have wine, you can give them tea with a good tot of rum in it, they'll all take a sip of that. Supper? They wouldn't touch it. And as for cake, they'll just break off a little piece and peck away at it all evening. I had some sweets and chocolate waiting for one of them. She took the whole packet and stuck it into the pocket of her skirt; she wouldn't even glance at it in my presence. They've got good manners, these people. But if you can implore them to get the first glass down, then you're away.'

You can have a good conversation with them about all sorts of things.

'For example, where they were on Sunday. What was the dance like? Who are their girl-friends? In short, everything except work, because that might remind them of who they really are. And you mustn't mention their mother either. You can talk about their father, brothers and sisters and even their grandmother, but don't bring their mother into the conversation, old chap, even by accident; that's my advice. If you do, it's all up and you can begin again at the beginning. But best of all they like to sing. I've had some lovely evenings like that. She comes in and sits in the corner, well out of the light, and sings away to herself and laughs quietly, according to how much you can get her to drink. When I was working over the way at B., I had a room in the estate manager's house and he had some unmarried daughters... so I had to be careful, I couldn't make much of a row. But the farm girls there were always wanting to sing, so in my room they just hummed away under their breath and it was as delicate as the twanging of a thread of cotton. I've never felt so much at home with anybody, not even with a fine lady, as with these little girls as they sang; I could have listened to them till morning. Afterwards they began to grow sleepy. Particularly after they'd had a bath, because I made them have a bath too.'

They do not abuse this confidence; there are no such cases. It is just as I had surmised. Indeed those who accept the invitation are all the more diligent and obedient. 'It is as if they want to keep in your good books... They're all the more ready to take your orders, as if something might come of the affair... In short, they're women. But in the presence of others they wouldn't admit for the world that there is anything between us. Or rather they betray it when you meet them at work by looking down at the ground and their hands move like lightning— at least that's what happens in these parts.'

I could have listened to expert lectures on the customs in various districts, and about the difference between areas of clay and sandy soil, for this difference appears in their morality also. Where the puszta has a clay soil and consequently much effort is needed in hoeing, the folk tend to be reticent and sullen, and can hardly wait to fall into bed in the evenings. But where the soil is sandy and the hoe glides along almost by itself, there is no end to the romping every evening and all that goes with it. Then there was talk of the more refined disposition of our region of Transdanubia. Here the folk still manage to preserve their primeval nature. (Coming from such lips the word 'primeval', you will certainly realise, must be taken to mean slavish, animal and everything that offends the human intellect.) Not so in the upper reaches of the Tisza, where the people cannot even keep their womenfolk decently clothed, but will go out for the blood of anyone, even a gentleman, if he so much as casts a glance at a woman. Then I heard more detailed accounts of certain customs; for example in Fejér county the girls get undressed, but in our district you cannot get them even to take off their aprons—they are so bashful that they cover their faces with them. (The very next day I noted the opposite of this truth. I was sitting on the couch in the room of one of the farm officials when in came one of the girl share-croppers. She had refused to carry away the chaff after threshing because, she said, her shoulders ached. But this had happened a couple of days before, and now she could not have had the faintest idea why she had been called in. My friend was concerned with health and hygiene; it was he who decided who was unfit for work, who should be sent to the doctor in the village. He said to her, 'Take off your blouse!' and went out of the room to do something else. The girl glanced at me, then blushed furiously as if she had suddenly realised something. When I looked up from the book I was reading, there she stood in front of me, in her chemise only. I got up and put my hand on her bare shoulder, then in my confusion I quickly made my way out. So clumsily did I reach for the latch that I broke the bottom pane of the glass door and cut my wrist quite badly. The girl, seeing the blood, came over to me in fright and almost followed me into the yard just as she was.) Elsewhere, there was talk of the real or pretended susceptibilities of the farm girls, illustrated with highly-spiced anecdotes. 'They behave like a block of wood, old chap ('but one with branches!' interrupted somebody with a guffaw). To them it is the most terrible disgrace if they betray their share in the proceedings.' And then I heard of the ingenious attempts to cover up the really big scandals that occur but rarely. Either they marry off the girl, or they give one of the farm lads a free hand with her and, well, 'let her get her maintenance allowance out of him!' Elsewhere I learnt of the unbelievable stupidity and credulity of the puszta folk, which allow even those who are rather proud of their exploits and bridle against such ideas to lead their betrothed to the altar with head held high. 'Well in this, old chap, they're incredibly stupid, that's certain. For example, there was once a girl who used to visit me regularly for at least two months. Of course they talked about it. One or two folk actually saw her coming too. One fine day her boy friend comes to see me—of course with his cap in his hand—gently does it!—and standing to attention, as is right and proper—and stutters something about having heard this and that, with respect. It was too late to deny it. But I felt sorry for him; why should I make his life miserable? "Yes, she's been to my room," I say to him, "but it was only for a chat." And what do you think? He believed me straight away and even thanked me for my kindness... And they're clumsy and greedy as animals; they've no refinement at all. Some time ago at a dance one of the girls nearly knocked the eyes out of a lad. They came up before me—it all happened in the stackyard where they had slipped away from the dance. I couldn't understand the affair. If the girl had gone off with that particular boy, why did she go for his eyes? "He wanted to bully me," said the girl, but not using that word, of course. I had a private word with the boy. "What did you want to do to her?" I asked. "Just that," he replied. "Did you kiss her?" At this he was amazed. "Do you mean I ought to have kissed her as well?" he asked. They don't know as much as we do about their own wives. And yet they have a good proverb: "You can't deceive a cow or a woman." Do you understand? You've got to give them both their due.'

This was the kind of thing I heard. I recall those faraway stifling evenings which the next morning had leapt a frightening distance away and, like the bits of coloured paper from the bottom of a kaleidoscope, there race before me, one on top of the other, tales which are bizarre in their very dullness, anecdotes without any point and the ghostly guffaws which burst forth without any rational cause. There emerge lady-killers

reminiscent of the heroes of the young Móricz,* artful amusements which vie with the orgies of Montmartre, the faces of farm girls fainting on their temporary bridal couches, slaps and bloodstained sheets, interrogations in the course of which 26 lads admitted that they were in love with the same girl, unmarried women who had risen to the height of 'waitresses' in Budapest; there were pusztas whose entire male population had been ordered to another part of the country for a whole year, where now (and this evoked the loudest laughter) all the children strongly resembled one of the farm officials present. I heard of abortions, the killing of children, the jocular listing of rules governing the parts of the girls' bodies which could be touched by hand (the breast came last of all), and the sudden death of women. I leave it to the imagination of the reader to put them into some sort of order, for this is surely not the first time he has heard of such matters. To one of the pusztas the sheep-shearers used to come from the market town of Sz. on the Great Plain. Every year they had to bring for one of the farm officials a 'pupil', who was to be a particularly beautiful virgin girl. They found it difficult to convince me that there are still fairy-tale occurrences in this world, with virgins and dragons, but lacking precisely the brave knight who comes to the rescue...
In order to decide on their ability to work, the estate at Cs. ordered all labourers offering themselves for hire to undergo a medical examination and extended this practice to those already employed. The rumour went round among the girls, who were all called in on the first day, that their virginity was to be examined. Out of the whole puszta (and here again there was a roar of laughter) only two girls dared to put in an appearance. But now even these folk are beginning to become impudent; they are going from bad to worse, like the whole world in general. Mr W., the accountant, had a beautiful 'daily woman'.

* Zsigmond Móricz (1879–1942) depicted country life in his novels with stark realism.

('Yes, I taught her!') He made her swear not to have any dealings with anyone else... They lived in a paradise of happiness; the girl was a mere fledgling, the very embodiment of animation. Two weeks later he discovered her at the foot of a haystack with one of the boys. 'I had a sudden fit of anger. I lifted my hand and all she did was to step back pertly and ask me insolently what business it was of mine.' "Nobody orders me away from my pleasure," she said, using the expression normally given in reply to gossiping old women.'

'That's just like these folk, old chap; they haven't the faintest idea of what honesty means.'

It is not usual to give presents. 'In this respect at least they still have some feelings of honour.' The truth is that the girls dare not accept gifts. For while it may be common knowledge that someone has the 'right of access', gossip really begins when there is some material proof of it, and then it is utterly cruel. 'They're jealous; that's why,' declares one of the milk inspectors who makes his rounds from puszta to puszta and cheerfully boasts that there is a family waiting for him in each one. When he started, he once gave a girl a woollen scarf. The next evening at the well the women tore it away from her with much quarreling and brawling, and trod it into the mud. From that time onwards they called the girl a whore, even out in the open. So did her mother at home.

In all these tales there is certainly a good deal of masculine bravado. The defencelessness of the puszta girls, indeed, may well be greater than that of girls working in the towns, but only in proportion to their isolation and lack of education. It is highly likely that if someone were to describe the situation of working women in a factory the picture would be no brighter. True, the people of the pusztas are far more restricted. They cannot leave their place so easily from one day to the next, or even from one year to the next. The farm servant with eight or ten children does not give in his notice, pile on to a cart all his hen-houses, furniture and a piglet or two, and then go off into

201

the world to find a new job simply because one of his girls has had a sudden desire to move. And suppose he were to get up and out at the end of the year, would there be a different fate in store for them elsewhere? Moreover, they do not know any other way of making a livelihood except by being farm servants. And in the black night of ignorance, destitution and barbarism there seems to be no other way of escape but submission or death. They do not often die of it. There might remain the solution so beloved of middle-class novels—the death of the seducer, but not even the oldest folk on the pusztas can recall such an event. Very very rarely, say once in a century, somebody in a fit of anger may perhaps strike a bailiff or assistant, and then it is not because of a love-affair. The farm servants forgive these seducers of extraordinary power and fascination; indeed they even pity them with that sensitive, often excessive eagerness to show sympathy which is such a characteristic trait of the poor in their relations with the rich. 'After all, he's a human being too,' they say of some trouble-stirring farm official, 'it's just his nature. What else can he do?' There is some truth in this. What can a young farm official do? Sometimes he is stationed for years in some puszta at the back of beyond and can count himself lucky if he gets within sight of a town once a year.

Of course the girls of the puszta, not content with the two possible solutions of submission and death, sometimes attempt the impossible third one. However, many gallant escapades I heard from the lips of the overseers, I also heard of almost as many heart-warming tricks from their chosen sacrifices, of how they succeeded in evading their conquerors if for some exceptional reason they were not to their taste. On such occasions, the puszta would turn into a magnificent comedy, staged every night for weeks. There were enigmatic schemers, endless and interwoven entanglements, wigs, girls made up to look like old women, if it was a question of rescuing somebody and there was some hope of being able to keep them for themselves...

These plays, in which I myself once or twice took part at least as prompter, if nothing else, would be followed by tremendous merriment and grateful expressions of thanks, not to mention the comments that went on for months. It was here that I learnt that one can fight, even if it is only grim humour or self-mockery which is liable to backfire, and the only satisfaction gained from it is that of the child who grimaces and catches his breath, yet impelled by irresistible desire still goes on pulling the scab from his wound.

CHAPTER THIRTEEN

Culture on the puszta. School and church life. Poet-reporters

Uncle Hanák's landlady opened the school door at half-past seven in the morning. I have happy memories of school. What was it that I picked up there that now, years later, brings out great pleasure in me, rather like those medicines which send one into a fever days after taking them? The more zealous pupils who arrived at half-past seven were divided into various main and subsidiary groups. The most pleasant one was to carry water; Aunt Pápa, the landlady, allotted six boys and four girls to this group. We boys paired ourselves off and got hold of a can or tub, then sauntered to the puszta well, telling each other jokes on the way. In four or five trips we had filled the big wash-tub in the kitchen and the three butts in the garden, from which the girls poured the water into the tiny troughs for the bees and the cleverly-contrived little channels in the tomato-beds. For Uncle Hanák was a model gardener and was famous throughout the county as a beekeeper. Meanwhile the second group of children chopped mangolds for the cows and fed the pigs and poultry. The next little group husked maize. Some children also found employment round the chopping-block, but with a bad grace, because nobody liked it. Yet one had to obtain permission to transfer from one group to another. Discipline was firm. The proverbial state—that half the school hoes the master's garden as a punishment and the other half as a reward—came true only rarely, after the gentle rains of May.

All this activity lasted for exactly one hour. After we had finished our morning chores, Uncle Hanák appeared in the classroom, by which time all six classes had assembled. We welcomed him joyfully. The girls sat in one row of desks, the boys in the next; it was a co-educational system. Lessons began.

Those who wanted to learn could assimilate an enormous amount, and whatever they pleased. They had a rich choice at their disposal. Uncle Hanák began by teaching the first class, then went on to the second and third classes and so on. While he was occupied with one class, the rest prepared their lessons or even then perhaps fetched water if, for example, it was wash-day in the house. The principle of free competition was used in answering questions: those in the lower classes might offer to answer questions put to the upper ones, and Uncle Hanák took their answers into account when he reported their progress. This is probably why I had an extensive knowledge of constitutional law when I was in Class 1, for this was among the subjects taught. On the other hand it was not until the eve of the matriculation examination that I finally resolved to acquire a knowledge of multiplication and basic arithmetic; I was a-fraid that the examiner would not understand my occasional moments of perplexity, as a result of which I often found during my eight years of schooling that I could not perform a simple multiplication, though I was better than average at mathematics. With Uncle Hanák we practised mainly the prayer of confession, at an incredible speed. Watch in hand, Uncle Hanák kept an eye on the tempo and conducted with his stick, urging us to go even faster. Answering questions on this developed into a competition, and there were some real champions among us.

Ecclesiastically, as I have already mentioned, the puszta belonged to the parish of Pálfa. Once a week a carriage was sent for the parish priest from Pálfa; sometimes it brought him back and sometimes it did not. At the end of the schoolroom opposite the dais, big folding doors hid a small chapel with a proper altar, on each side of which there were forms for the local dignitaries to sit on. On Saturday evenings we opened the doors and turned the desks round to make a church of the schoolroom. On Mondays we shut the doors again and only the more sensitive souls like myself could not forget the proximity of this consecrated place. The room, where the keen-scented could still catch a whiff of incense several days afterwards, was also used sometimes for dancing. Here too the low comedians who occasionally found their way to the puszta took the stage, amusing their audience with the crudest possible jokes.

On the Saturdays preceding the great festivals we might be honoured by the presence of both the parish priest and our school supervisor. On these occasions the whole puszta came to confession and next day received communion. It was said that once upon a time the count himself made certain that all his farm servants performed their religious duties satisfactorily. Both the Apponyis and Zichys were true Catholics and had a concern for the souls entrusted by God to their care. Such mass confessions at Christmas and Easter remained customary even under the régime of the Jewish tenants.

From the chapel door the farm servants stood in a long single file through the schoolroom, out into the yard, indeed almost as far as the ox-stables. They chatted together, while cigarette smoke and uninhibited girlish laughter rose here and there from the queue. The young men threw sparkling kreutzers high into the air as they gambled, for when they had a little free time and two or three of them were gathered together they always gambled. Uncle Hanák would look out of the window from time to time to see how many of us were still to come. In one single afternoon from one to two hundred folk would make their confession. And now it became clear why we had to practise the rapid muttering of the prayer of confession. We schoolchildren were the first to come, panting out the

206

prayer with dangerous haste, together with the list of sins which had taken us so much trouble to compile, usually helped by our mothers when we grew desperate.

The parish priest was severe, and just the type of man required for the people of the puszta. He was more like a soldier, in his tone, his looks and even in his gait. He was rather the servant of order and discipline than of humility. Confession resembled an interrogation. Were not all those present guilty in advance and deserving of a severe sentence? There were no confessional boxes. The priest sat in a simple armchair, his back straight as a ramrod, legs crossed and hands tightly clasped. He shot a sharp glance at each newcomer. We tried to get over it quickly, thinking of the others waiting outside. Sometimes he would look us up and down, and occasionally reprove us with a brief, carefully-chosen phrase, for he too was in a hurry. We poured out our souls and he, like the good shopkeeper who automatically knows the price of everything, doled out the appropriate penance without a moment's thought. He would then hold out his hand to be kissed, thereby signifying that we might go. And so we went, almost at a run.

On Sundays I was a server. At all seasons of the year I had boots which I could wear before the altar. 'Ad Deum qui laetificat juventutem meam...' I began and he continued the phrase. The peculiar sentences of the liturgy crackled out like words of command. Once in my excitement I spilt some of the wine. 'Idiot!' he growled at me so that the congregation could have heard him if they happened to be listening. I crouched down, terrified of the God who had such an interpreter. With my head well down and in heartfelt fear and humility I offered him the censer on its chain.

How did Uncle Hanák, who was a revolutionary, get on with him? Uncle Hanák, we knew, had been transferred to the puszta from somewhere in Upper Hungary as a punishment, but even this did not break his spirit. Before he came it had been the custom that the children of the farm officials did not sit in the same desks as the other children. Places were reserved for them beside the teacher on the dais. Uncle Hanák put an end to this with a single wave of the hand. As a result, it is true, he was promptly struck off the list of those perquisites awarded as presents by the estates to the intellectuals of the puszta. But what did he care? He had his bees. Did the parish priest also keep bees? After he had finished his official business he would have long conversations with Uncle Hanák, who was obviously talking to him about bees, because he had no other real subject of conversation. Sometimes the two of them would stroll over to see us and do us the honour of sitting at our table. My father would run quickly over to the vine-dresser, who always had a spare bottle of wine or two. When not on duty, the priest was friendly or even inclined to be matey. He would raise his glass to the light, smack his lips and roar with laughter at the anecdotes; he would put his hand on my father's shoulder and joke about my mother's heretical origins. I gazed at him in astonishment and fear. He was the first person I had met who behaved in two utterly different ways. It was as if he embodied two souls, two quite separate people. His clerical garb awoke endless respect in me; I felt that he held my fate in his hands and could thrust me into eternal damnation with a single nod. I preferred him when he was stern and unapproachable to the times when he wiped his mouth with the back of his hand and cheerfully took a second helping of stuffed cabbage. There was something eerie about his informality. I should not have been surprised if he had suddenly given himself a shake, turned into an eagle and flown out of the window.

Both to him and to Uncle Hanák I owe a debt of thanks. They were the first who presumed—on what basis I do not know—to discover my intellectual abilities. I drew with 'astounding' skill, chiefly from memory, but at any time of the day or night, even if I were suddenly woken up from sleep. Most of all I liked to draw steam-ploughs. 'Marvellous!' shouted Uncle Hanák after the third glass of wine, 'it's even got a pressure-gauge as well!' I was also an excellent reader. Though I stumbled from time to time, my pronunciation was correct and natural, and 'it was clear that I understood what I was reading.' I became a child-prodigy, like all children, without exception, who are under observation. This opinion slowly gained ground in the family until it caught up with me and began to infect me. I became proud, yet was scared stiff lest they put me to the test, for the rumour went around that I was an excellent mathematician too.

True, I loved going to school. There was no day-nursery in the puszta, and my mother let me go off to school with my elder brothers and sisters long before I was of school age. Naturally I had no books, but so that I should not go empty-handed, my mother gave me a fine agricultural spare-parts catalogue. I held this up in front of me while the others spelt out their words at the tops of their voices. A very great deal that I happened to hear thus stuck firmly in my mind. I did not yet know how to read, but if they stood the catalogue in front of me, I would recite whole pages of verse and readings I had heard in school. Educationalists say that there is no method so bad that it cannot be used to teach a child spelling sooner or later. Even under the guidance of Uncle Hanák I had acquired the knowledge of reading. What is more I quickly learnt to write—indeed I soon became a famous writer.

I wrote on fences, it is true, but most of all I liked to write on nice, whitewashed walls. I published various simple physiological facts and plain, direct advice in the largest possible letters I was able to make by using the full extent of my arm. I also carried on a news service, consisting chiefly of invented engagements, but I was not afraid of launching a few personal attacks, complete with a pithy adjective or two. I have already mentioned my prowess at drawing. Unfortunately—was it the itch to play a role or the vanity of an author?—my products, though only one or two of them could be regarded as all my own work, were all without exception signed, because best of all I loved to practise my own name. In those happy days I seemed to feel in my fingers the sensual joy of writing. This led to a continual stream of serious conflicts. And as if this were not enough, with half a day's diligent work I produced a whole market of steam-ploughs on the newly-whitewashed wall of the bailiff's house. Just imagine a herd of horses in which every single figure, horseherds as well as horses, and even the storks flying above them, all happened to be relieving themselves.

My ability was beginning to degenerate.

Nobody had a good word to say about the school. Within the meaning of the Act, the estate bore its costs, yet what good did it get out of it? Certain agricultural operations, in the opinion of the eminent experts of our age, can best be performed only by children—for example, shelling beans or lentils. Their nimble, pliant bodies are suitable also for picking caterpillars, for they have not grown far from the ground. With proper supervision and instigation they can weed at twice the speed of adults.

We roared our approval when we arrived at school in the morning and were told that we were going into the fields that day instead of having classes. We marched out and picked off caterpillars. It was a day off, but this does not mean that we learnt absolutely nothing. We were learning the ways of life. Uncle Hanák did not accompany us; his task was taken over by the regular overseers of the estate, who in one single day were naturally unable to get out of their usual rut, so they treated us as they did the adults. They walked behind us with sticks, raining short but well-directed blows on our trousers, which were strained heavenwards as we bent down. They also used commands to keep our enthusiasm of the morning trained in the way it should go. It is interesting that the slightest tap of Uncle Hanák's hand was enough to produce a terrible bellow of pain in the classroom, but here you could have heard a pin drop. How was this? Was it a sense of duty or the effect of fresh air? Was it the gentle whisper of nature that here one must stand up like a man, sweat and weep as we might? We scoffed at those who broke down easily, indeed we secretly added a few blows of our own to them. It was as if they had broken the rules of a game whose rules we had already divined.

The estate employed children for such work at daily rates. We received 10 or 20 fillérs per day, and had the satisfaction of getting up at the same time as the men, in other words before sunrise. We carried the same sort of haversack for our food as they did.

Grandmother approved of our going out to daily work. (She still did so much later, when I was attending the upper forms of secondary school.) 'Just let them get inured to it,' she would say, 'they will earn all the more respect if they happen to do well in life.'

In general the parents themselves could not abide the school. They regarded it as the stupid idea of some distant authority which had no close knowledge of affairs as they stood. They received no daily wages for children who went to school, but they did for those who went pea-picking. They could hire out children of 9 or 10 years old. Their children were sent to school as if they were doing a great favour, or sending them to work for nothing. At all events they gave them no lunch, though most parents would have been unable to do so even if they had wanted to.

About half the pupils came from the far side of the puszta, which was so distant that they could not go home between morning and afternoon school. What did they eat? Nothing. Those who brought a round of bread or a handkerchief full of boiled maize were rich, and at the cost of a carefully-measured morsel or so could lord it over the others and do exactly what they wanted with them.

Besides all this, the puszta school was a place to be ashamed of... no gentleman would send his children there. The intellectuals of the puszta sent their children to the village or town schools. There was a great deal of discussion about this in our family too, not because we wanted to put on airs, but because grandmother thought it important for the children to learn something and not just wear out their clothes and have their jacket dusted for them. She went on a round of the villages. The news she brought back was not reassuring. In K., the method of the schoolmaster was to load his waggon with manure in the morning, stop with it outside the school, cane the whole class and drive on out to his fields. He was an excellent farmer. About eleven o'clock, on his way back, he beat the class once again. He taught only when the weather was bad. In D., every child had to bring a log every day and lay it on the dais by the teacher's desk; those who brought two logs were exempted from all mental endeavour for the day. And in V., everywhere the situation was much the same. There remained Ozora, where the Catholic school was the subject of much talk, perhaps because it was two-storeyed. My brothers and sisters were already at school there. It looked as though I was to share the same fate. My mother packed up my belongings and we set out. At Simontornya I was given some new boots, and we continued our journey. But on the outskirts, by the second bridge over the Sió, my mother came to a sudden halt. She walked up and down for some time, then suddenly took me in her arms, the tears streaming down her cheeks. 'Do you want to leave your mother?' she asked. 'No,' I replied solemnly. How did I know what was in her mind? Ozora meant not only the spirit of my father's family, but also estrangement from my mother, even at that age. We turned back. 'I know how to read already,' I said later. I was entered at Rácegres in the second or third class.

As far as reading went, everybody learnt to read at school, and many folk on the puszta know how to read. It is through them that European culture filters in. It is something of a mystery how it penetrates, since newspapers, for example, are not taken in the farm servants' dwellings. The drivers who cart goods into the villages occasionally read a copy and this is passed around. Otherwise print arrives only in the form of wrapping-paper, almanacs and those little books entitled 'Duties of the Best Man'. These can be found even today in every family. But just as the waste from a little village tannery can destroy all the fish in a lake, or a tiny drop of paint change the colour of a bath, so the fluid from these slender channels has obscured, confused and finally killed the culture of a whole stratum of society. So far in the puszta this is the only result of the struggle against illiteracy, which is regarded throughout the world as a standard of culture; we may as well admit this if we look at it objectively. I wonder when the people of the pusztas were more educated: when they had never heard tell of printing, or now that they have? I certainly could not give a ready answer to this. Now they are certainly not educated.

Not long ago, for example, this very region of which I am writing poured forth a stream of folk art as rich and inexhaustible as the geysers in Iceland... Bartók—to call in a higher authority—collected almost a third of the epoch-making material for his *Hungarian Folk Song* at Ireg, near Ozora. Nowadays the farm servants sing pop-tunes; such is the way of things. They do still sing folk songs, but those who subscribe to culture and want to get on in the world fill the air with the ballads of the capital. This is the way of development, they say. This throws me into a quandary. They still talk about 'historical necessity,' but the use of this term in other fields has long ago coupled it in my mind with the impotent stupidity of a generation, and when I hear it I swallow hard. What good can be expected from a culture at whose distant breath all that is of real spiritual value withers away and disintegrates? I have no need, I think, to proclaim my faith in 'progress'; my readers will understand that it is not the spread of reading and writing that grieves me, but only their present form. Have they served the cause of enlightenment? Must I produce examples to prove that the press has disseminated among the farm servants far more numerous and dangerous superstitions about the world and society than any old witch with her peering glance? In the pusztas the printed word spreads clouds of rubbish, well-tried and tested internationally.

So we still have something to be thankful for, even if it is on the decline. The gutter press, in whose columns some gentleman, who is thrice as servile and spineless as a swineherd on the puszta and ten times as uninformed about life or even Hungarian style, informs the said swineherd of a successful hunt, a prince's wedding or a hair-raising sex murder, does not inspire me to gladness at the passing of an intellectual age when the daily news still arrived on the puszta on wings of song and in this form:

> 'Have you heard what happened down in Sárbogárd?
> Feri Kis was killed there, in the little yard...'

and so on up to the point where the mother of one of the murderers sends the message to her son in prison:

> 'Rest his weary head upon his curly hair,
> Use it as a coverlet to cloak his courage there.'

It was the poets who carried on a news service. And they were hawk-eyed sociologists, who got right to the heart of the matter when they commented on the most trifling incidents.

If only the printed word had taken this over! Unfortunately it retained only a minute part of it. Yet the spirit of the puszta made an attempt to conquer the spirit of the printed word, not

214

suspecting that this too had its own special regulations. The results of this clash could be seen in many interesting blends.

Most of the folk on the puszta who could write as well as read were writers in earnest. I do not know what the situation is elsewhere, but on every puszta in Tolna and Baranya there can be found at least one poet, sometimes two or three. They are particularly numerous among the landless peasants in the villages, because there they have even more time to devote to writing. They write on little bits of paper—if indeed they have any paper at all, for this is not essential. Usually they just 'say their fill' in four to eight lines, which either survive or perish. They call themselves poet-reporters. They are not concerned with national news; they do not roam the whole country unless perhaps they hire themselves out as harvesters. They are tranquil folk, who work normally but while they are doing it they think up poems. After the First World War when there was plenty of money in the villages, some of them had their works printed, in four-page newspaper style. It was only then that it transpired how many of them there really were. In the printing works at Dombóvár it was not unknown for the machines to be clattering away at night also. The ordinary peasants who, where writing was concerned, remained just as tight-fisted when there was plenty of money about, laughingly and proudly bought and read the pamphlets which had originated from among them and contained news of their own life. The village of Görbő had its own poet, so had Nak and Egyházbér. In Döbrököz, István Nagy Kovács was active, in Szakcs there was József Tóth-Pál and around Mocsolád someone called Keresztesi... And how many others were there, prevented from public appearance by the tradition-al modesty of the poet? The whole area buzzed with creative activity. In my own family I am not the first writer.

In many respects they were innovators. They broke through the rigid rules of prosody. Here and there an important statement or substantial observation would extrude a large bump on the traditional form of the verse, like a piece of hard filling in a sausage, but these were the tastiest morsels of their products, though it is true to say that only the real experts could savour them fully. 'Ear Bitten in Baranya' proclaimed one title. 'Orphan Girl in Regöly Jumps Down Well' said the next. 'In Tamási Even the Girls Shave', 'Seven Litres of Milk in the German's Stomach', 'Virgin Bride in Egyházbér', 'Love for Fourteen Kreutzers', etc., etc. 'A Little Blossoming Rose in the Devil's Hands' told how a retired assistant farm manager raped a thirteen-year-old girl in the stables at Sütvény-puszta. Every verse published an exact item of news, briefly and to the point.

'A storekeeper of Nagyszokol, a butcher in Ireg
Went out on the spree with the lovely actress...'

Lines like these are typical of Tóth-Pál. And as for his brevity, the following lines about a knife-grinder are typical:

'Down in Nagyberek, a dealer turned the stone,
While his neighbour held an axe for him to hone.
When the axe was sharp, he hurled it in his face,
For he'd seen the dealer his own wife embrace.
Red blood spattered forth upon the grinding-stone.
Let everyone beware of lust too great to own.'

Nor was profundity lacking, as well as drama:

'A Látrány man loaded his Lancaster rifle with shot
And into his very best friend he emptied the lot.
The news of the shooting went quickly around that day.
When they meet in the next world I'd like to know what
they will say.'

But it was not only ballad-like events that they published. Most difficult of all, they glimpsed and noted the vibrations of the

216

spirit of the people. Psychologists and ethnographers alike will certainly find a precious gem in the following six lines:

'Among the boys of Kurd, this is the latest craze:
In the pockets of their coat they put a little maize.
This is why they deep within their pockets stow it—
Later in the spinnery at the girls they throw it.
All the girls of Kurd, they like the latest fashion;
When a boy throws maize, it signifies his passion!'

They also cultivated the epistolary style, in a modern idiom. 'Poetic Epistle to the Workers of Mocsolád' was written by the poet of Döbrököz to console those whom the priest had had jailed, because:

'Coming home from work, we were singing in the street
When we met the priest, who most rudely did us greet.
All of us he caught he struck at with his hand,
Till he was chased home again by our little band.'

'Poetic Epistle to My Legally Divorced Wife with 70 Acres, Alsónyék, Tolna' discloses revelations about the poet's mother-in-law. The author married into a one-child family from Sár-köz in the depths of winter. But

'Scarcely had the month of March begun to bloom above
Than there came an evil worm to poison all our love.
Such a monster worm it was—I've never seen another,
Vicious, weird and horrible—for it was your mother.
I'll not hide it from you; her crime to you I'll tell:
Reprobate she was, for *she* desired my love as well.'

The poet was hounded away and later prosecuted for this poem. He shouldered the responsibility for his work. 'Poetic Thanks to My Cruel Enemy' touches on an eternal truth at the end:

217

'For he who's born a poet
Does not grab a pitchfork for to thrash an evil wife,
But through the printed word
Pours out all the inner secret truth he's learnt from life.'

In the poetic epistle sent 'To My Friend János Balaskó who
Has Emigrated to Canada', we have a really captivating, artistic picture of a forsaken dwelling. This poem discloses a decided talent. Here we may see what could have become of the
author—indeed, what could become of all these folk if they had
a chance:

'Now around your house it's silent,
Not like yesteryear.
There's no straw within the garden,
Nor a haystack there.
Nothing moves within your courtyard
Where the clods congeal.
Last summer horses' hooves did not disturb it,
Nor the waggon wheel.
Still in piles lies all your firewood
Waiting to be chopped,
That you got at Csurgó in the winter
When the prince's trees you lopped.
Your poor wife's in trouble. She's no
Wood to make a blaze.
She must cook her meagre supper
On the stalks of maize...'

I knew a lot of poets. Some of them could not even write, but
could turn any given theme into rounded cadences after a few
moments' thought. We had a poet too, Uncle Gondos. I used
to settle down beside him fascinated; rocking with laughter on
the seat of the ox-cart, I enjoyed his creations at the moment of
birth as he reeled them off. In them there would glitter side by

side a stork's nest, a molehill, the moon, and what was under the oxes' tail. 'La poésie n'a qu'une ennemie: la littérature'— the puszta poets worked in accordance with Léon-Paul Fargue's excellent maxim. You think perhaps that I am saying this with my tongue in my cheek? Not at all. Real poetic works come to birth as easily, unconsciously and innocently as possible, or if they have to struggle through the ever-inimical past of literature, with the greatest possible exertion. The imagination and creative methods of Max Jacob can be compared with those employed by these anonymous poets of the puszta.

They were poetic yet realistic, coarse yet ethereal in their ordinariness. Of course there was a lot of dross in their efforts. But I believe that if they were to edit a paper they would produce not only something interesting to read, but—with practice—something of undoubted value. Even from the examples quoted it can be seen that they are far above the verse published in the Budapest papers. I learnt much from them.

Was it they, I wonder, who revived the parched relics of ancient folk customs and filled them with new content? Or did all the folk in this warm nether stratum still live their art at first hand? It is a pleasant thought: that the vocation of the Muses is to console the poverty-stricken masses. The finest creations of folk art float on the surface of the most stench-ridden squalor, like certain beautiful flowers in a morass. The only folk who have time to occupy themselves with beauty are the very rich and the beggars, who are no longer tortured by worldly cares. The shepherds of Rácegres, as soon as they were able to sit down, picked up a knife and in a couple of hours had fashioned a carving worthy of a place in a museum. The carters would sit well out on the pole of the waggon between the oxen as they wandered peacefully through the fields, whittling away at the curved yoke until it became a triumphal fairy arch.

From the houses of the well-to-do peasants folk art had been long banished, like an over-fastidious spirit enraged at the sight of their middle-class desires. Thoroughly offended, the old noble tastes had given place to shoddy goods and ideas, while the people of the pusztas were still carving cunningly-contrived boxes, taking over from each other the ornamental designs on their whip-handles, and running to listen to a new song. The old folk handed down their superstitions and beliefs to their successors with all the tortuous detail of folk making their last will and testament. They used fear and if necessary castigation to implant their customs into the new generation. This was the true culture of the puszta, this was what linked folk together and made reply to disturbing questions. These customs and beliefs conducted the farm servants over the difficult stumbling-blocks of love and death, and around the dangerous bends of life. These consoled them during their hungry, thirsty pilgrimage through each barren year. And it was these customs and beliefs that first touched my soul and rubbed off its edges for life on the puszta, not Uncle Hanák's school. It was not the culture of Europe, which was unable to conquer the barbarism of the puszta folk because most probably it had nothing better to substitute for it.

This was the world where I grew up imperceptibly. First I reached table-height, then I could touch the top of the dresser, and suddenly one morning, with a certain amount of stretching, I reached the top of the cupboard. First it was only a dog that obeyed my commands, then a sucking-pig and then a cow, until in the end I once drove a four-ox cart home from the fields without any undue trouble. I had more or less finished my schooling for life on the puszta.

CHAPTER FOURTEEN

The smell. Strangers on the puszta

Sometimes guests arrived on the puszta from mysterious distant regions. They walked around as if they had stepped into a swamp or were picking their way through broken pottery. Out of their element, they would glance all round suspiciously. If they once stopped, they found it hard to move on again in their timidity. They had to be reassured. They would peep through the windows of the servants' lodgings, but they refrained from going inside. Guided by the farm officials they would walk down the broad alleys inside the stables, delicately avoiding the dung. From a respectful distance they viewed the bulls, cows and sheep—and us too. From a respectful distance we also gaped at them. We thronged behind them as they went along, but left a wide gap in between, as if we were afraid that they would suddenly turn round and jump on us. They held handkerchiefs to their noses; I well remember one group of which every member kept his handkerchief permanently to his face. They found the oppressive atmosphere difficult to bear.

Nor was it easy. Later I myself had this experience when I had the opportunity of crossing from one social stratum to another and believed I could do this without losing my balance. It was impossible; in society, just as in nature, height and depth have their own distinctive atmosphere. After a sudden change of this kind I observed in myself the same physical symptoms as when I had been down a coal-mine or when the lift suddenly stopped on an Alpine peak: my stomach was in turmoil, my pulse beat faster, my senses were numbed, and I staggered, gasping for air. It was then I realised how difficult a thing is equality and how far one is tamed by one's social status, which keeps every atom of one's being in its thrall. I had particular trouble with my nose, even when I was quite young, as grandmother's hawk eyes soon noticed. She had no objection to the adolescent way I tied my tie, nor to my ostentatious shoe-cleaning, but she followed my rapidly-growing fad for fresh air with suspicious anxiety. 'Shut that window now,' she said, shivering as she pulled the century-old shawl over her breast, 'or can't you bear our smell?' True, I did find it difficult to bear, and I blushed because of it. I tortured myself with self-accusations and felt a miserable traitor. The scents which had once been dear to me became torturing monsters and stifled me. When I came home for the second time the intimate atmosphere of the common room literally knocked me back at the door. The familiar smell of home, for which I had yearned far away, had become a stale, musty mixture of soot, cold vegetables and linen drying in the room. That dear apron where once I had been so glad to bury my face now revealed a rancid smell of washing-up water. But I could not mention this; how could I have said anything? At grandmother's first command I closed the window and sat down at the table once again. But in the dark corner the freshly-dubbined pair of boots began to work like an octopus; they stretched out their tentacles and piercing the submarine density of smells—the smoky oil lamp, the cabbage fermenting in the barrel and the sweet pieces of pumpkin sizzling in the little stove—wound themselves round my neck. I got up and went out. As I was closing the door I heard grandmother say 'Quite the gentleman, isn't he?' to my grandfather, who was bathing his feet in a mixture of garlic and spirits. I looked up at the stars and pondered on the course of human progress.

Progress—that famous idea whose achievements for the moment merely increase the distance between human beings. In the Middle Ages the lord of the castle had his serfs guillotined, but if Fate so ordained it, he could stay with them in one and the same room. When were folk nearer to each other? An English traveller was incensed to recall the Chinese mandarin who had all the coolies in an inn-yard beaten because when he came in he did not receive the appropriate salutation from them. Half an hour later the English traveller came across the mandarin among the dirty coolies, playing a friendly game of dice with them on the bare earth. 'He might well do so,' says the keen-scented Englishman, perhaps enviously, 'he smelt just as bad as they did.' The smell had not driven him away. Oh, the nose! And democracy, the strapping infant of the eighteenth century, was not figuratively but in reality drowned in bath-water, through one section of society being provided with baths and the other not. Is it such trifles that bring holy ardour to a standstill? Yes, unfortunately. Fraternity gushed forth; the gentry offered their right hand to the people and smartly retired three paces, eagerly waiting to be able to wash their hands. Such traits, of course, are observed and noted more often by a social class than by the individual. The farm servants suspected that once again some change had occurred in the world, and that it would be to their detriment. They gained nothing on the swings, and once again lost what they still had to lose on the roundabouts.

Grandfather from Nebánd thought the old gentry to be the real ones. Was he right? In the old days, when Börcsök arrived with his satchel of silver in Vienna, the prince himself would often take him into his room, sit him down on the same sofa and chat with him. But now when the farm servants had any business to do in the manor-house, they got as far as the passage or the hall and no further. The master came out to meet them there and dealt with the business as quickly as possible. I knew a farm manager's wife who had never seen the inside of the farm servants' quarters in her life. Yet these dwellings were not really dirty, nor were the farm servants themselves. They

223

wore their underclothes usually for a week or two, including nights, of course, for they knew nothing of night-shirts. Their idea of dirt was what showed, in sharp contrast to the basic colour of body or linen. And of this they attempted to rid themselves immediately. Old carters would fastidiously beat the dust from the knees of the uncertain-coloured trousers they had worn since before their marriage, if perchance they had to kneel on the ground. They had a feeling for cleanliness, and as far as possible they looked after themselves. According to those who fought in the 1914–18 war, it was not the peasants who were most steeped in grime; they would wash even in ice-cold water, and when the weather was freezing still took off their shirts to delouse themselves. Incidentally distinctions were made at home between various insects. The louse was a scandal, but they would hunt fleas quite calmly and with a certain amusement when in company. Lavatories existed only in the manor-house and in the houses of the chief officials. The farm servants, however, would not have stepped in them even if they had been given special permission to use them, and they had every reason—they simply could not abide the stench.

There is no need for me to say anything about the idle superstition that the peasants and the poor in general do not heed the words of the gentry. Anyone who has ever got into conversation with the poor and has succeeded, however imperfectly, in 'getting on to the right wavelength' will know how they receive not only enlightenment but advice in the most delicate private matters with great attention, and with all the joy and gratitude of a thirsty soul. I know next to nothing about pig-breeding, but the travellers in a third-class compartment once tried hard to prevent me from getting out of the train at Kaposvár after I had given them an hour and a half's seminar on the strength of my knowledge. They would have paid my fare on to Somogyszob and indeed back again. The peasants and the poor in general are only too ready to listen to the gentry. Perhaps this is why they realise so soon that the gentry have very little idea of things and talk in an airy-fairy manner; this might not be so bad—indeed it might lead to an interesting discussion—except that they imagine themselves high in the clouds, to make matters worse. The poor folk watch the faces of their superiors with the gaze of a psychologist and learn more from a movement of the mouth or eye than from the sus-piciously benevolent phrases which are usually difficult to comprehend not because they are high-flown, but because they are too low-pitched and confused.

Even so, it is difficult to live among them. Guests arriving on the puszta may well have felt that they were on a stage and had to play a part. They acted badly. They were attacked by stage-fright and were none too happy to emerge from behind the scenery. Life on the puszta! The landowners were scared of the air of their own pusztas, and not only because of the everlast-ing stench.

I never set eyes on our own landlord. Where did he live? Nobody knew. It was said that once upon a time, when he in-herited the estate, he determined to visit all his pusztas. At Rácegres there were months of preparation for his reception. The noble gentleman never came; before our turn came he had grown weary of travelling all over the place. But one of his nephews once paid us a visit, engraving his name and that day once and for all in our family history—with sad letters, un-fortunately.

For weeks before the event, the puszta was in a fever at the news of his arrival. Stables were whitewashed, trees lopped, and everything swept out. My brother and I were given red hussar's shakos, but whether it was in honour of the occasion, I do not know. In the manor-house secret preparations went on from morning till night. Finally one day at noon two coaches-and-fours appeared on the hillside. In a moment we all thronged round the entrance to the puszta, while the farm officials feverishly lined us up on each side of the road.

My elder brother must have been about nine or ten years old at this time. He was a lively, agile boy and quite beside himself with excitement. He jumped up and down, twisted right and left and kept running out into the middle of the road to see whether they were coming yet. Nothing could dampen his good spirits, not even the couple of smacks he received from one of the bailiffs. He had never seen a count in the flesh, but how many tales and legends had he not heard about them! When the clatter of the carriage could just be heard, he began to clap his hands and leap around, uttering little shrieks of delight, his eyes shining. The coach rolled along in a huge cloud of dust between the silent, bareheaded ranks of farm servants; it might have belonged to Mars or Jupiter, or indeed to a god of absolute and invariable power. At last it reached us. Feri shot high into the air with a loud shout and—obviously as a mark of his respect—hurled his red shako firmly and accurately between the first pair of horses. He was a good shot.

One of the magnificent steeds reared up; the other leapt forward, so the first one staggered, turned round on its hind legs and fell between the rear pair, which likewise reared up. There was a crack. The pole broke and the carriage hit the horses' hind legs. Feri naturally took to his heels at once and, as was his custom whenever he had done anything worse than usual, did not stop until he arrived at Nebánd. He did not see a count this time either.

In any case the count was in the next coach; the first one contained three ladies dressed in white. They jumped up from their seats and one of them pointed at me with her parasol. 'That was the one!' she shouted, with rare ingenuity discovering the perpetrator of the crime in me, seeing that I too had a red shako on my head. I will not continue the story; suffice it to say that I did not see the guests either.

It was only from the farm servants that I heard about them. They had long names, impossible to spell, like those of most landowners and tenants, and the servants could hardly pronounce them. They twisted and twined them round their tongues in different ways for different sentences; with good intentions worthy of a better object they tried to turn them into some comprehensible Hungarian form, but this merely increased their respect and admiration. In general the gentry had appropriate-sounding names too. They were extraordinary and unapproachable, almost as if they had come from another planet, and not from this ordinary valley, with its acacia trees, dock and towering well-poles.

Sometimes hunting parties also made an appearance, usually at the beginning of winter. We rarely saw them either. As soon as they arrived and the first shot rang out in the fields, mother simply locked us in the kitchen, hammer away at the door as we might. She would not allow us to go near them even when the hunters had returned with their spoils and could be stared at in comfort through the railings of the gateway to the manor-house. The hunters carried guns, and mother had a genuine gun-phobia. Somehow she had the idea that loaded weapons had a life and mind of their own; they had the power to aim from a table, for example, or from the shoulder of a huntsman, and like a good bloodhound would fire away of their own volition at an unsuspecting spectator, and particularly at children.

When the tenants took over the puszta, guests came more often. There were artesian-well borers, relatives, a rainfall-measurer... I am also happy to recall the visit of the socialist leaders too.

The company which rented the estate entrusted the management of the puszta to an exceptionally tall, bent and ugly-faced, red-haired man, who was very friendly and had a humane way of talking. We had to call him 'Mr Fantusz' and not 'Mr Manager' or 'Mr Bailiff', as a result of which for a

227

long time I regarded this as a high and most distinguished title and not a surname. He wore *pince-nez* and was renowned throughout western Hungary, I imagine, because he never beat anybody. On the contrary, at Easter when we went in a huge band to wish him the compliments of the season, he would stand on the steps of the office like a king and scatter a handful of freshly-minted, gleaming one-fillér pieces among us. Were the socialists his friends? Certainly they came to see him, either as his guests or on study trips. The four-in-hand was sent to meet them, which proves that even a Fantusz has a sense of humour.

There were three or four such leaders; I cannot recall exactly how many, nor do I remember their names. During the revolution of 1919 my father recognised eight or ten of them from the illustrated papers and somewhat surprisingly, despite his royalist feelings, he took them under his protection, though before this he had only seen them at a distance. The leaders talked first of all with old Uncle Sövegjártó, who immediately kissed hands... Uncle Lukács did the same, and the womenfolk also knew how to behave towards folk who arrive in the big carriage. The leaders tucked their hands away in embarrassment and clumsily walked among the labourers who all stood stiffly to attention and answered their questions with military precision and Hungarian frankness—'Very good, sir,' 'Excellent, sir.' 'Things couldn't be better, sir.' I can just imagine the state of mind of the leaders, for I too have arrived by carriage at a puszta. They stayed among us for three days, but spent only half an hour round the farm servants' dwellings. They withdrew to the manor-house. One afternoon they all came out to go fishing, which caused general amusement, for everybody knew that the Páskom branch was just an overflow, and the fish there had long been killed off by the dung that had seeped into it. But nobody told them to go a hundred yards further on to the Sió, where they could catch as many fish as

228

they wanted. It was this incident, I believe, that gave rise to such happy recollections of their visit.

The people of the pusztas heard very little of the movements that were to change the world. Sometimes there arrived by unfathomable routes appalling prophecies concerning the impending punishment of the gentry, the Jews, or quite simply the whole world. The farm servants would nod and resign themselves to their fate. The more mythical the prophecy, the more they credited it. They were more ready to believe that the world would be destroyed from one day to the next than that it would be changed. Aunt Beszédes affirmed with all the conviction of a paid sociologist that there must always be gentry, but that spring when Halley's comet appeared she refused to sow beans because by autumn everything would be over and done with. But when the social unrest fermented into revolution, the farm servants with astonishing speed got the gist of the complicated phraseology of the posters and speakers arriving from Budapest and the local towns. After the official discussions they held a separate meeting and scratching their heads tried to work out what should happen to the land so that everyone might be treated fairly. They viewed the village-folk with suspicion, for these were sniffing round the estate during that winter of 1918 like hungry wolves to find the best morsels for themselves. The farm servants feared for the land; they were rightly afraid that perhaps there would be nothing left for them, for not even at that time, of course, was their case brought to the fore. The greatest 'revolutionaries' were the large farmers. So it happened that the people of the pusztas, probably out of sheer anxiety, wanted immediately to take into their own hands both the puszta and the manor-house too. Just as in 1848, so now too the revolutionary government had to use bayonet and bullet to convince them that they must wait their turn. So they waited. And we all know well the events of 1919.

Beggars turned up every day without exception, and sometimes there were several of them. The majority of them were mendicants pure and simple. You can guess their state; they were ready to weary themselves with a walk of eight or ten miles to strike up their prayers and hymns of woe at a farm servant's kitchen door. They would get a crust of bread or an onion... they never got enough to cover their daily needs. Most of them we knew well. They were old farm servants worn out in service, or incapable of working owing to some accident. They made a well-defined circuit of the countryside, turning up again punctually, as if they were the paid apprentices of suffering. 'Where's Uncle András got to?' we would ask if one of their number failed to put in an appearance for some time. The cold winter had carried him off: he had died on the bank of some ditch... Once the dogs brought a chewed foot back to the puszta.

With them were associated the tramps too, though these did not beg from door to door. They arrived in the evenings and asked only for lodgings. They had their customary place—the little lean-to at the end of the calves' sheds. The foreman of the puszta would take them there after he had carefully searched them all and removed their matches, pipes and knives. They were strong, healthy folk, some of whom even dressed like gentlemen, as far as their wanderings over the pusztas allowed such traces to remain on their bowler hats and striped trousers. They sat out on the doorstep and told stories of the wide world. The world was mysterious and terrifying. I would glance anxiously into that distant world, from which people arrived either by carriage or staggering with hunger and thirst. We heard dreadful tales of fickle wives, cruel brothers and sisters, heartless merchants and prisons. The farm servants shook their heads and felt glad that they had at least a roof over their heads. The tramp sighed and with a long, silent glance accepted the jug of sour milk or bowl of soup which one of the women would finally offer him. There also arrived prophets, with hair down to their waists, lunatic faces and huge bibles in their knapsacks. Then there were poets who recited their own works, sword-swallowers and musicians.

At rarer intervals we had knife-grinders, dancing bears, and once a man with a monkey on a brass chain; it snatched the tomatoes ripening in the windows and ate them all up. There were poultrymen, rag and bone men, and once an actress with a feather in her hat. She also came on foot. She turned out to be an itinerant prostitute and took her pay in kind, just like the itinerant shoemender. There were Bosnians, gelders and fruitsellers in a huge beehive of a waggon who for a basketful of wheat gave a basketful of plums, for the farm servants naturally have no fruit of any kind. Apart from these there were pig and calf traders and all kinds of gipsies: tub-makers, carrion-eaters, fortune-tellers and those who had no special title but just stole. There were merchants and wedding-parties careering through the puszta from one village to another, who threw out cakes and pretzels. And there was an itinerant huckster.

He was Uncle Salamon from Dorog. He arrived every Monday afternoon and always heralded his appearance with a whistle. This was more of a tradition or for his own delight than anything else, because everybody knew perfectly well what his business was. He supplied the puszta with everything from thimbles and lace to axes, in exchange for any conceivable object. His pack grew bigger and bigger. I am reminded of the ant which can carry three times its own weight when I recall Uncle Salamon going along the hill paths under his fearful load. His steps were light and nimble, as if he were clinging to a balloon which floated towards us or away from us. Grandmother was fond of him and even when she was in the midst of her work she would have long talks with him. She set him up as a model (as she did everyone who had got on in the world) before the male members of the family, to their considerable chagrin. She thought him an educated man and

231

accepted his advice, especially in the complicated problem of selling the sucking-pigs. Indeed, everybody on the puszta liked Uncle Salamon. I cannot recall a single sarcastic or offensive remark about him. The farm servants rather took him under their wing, like all strangers and tramps who had 'neither home nor master'. He became a Jew to them only when at the logical end of his career he opened a business somewhere in his own house. His son who called everyone 'sir' and continued his father's activities in a waggon was despised and regarded as a beggar. He was deliberately sent over a rotten bridge and when it collapsed satisfactorily, they did not lift a finger to help him.

Once we even saw an airship. It was the size of a small rubber ball, gleaming yellow in the evening sunlight as it hovered far away over Vajta. The whole puszta turned out. We gazed at it as if it had come from another world.

CHAPTER FIFTEEN

Quacks and healers. Health on the puszta. Surgeons.
Folk cures

The 'wise folk', as they were known, came in secret. This was all part of their trade, although the news of their arrival spread like wildfire through the puszta. 'The man from Igar is here; he's at the Hajases!' the news flew round, and we should have rushed to the Hajases' door in our excitement, had not some mysterious command prescribed that we must keep quiet about this unusual event and only glance occasionally at the Hajas house from afar. Yes, the man from Igar was really there, sitting barefoot in the kitchen. On other occasions the woman from Udvard turned up, or Menyhárt from Szilas. All of them were concerned with cures, for body and soul alike.

This journey of theirs was an unselfish act on their part, for after all there was plenty of work for them to do at home. The villagers went to visit them in droves; sometimes three or four waggons would be waiting outside the house of the wise man of Szilas. The farm servants, on the other hand, did not find it easy to move around. The occasional farmhand's wife who undertook the journey to a quack-doctor acted as postman for all the puszta's complaints and requests for help; she would ask advice not only for herself but for at least another thirty problems. The wise folk performed their cures from a distance and by sending messages also, but if they possibly could, they visited their flock in person. They would stay at the home of one of their intimate friends. The room immediately became transformed into a holy of holies. The farm servants followed on each other's heels. They visited the quacks in a previously arranged order, the women by day and the men after dusk. The bustle and commotion, muttering and whispering went on until dawn. The healers usually stopped for only one night, though the farm servants would gladly have kept these shrivelled old women with the sing-song voice and the pious-faced old men for months on end. They were not all old. The man from Szilas, for example, was a fine figure of a man in the prime of life and had no beard. The only sign of his profession was his way of speaking with his eyes closed. They could never spend the whole night in one place, because if they went away in broad daylight, their words lost their power.

Naturally the people of the pusztas were as far removed as it is possible to be from what townsfolk generally term 'the forces of nature'. Nowhere have I heard so often the phrases 'I'm a bundle of nerves', 'Don't get on my nerves!', as amongst them. They were indeed nervy. Nor was it their nerves only that gave them trouble. They had pains in their lungs, their eyes, their teeth, their hands and feet, and particularly in their stomachs and ears. And as old age crept on, they had pains in every part of their bodies, just like mortal men everywhere. But in some quarters it was widely assumed that they were not prone to ill-health. True, they were not normally sick for any length of time: they did not keep to their beds. They merely gave a sneeze and died, carried to the grave by a breath of wind. 'Poor man, he even coughed blood,' said the widow tearfully, after the funeral,' but he was used to that; he'd been doing it for ten years.' In other words, 'there must have been something else wrong with him, poor man.' Usually there was, too. It was all too plain from the faces of old-looking folk of 45–50 that three or four completely different fatal diseases were at work within them, competing with each other to reach the goal and hear their splendid Latin name from the lips of the doctor, who would say with an appreciative nod, 'I've never seen such a case; why, she had cancer even in the roots of her hair!' 'When did she take to her bed?' he would ask. 'Yesterday evening. In the morning she was busy in the house, poor love,' replied one of the sad relatives. 'Well, couldn't you see that she was ill?' A shrug of the shoulders. 'All she asked for was a little tea, or a brick for her stomach; she had consumption.'

The doctor suspected that some quack had treated his patient, but he could do nothing about it even if he wanted to. To the people of the pusztas the doctor counted as one of the gentry, and unless he had passed the impossible examination to win the sympathy of the people—complete equality of heart, nerves and pores—they did not trust him. They did trust the 'wise folk'. It was not only because they were of the same stock and spoke in a humane language which could be understood, but also because they did not recognise any case as hopeless. The quacks never gave anybody up. They never shrugged their shoulders, put on a pious look and informed the relatives that only the Lord could help them now. They would help anyone. Thirty years ago Uncle Takács had been on the verge of death when they sat him down in the shadow of a black hen with some appallingly strong root between his teeth. He got better without knowing what had been the matter with him. For it was proper to take to the quacks only those illnesses of which nobody knew the origin. For lesser diseases there were folk on the puszta who knew how to deal with them.

Those who understood the diseases of animals had the full confidence of the people, who would take their own troubles to them. The drivers poured the same brew of wild chicory into their horses and into themselves if they had stomach-pains. For dysentery, which was quite common among them, they used a brew of burdock. For colic there was Spanish garlic, and for hardening of the arteries garlic in brandy, with suitable incantations. At the Szerentséses I myself was given a gruel of ground maize with honey for my cough, after I had turned up my nose at the simplest and most potent cure—gargling with urine. When a horse had cataract, the drivers would blow into its eye a powder of finely-ground glass mixed with sugar, and this ate it away. They used roots of snakeweed for any painful tumours in their animals; for these caused inflammation and collected the pus. The drivers pricked the hide of their animals with hands as sure and steady as those of the shoemaker at work on the sole of a shoe. They were just as adept with human beings too; indeed, they were more and more restricted to them, for the estate did not appreciate their knowledge and engaged a veterinary surgeon. Slowly the farm servants and peasants began to take their animals to the vet too. They themselves continued to swallow potions, but they now put on anxious faces and called in the representative of official knowledge if their cow was sick. Incantations and superstitious treatment disappeared first from the realm of animal surgery, or rather it was only here that they ceased to be used. How had this come about?

Uncle Leperdi came to the conclusion that it was a waste of time to use incantations upon animals because 'the animal can't understand what you say to it anyway; it hasn't got a soul.' But he himself—whose aching feet had been cured by the woman from Udvard by means of a bath full of horsetail—had a soul. He was an old cowhand, and though he knew very many incantations, he no longer used them, for he was an educated man. Moreover he believed only in one such custom: you take a live mole, press your left thumb on its heart and walk round in a circle saying your prayers until it dies. By this means you can rid animals of scurvy.

Surgery was the province of the shepherds. This was a matter of fact, and everybody recognised it. They were excellent surgeons. When it came to cutting a hole in the skull of a sheep,

236

grandfather was called in, not only by the estate, but also by the veterinary surgeon at B. 'Uncle Jani's got the knack of it,' he said, instead of saying that Uncle Jani, otherwise grandfather, was not in the least afraid of digging around in living flesh and bone.

Nor was he. The threshing-machine, as had become its custom practically every summer, caught the hand of a lad who was feeding it and battered it to pulp. The previous year's victim had died from just such an accident. It was certain that this lad too would bleed to death before he could reach a doctor. The manager sent for grandfather. 'Well, my boy,' said grandfather to the lad, who was deathly pale, 'you're fond of life, aren't you?' 'Yes, I am.' 'Well, then, shut your eyes tight, as you'll faint anyway,' said grandfather and twisted off the boy's arm from the elbow so skilfully that he even left a piece of skin to cover the stump. He did it so well that the head doctor in the hospital at Szekszárd asked the carter who took the patient there, 'Which doctor made such a fine job of it?'

My father acted as grandfather's assistant only in his youth, but he too had an instinctive feeling for surgery. There was no surgical problem brought to him but he knew immediately what should be done. Once I got a splinter under the nail of my right thumb. This accident occurred in circumstances I preferred not to mention at home. (We were putting up a plank to get into the loft of the vine-dresser's house, where the grapes were stored to dry.) My parents realised that something was wrong only when I could not hold my spoon in my right hand. My father felt the swollen thumb with an expert hand. 'Let it develop for another couple of days,' he said. Two days later he stood me between his knees and cut the nail open lengthwise with his pocket-knife. The pain, which at the time I dared not scream out, is engraved for ever in my memory. At the first sign of a squeak from me, my father looked at me disapprovingly; it was the glance of someone disturbed in the midst of his work. Then he lifted the two pieces of the nail as calmly as

237

if he were pulling off the two wings of an insect. He cleaned up the pus and blood and had finished the job in a minute.

At that time the estate already had an agreement with the doctor in one of the neighbouring villages. For a yearly sum in cash and in kind he looked after the farm servants and their children up to the age of twelve, but unfortunately his stock of medicines was hardly more varied than that of the quacks. These doctors did not really prescribe anything but purgatives and aspirin. If a tooth ached, they pulled it out. The estates employed them chiefly for the sake of discipline, so that the employees should not be able to withdraw their labour on the pretext of sickness. It was the estate carriage that brought the doctors out to the puszta, where their appearance was like the sound of a passing-bell. In Rácegres, at the sight of the 'doctor's coach', the women would cross themselves and murmur a swift prayer, for the sick man could not hope to live much longer. Only at the last moment would the relatives ask for official aid, by which time the patient had turned black. 'Please get the doctor to come quickly,' a solemn-faced father or son would mutter, 'I shouldn't like to get into trouble.' All the same there were cases where a younger and still conscientious doctor would report them for criminal negligence.

According to the law, the estate must bear the costs of treatment for its sick farm servants up to a limit of 45 days. It was unusual, however, for the farm servants to claim their right. In recent years most of the estates had all prospective employees medically examined and employed only those of iron constitution. Those who had fallen sick during the year were dismissed. On the neighbouring estate of X., which was owned by an internationally famous industrial concern, they wanted to introduce a local regulation that any farm servant who absented himself from work for more than eight days on any pretext whatsoever must give in his notice at the end of the year. Most interest-

238

ing of all was the reason for this. In other countries the firm had been compelled by workers' welfare institutions to make so many sacrifices that wherever possible it had to practise the strictest economy; in X. it was possible.

It was possible almost everywhere, with the exception of one or two areas—notably on the pusztas belonging to the Counts K., in whose centre the owner had erected a truly excellent hospital. The people of the pusztas were terrified of sickness not because they might perhaps lose their lives, but because they would certainly lose their jobs sooner or later. There was little compassion for the sick: perhaps I ought to allude here again to animals, of which so many were lost from one day to another, representing so much monetary value... Or shall I mention military discipline, and compare the spirit of the puszta to that of an army engaged in perpetual warfare? What would happen if the general were to mourn every fallen soldier? The lords of the puszta, perhaps with regret, but certainly with a toughened spirit, commanded those who could not stand the pace to fall out, and cast them aside. This behaviour of theirs, their superior and aristocratic lack of concern, filled me with the same astonishment that I had felt when I observed their happy, clear glance sweeping unscathed over the moral mire around them. For two months we had been expecting one of my dearest relations to die; only then, in his last days, after so many years of misunderstanding, did I come to realise what a great man he was. On a puszta at the back of beyond, he lay convulsed by a terrible disease and by the worry of how much longer he could afford to pay the doctor who for five pengős floundered through the bottomless mud of autumn to inject him with pain-killing drugs. He was not to be consoled, by the document which his son pressed into his hands as the first and tardy sign of his love —a document concerning a literary award of considerable value. Everybody knew that he would die, except himself. The owner of the estate got to know it too, hence his visit to us. The old man's wizened, yellow face was suffused with a devout and

239

happy light and his large white teeth gleamed in an ecstatic smile from beneath his thick, greying moustache when the tall fur-coated guest offered him his hand. After greeting him, the visitor briefly informed him that unfortunately he must hand in his notice. It was November, and in the new year another man would be engaged in his place. With this the guest departed. 'Well in that case I'm dying,' said the sick man after a brief silence. In vain did I try to console him. The most awkward family problem was thus settled simply. 'I must make my confession,' he said in calm, straightforward tone.

In general even the relatives showed very little sympathy. Nor do soldiers waste much time in compassion for a wounded comrade. 'Your turn today; mine tomorrow'—a hard fate first and foremost hardens the heart. When Uncle Nagyvadi took to his bed, his son-in-law began to wear his fur cap. The old man raised a terrible storm. 'You might just as well calm down,' his wife threw at him, 'you won't live to see the winter anyway.' 'But by heaven,' said Uncle Nagyvadi, 'you're not going to rob me!' And he got better, probably just because of that fur cap, as he himself used to relate with roars of happy laughter.

Was illness a disgrace? Certainly everybody kept it secret as long as possible. The farm servants would groan, catch their breath and complain of pains in their sides; occasionally they even pretended to be ill, but the words 'I'm ill' did not come easily to their lips. They had a horror of the sickbed. Those who lay between the sheets by day were regarded as lepers. And those who did not stir from the house for weeks were as good as dead and buried in their minds.

Yet with the quacks they were frank. They opened their hearts to them, knowing full well that their confidences would not be passed on further. In any case, the quacks saw into one's heart. The woman from Udvard told Aunt Horváth as she came in that she had come from the east and that 'her heart was

240

growing dark'. And she told Aunt Takács that her troubles were due to a man.

The wise folk certainly did read people's minds; I myself know of very many cases where they effected a cure. They were not only doctors, but priests and judges also. They pronounced sentence and granted absolution. When the man from Igar settled down in the Hajases' kitchen, one could sense in the puszta not only the throb of some indefinable hope, but also the atmosphere of the summary court of justice. How did the man from Igar achieve this? He compelled all who came to consult him to be utterly frank with him—more so than they could ever be with their partners in marriage, or even with themselves in their dreams. After all, a single untrue word or lying thought took away the efficacy of the curative herbs and incantations. (Where they failed, the patients without exception blamed themselves.) One had to believe. The wise folk had purloined this from the Nazarene.

Those who believed were cured: what is miraculous in this? Uncle István Nagy's wife had such a throbbing pain in her thigh that for weeks she could not get a wink of sleep. She went to the doctor, but no medicine did her any good. The woman from Udvard drew criss-cross lines on the aching part with the edge of her palm. Then she turned to the wall for a good half-hour. She gave her nothing. 'Come again in nine days' time,' she said finally. Aunt Nagy went merely to show her gratitude with a couple of hens, for in the meantime she had made a complete recovery. It was not wickedness that caused the Szabó boy from Alsómajor to think of leaving his young wife for an 'accomplished' city girl, but the playing of the moon-beams on the stable window, if I remember rightly. The quack ordered medicine for him and for his wife, and they took it until everything turned out right again.

'They really knew something about medicine,' said the farm servants of the quacks. They prescribed cures which made the patients see stars when they took them—but was not this, I wonder, the real cause of their cure? It is impossible to be rid of anything without some sacrifice, and this medicine was a real penitence. The old village doctors laughingly instructed their young assistants to prescribe bitter medicine as far as possible for the farm servants—the more bitter, the better. And if possible everything was to be in liquid form. They might trust liquids and take them. Powders they did not like.

The root of the trouble was that only in the rarest instances did the farm servants follow the doctor's orders. When Aunt Gallé died after having her ninth child, they found in her straw mattress all the medicine that the doctor had prescribed for her during the previous two years. And as for Uncle Szabadi, everyone knew that he had been cured by a blow from the bailiff. He had been constipated for an incredibly long time. Every day he was sent castor oil from the office, but he still did not turn up for work. In the end he was called in. Uncle Szabadi turned up with a pint bottle under his arm. In it he had carefully collected all the daily doses. They wanted to pour it into him on the spot. 'Take it, or I'll box your ears!' shouted the bailiff. He gave him a blow and ordered him to work next day. Uncle Szabadi bowed and never complained again.

Naturally they did not keep to a diet either. Indeed they did not obey the most elementary orders. They would give sauerkraut to a patient with typhoid, racked by a 40 centigrade fever, and potatoes seasoned with paprika to those with an ulcerated stomach. 'He did so want it, poor thing.' They had not the heart to refuse.

They observed the words of the quacks. At their command they would even take a bath, which was a very tiresome process. The farm servants had no provision for bathing. Most estates had impeccable cemented pools made for the pigs, with artificial sandy banks and even trees to give them shade. The farm servants at the very most might steep themselves in the Sió, and then, of course, only in summer. But they regarded bathing as one of those frolics suitable for the young; splashing around

242

was not proper for a married man. If they went to all the trouble of hauling the wash-tub into one of the rooms and began to heat the water on the stove (from which it had to be carried a can at a time), everybody knew at once that they were preparing to fulfil some 'prescription'.

If a doctor wanted to achieve success, he too had to be something of a quack. There was nothing legendary in the story of how the chemist at E. grew rich. He made up the medicine according to the doctor's prescription, but in handing it to the peasants, he would whisper confidentially that it would be effective only if the patient took it at midnight, standing in the middle of a circle drawn in the dust at the cross-roads; he was then to throw away behind him the stick with which the circle had been drawn, and run home without looking back. He prescribed 'silent water'—water brought without a word from the stream—for dressings, and the farm servants were quite willing to obey him. With every medicament he gave appropriate instructions for use. They flocked to him from miles around.

Usually the farm servants fought shy of the chemist too. The 'wise folk' prepared their own brews. It was the itinerant merchants who were chiefly responsible for passing on to the puszta such medicines as civilisation had discovered for the consolation of the human race. Uncle Salamon sold ointment for various aches and pains, ointments for growing and twirling moustaches, and vast quantities of mercury ointment. But occasionally we heard news of some sensational discovery. Agents would arrive and offer us not only boxes of toilet soap, but also the latest infallible miracle-cure for pains in the chest, rheumatism and pregnancy. We were not behind the times. Opticians came too: everyone chose glasses for themselves from his box. There were also beauty specialists, who after the First World War sold chiefly contraceptives.

To conclude on a cheerful note, let me mention the itinerant radiologist. He carried his equipment in a huge box on his back. It could be used to give shock treatment, and also showed the 'state of the blood'. Those who became intimately acquainted with him during his experiments were X-rayed in great secrecy by night. He was said to have placed a lighted electric bulb into the patient's mouth and squinted into him from the other end. Or would it be more fitting for me to feel sorrow at this? He allegedly X-rayed Uncle Takács and Uncle Vadócz for four eggs apiece.

CHAPTER SIXTEEN

*Seasonal labourers, harvesters, day-labourers. Their income
and life on the puszta*

To be quite fair, the monthly and seasonal labourers, harvesters and day-labourers from the village, who were engaged for
varying lengths of time, were outsiders, but this was not what
we felt them to be. As soon as they arrived and threw off their
sheepskin coats, taking from their shoulders the cooking-pot,
scythe, hoe and wooden fork all tied together with a string, the
world of the puszta caught them up and mingled them with us.
The men were all on Christian-name terms with each other, as
well as with the women and girls. The great democracy of work
and poverty demolished in a twinkling of the eye all the barriers
dividing natives from newcomers in morals and customs.
Foreign languages were no hindrance, indeed they instigated
all the more kindness, attention and merriment. During the
war Russian prisoners of war arrived there and they too found
a kindly welcome; one of them stayed on. He got married and
was allotted a kitchen to share with the Szulimáns, who were
obviously descendants of some Turk who had likewise stayed
behind. From wherever the strangers came, the people of the
pusztas regarded them as their own kind.

The sharecroppers came from the neighbouring villages, the
monthly workers and seasonal labourers from Vas county or
from the uplands. Both groups had their origin among the
landless peasants, but only to the superficial or absent-minded
observer had they anything in common. Down in the under-

world of poverty class-distinctions are perhaps even wider than up above. Heaven and earth divided them. It was only on the puszta that they made contact while hoeing maize together. It was rather like a meeting of aristocrats and bankers on neutral ground in some fashionable salon.

Towards the end of February, one of the estate officials (who also held the job of selling stock) set off on a journey. Sometimes he was absent for a week, going round the villages and looking over the folk in the counties of Gömör, Ung, Bereg or Borsod. The men, formed into bands under the direction of a gangmaster, waited their opportunity to descend on the more fertile parts of the country, like the *kuruc* soldiers of old. The estate official finally struck a bargain with one of the gangmasters and drew up a proper contract with him. At the same time he would make a contract with a gang of reapers from one of the neighbouring villages. When the weather improved, the cattle were driven out of the sheds where they had spent the winter and turned on to their summer quarters. The straw and dung were cleared out of the huge sheds. We waited daily for the 'country folk' to arrive, excitedly wondering whether they would be the same ones as last year. One or two of the youths and girls even dared to ask at the office who were coming and when, and where they came from. The folk serving up at the manor-house would look at each other, shaking their heads; a well-built bailiff's wife would sigh from the depths of her being: 'What a mob!' For sometimes love affairs developed between the native and the 'foreign' young folk, and they did not see each other for six months on end. At last they arrived. Even if they were the same as the previous year, we scarcely recognised them. They had become lanky and lean, living from hand to mouth, and really had to be set on their feet again. The estate did not object to this, for it was commonly believed that such folk made the most diligent workmen. They asked for their first monthly instalment immediately and sent it home, they even brought folk with them to carry back the big bundles of produce. Next day they demanded the next month's portion. The officials shook their heads and smiled—by now this had become the regular custom. They had two days to put their lodgings in order and settle in. Meanwhile they ate.

How did they live at home? How did they drag out the winter? It still needs one of them to write this up. As we have seen, the poet-reporters supply a picture of them which, despite its fragmentary character, shows evidence of a sharp eye for detail. I could not describe their quarters on the puszta better than István N. Kovács of Döbrököz in one of his fly-sheets in verse:

Now the puszta's silent, sounds of work are none;
God alone can tell where all the folk have gone.
Where at height of summer the workmen made their camp,
Now the master's oxen weather winter's damp.
From the wooden rafters hangs a suit or two,
Ragged coats and trousers, hats for mice to chew.
On the shelf a loaf of mouldy bread decays,
Where the mice have camped for many empty days.
Down there in the corner, what is there to see?
Just a heap of crumbling wooden boxes, two or three.
From their rotting planks a mouldy dust exudes—
In the stinking cowsheds woodworm ate them through.
When in future days again the spring will come,
Then upon the pusztas work will be begun.
From the sheds they'll sweep the rotten bits of wood
And into the cowsheds labourers will flood.
Hear the ancient cowman shout with lungs of brass,
'Time to change your shift now, out you go to grass!
Hey there, devil take you! There's the door and out you go!
Labourers will take your places when you go.'
This is how they find poor labourers a house—
They exchange their lodgings with a herd of cows!
Education's great and culture grows apace,
Here the workers' poverty should not find a place.

They were indeed quartered in the cowsheds. There were one or two places where a special workers' colony was built for them; this was a clay-built lodging, half dug into the earth like an ice-pit, with a long wooden bench inside along the wall, where they all sleep together. The cowshed, however, was the usual place. In front of the mangers there was a long line of sleeping-places for the labourers, just where the oxen stood in the winter. Four little stumps were driven in where each animal stood, and on these were placed boughs, lengthwise and crosswise, then straw and a blanket. It was impossible to air the sheds properly through the dim little windows, and naturally they cannot be heated—whoever has seen a shed with a chimney? There was no washroom in it either; in other words it contradicted with almost painful precision paragraph 7 of the legally confirmed Contract of Employment, which stated: 'The employer must provide for the employees proper accommodation which fulfils the requirements of public health and morals; the sexes must be separated, and the accommodation must be capable of being heated in cold weather; the labourer must also be able to keep himself clean therein. The straw used for sleeping purposes is to be changed as necessary. Cowsheds, sheep-folds and Dutch barns may not be used as lodgings for labourers without suitable modifications.' In principle, separation of the sexes existed. At the entrance to the sheds on the left and right there were generally to be seen little wooden boards provided with arrows and the inscriptions 'Men', 'Women', in addition to other witticisms inscribed there later. But the majority of the men and women were at the same time husband and wife, who settled down happily next to each other and sometimes even slept in the same bed. They also made room beside them for their children. Thus whole families were to be found in the sheds, and the labourers did not keep the legal three metres apart from each other, because if they did there would be no room for them all. The single youths and girls who came alone soon came together on a friendly basis.

'I should have been only too glad to sleep in a place like this every day during the war,' said one of the farm managers after he had explained very shrewdly that the estate could not consider any other accommodation. 'Perhaps we should build them a hotel?' he asked. 'This is good enough in summer.' The one reasonable objection might well be that even at home the labourers did not live in such luxury as this. 'They're only too happy that such places exist!' And this was true.

In this realm, and in the realm of servants' lodgings generally, conditions were most backward on the Church estates. (This was not one of my own findings.) The truly estimable explanation given was that the beneficiaries from Church estates normally got their land at an advanced age and thus, during the short time they still had to live, they refrained from all long-term investments and unnecessary expenditure.

Does there exist a deep degree of dire poverty whence it is impossible to look down any further with pity? The hearts of the farm servants really bled for the seasonal labourers who came from afar. They would look at them, shake their heads and try hard to help them. How? Where is the point beyond which man cannot help man? They helped them to get straw, did their washing-up for them, lent them blankets. They even entertained them. 'What, Sándor, you're not going without supper again?' asked the steward when one of them did not take his place at the common evening meal. 'I've already had it at the Szabós.' At the Szabós? He was a carter, and there were seven naughty children in the family; the Szabós were such beggars that, so rumour had it, they even licked the saucepan clean on the outside. Whatever could Sándor have eaten in their house? Some things in this world are inexplicable.

The kindness of the farm servants was matched only by their desire to banter—in other words they really regarded the strangers as their brothers. The farm servants' wives, completely forgetting how they themselves lived, would tell hair-raising stories of the morals of the monthly labourers, and particularly of the girls, of course. I listened with curiosity to their mud-slinging. Within me, I firmly expected these folk who came from afar to be quite different, and believed everything I heard about them. I soon came to realise what a vast difference there may be between two neighbouring villages, and how difficult it is to form a general picture of even a small country district. I also realised how the behaviour of a community can change from one year to the next, and this change may well depend on its surroundings each year.

When we talked of the 'folk from Kövesd', we meant not only those from Mezőkövesd itself, but all the gangs who came from that district; the men wore the characteristic tall hat and the women that slender-fitting skirt which was tied immediately below the breast. The folk from Kövesd were all good workers, diligent, clever and undemanding. Now among them there was one gang, from R., which outshone even the most colourful description. The girls would up and dance at the first hint of a whistle, and a smile was enough to entice them into the maize fields. In the warm summer nights the young folk all slept outside together among the ricks and till dawn there was no end to their giggling, singing and shouts of laughter. The young men on the puszta had the happiest recollections of them. The following year there arrived a gang from H. They were welcomed into the atmosphere of the previous year, for after all, they were near neighbours of their predecessors. But they were cold as ice. The girls walked around with stiff backs and heads erect, and blows rained unceasingly from their hands, like sparrows from the grape-vines. They lived like one large family; no stranger penetrated their ranks. Later the good old band of dancers returned, but in the meantime they too had changed. It seemed as though these gangs were always controlled by the temperament of one person alone. A single soldierlike gangmaster or solemn old man would keep the whole band under strict discipline and in dignified isolation, but sometimes the happy-go-lucky spirit of some girl or youth would prevail, and change the whole character of the band for the summer, like a pinch of yeast in a cask of wine. It was remarkable how these nuances could be sensed in the first half-hours as they arrived on the puszta.

Only one summer did there come to us a gang which justified the gossip of the farm servants' wives. They came from Vas or Zala—or rather they staggered in noisily, for on the day of their arrival they were drunk, the girls too, and we gazed at them in holy horror. Certainly women might drink on the puszta, but a drunken woman was condemned more sternly than one who prostituted herself. They were dishevelled and filthy, the men shabbier than gipsies. They did not bother to make beds for themselves, but lay around on the ground like animals. I know that it is impossible to draw conclusions about the peasant girls' morals from the way they talk; without the slightest embarrassment they will utter the filthiest words even in front of the young men. But a very great deal could be deduced from the words of these folk from Zala. They tore at each other day and night. For them love was no consolation. In the dirt of the dark shed they flirted coarsely and in each others' hearing. At dawn the puszta foreman would first shout at them from outside, then kick at the door, and only after this go inside, he was loth to find out who was with whom. The people of the puszta kept away from them too. Fleas leapt from them like maize from the gridiron as it is being roasted over the fire. Rumour had it that they were all afflicted with venereal disease. How then were they able to work? 'It hasn't any effect on them,' said the farm servants of their illness. In any case, such work as they did was tipsy, and not worth a brass farthing. The women became pregnant one after another, just to get out of the heavy work, in the opinion of the higher authorities. The estate nearly dismissed the farm official who engaged them.

The folk from Kövesd were clean, but is was not only in cleanliness and diligence that they outshone the people of the pusztas. They were kindly and polite. They were grateful for the help of the farm servants and knew how to express their thanks. In the spring they brought gifts—a little toy for the children, or an embroidered handkerchief for the wives. With us it was not the fashion to express thanks for a good deed. But if my mother happened to give a scone to their children as they sat around on the puszta, the folk from Kövesd would solemnly turn up in the evening and offer their thanks. I looked up to them and sought their friendship. I felt that they had some secret and would have liked to find out what it was. Later in my teens, when I gave my simple curiosity a more resounding title and announced that I was 'studying their customs', I spent several nights with them in the sheds.

I discovered nothing out of the ordinary. They knew who I was, sensed the fellow-feeling which took me to their midst, and instead of speaking themselves, got me to talk. Perhaps for the first time in my life I was carried away by the ecstasy of direct communication; I shall never forget the joy I felt as I chattered away happily, sometimes near to tears, in answer to their questions, as if I were bringing them some good news. Once I related in three instalments the contents of a French novel I was reading at the time.

I walked over to the neighbouring pusztas. I arrived in the evening and the foreman of the puszta, in accordance with the plan we had already made, found me a place among the labourers there as a sort of tramp. They were also from Kövesd. They received me in a friendly way, but I was unable to learn much here either. The men talked for a while quite freely and then went off to sleep; in the pauses during their rhythmical snoring I heard the girls chattering on for quite a long time. The tales told by the youths about the girls differed scarcely at all from what could have been said of the farm servants' girls. There was occasional talk of the intimacy which the overseers of various ranks naturally allowed themselves when dealing with the girls who undertook seasonal work. But on one of these excursions of mine I accidentally overheard a scene. One of the girls gave a young accountant such a dressing-down that he slunk away like a dog with its tail between its legs. She was a tiny little creature of about sixteen, who angrily rejected his boorish approaches with such a stream of language from her virgin lips that I was forced to turn away; she used coarse expressions for everything, including the ritual once performed upon the accountant, who happened to be Jewish. The male members of the gang smiled as they listened to the rapid fire of back chat. They did not intervene now, nor had done so earlier when the accountant approached her with words and gestures. Nor did the gangmaster say a word, though he was one of those responsible for discipline.

In all these gangs, even those which appeared to live in the utmost freedom, there was something of the tenacity and organisation born of necessity which is found among gold-diggers or marauding bands of guerillas. Did they feel themselves in a strange land? It was only in the rarest instances that dissension broke out among them. According to their contract, they had to obey the commands of the managers of the puszta, but they performed real work only under the leadership of their own gangmaster. From the estate they received every month 7–10 pengős in cash; then the full-rate labourers got 120 kilos of corn, 20 kg of bread flour, 10 kg of cooking flour, 3 $1/_2$ kg of fat bacon, 1 $1/_2$ kg of lard, 3 kg of beans, 12 kg of potatoes, 1 kg of salt, 3 kg of salted or raw meat, 1 litre of vinegar and 30 fillérs for seasoning. From this they must prepare their own food. They tried to save as much as they could of their daily rations. At home, a hundred kilometres from the breadwinner, a whole nestful of infants waited for their food. They saw to it that they consumed as little as possible of their rations in order to send all the more home. They practised economising in common. What little flour, lard, bacon and beans they received on the first of the month—and they could well have eaten twice as much for the exhausting work they performed day in day out—they put together; then with enthusiastic determination they commanded their cook, who was usually the wife of the gangmaster, not to use more than half of the lard, for example.

On Sundays they ate only at midday. They worked out an ingenious method of economising on bread. According to the amount of flour and potatoes received, each of them had a right to half a loaf per day. Those who did not take their share received instead a small piece of wood signed in ink by the gangmaster. These pieces of wood counted as money and when they were produced to the cook she would serve out at any time a certain measure of flour and potatoes. If it had occurred to anybody to attempt a swindle, he would have been punished with banishment for life, in accordance with their own special code. They did indeed take the food from their own mouths in order to amass 'capital'; some of them managed to acquire three or four loaves a month by starving. Bacon was doled out for the week, and here economy was practised through free competition. The number of pieces hanging over the sleeping-quarters plainly showed the victor of the week. They lived on soup. To be more exact, at midday on Monday, Tuesday, Thursday, Saturday and Sunday they each had a plate of 'meat soup', concocted by the cook for 38 people out of 5 kg of meat and small pieces of paste. On Wednesday and Friday they ate bean soup with dumplings. In the evening every day of the week they had bean soup, except on Friday, when there was potato soup, and on Sunday, when as I have said, there was nothing. They themselves insisted on including in the contract a clause by which the estate would allow the men at most 3 pengős per month of their cash payment, and the women 2 pengős. In addition they required their corn allowance to be handed over to them in their own village, at home. They did not even trust themselves sufficiently.

They too worked from dawn to dusk, with breaks of half an hour in the morning and afternoon, and one and a half hours at midday. They were allotted work that did not require animals, but needed agility and attention. They thinned out root crops, hoed and scythed, but did no reaping at all. The harvest was the task of the sharecroppers.

So after five or six months of heavy labour they took home five or six quintals of corn, 40 pengős in cash and some 20 pengős' worth of food that they had saved. In other words they had about 130–150 pengős in all, reckoned in money. This was what they took home if—contradicting their own avowed intent—they had not sent it home already. This enabled them to drag out the winter, if their relations at home had not already consumed it during the summer.

The sharecroppers appeared on the scene at about the same time as the folk from Kövesd. They came from the nearby villages. We knew them well, for even in winter they would look in from time to time to borrow a little flour. On the estate they performed the work that their serf ancestors had once done as villein services. In those days the serfs had received for these the right to use their own land. Now the sharecroppers received considerably less. They did the reaping.

Everywhere the estates used machines for ploughing, sowing and threshing, yet throughout the country reaping was still performed by hand, with scythe and sickle, just as it was centuries ago. This was the one single achievement of the agricultural labourers' movements in Hungary.

At the end of the last century reaping machines made their *début* in Hungary. They performed their work more economically, more swiftly and thoroughly, just like any other agricultural machine. A single mechanical reaper will do the work of a whole gang of human reapers in half the time... Naturally the estates acquired them immediately and they proved excellent. Suddenly the whole labour force available for harvesting became redundant, and at the worst possible time.

This was the era of the notorious harvesters' strikes and the peasant risings in the Great Plain, which were stifled in blood but not silenced by the rifle-fire of the gendarmerie. In vain did the government mobilise the army and the poverty-stricken Ruthenes and Slovaks from the uplands, who were assembled on state farms and sent in companies of 100 at reduced fares and under armed guard to those 'danger spots' where the Hungarian poor were pleading for an extra bushel of wheat. In vain did they promulgate the shameful 'harvest-strike' law, according to which, though everybody else might stop work like a free man whenever he wished, the Hungarian landless peasants alone must be compelled with bayonet and bullet to work against their will, because the seeds were dropping from the ear... The movement spread. And how would it have spread among the masses now unemployed as a result of the use of harvesters, masses who could not be pushed over to America in a matter of days? Apparently there were some who could picture this happening. The mechanical harvesters and reapers disappeared as quickly as they had come. I do not know whether there was a law about them, but in spite of the demands of progress I believe that in Hungary there was soon not a single harvesting machine in service. In my childhood I still saw one or two of them rusting away in the sheds at Rácegres. The sharecroppers growled as they passed them by and secretly kicked at them to hasten their disintegration. They might have kicked them openly; the estate regarded all of them as a heap of old iron.

The sharecroppers were organised in gangs to undertake work. They were allotted roughly 7 *hold* of autumn and spring crops 'per scythe', that is to say per couple. The tenth part of every harvested crop, in other words every tenth sheaf, was theirs. At one time this was all. The reapers cut the corn and returned home with a tenth, or earlier a ninth, of it. As time went on their share diminished. There were times and places where they reaped for an eleventh, twelfth or even a thirteenth. But the yearly reductions produced dissatisfaction and annoyance, sometimes even among the more humane gangmasters too. It was to the credit of the estate tenants that they succeeded in finding other ways of diminishing payments. They found several methods.

For example, in Transdanubia the tenth remained in force almost everywhere, but one had to work harder for it. The reapers now arrived in their gangs on the puszta early in the spring. In accordance with their contract they must perform various 'supplementary tasks' apart from harvesting until late autumn. They undertook anything merely in order to be able to harvest. Part of their 'supplementary tasks' they did virtually for nothing; not only did they receive no daily food for it, but they did not even cover the wear and tear of their implements with it. Thus, to give a single example, it is they who pulled up or reaped the flax. This is one of the heaviest agricultural jobs. It requires at least 16 days' labour to reap one *hold* of flax. According to their contract, the gang reaped one *hold* of flax for 70 kg of rye. If this was converted into money and divided in proportion, one reaper received a day's wage of 40–42 fillérs for this inhuman work from dawn to dusk—for naturally they too were bound to work 'from sunrise to sunset.'

It is they who picked the beans, peas, maize and potatoes and they who scythed the hay and lucerne. They coped with the root-crops too, from the first thinning-out to the final weighing. They also threshed. For threshing, bagging, stooking and rick-building they received 3—3¹/₂ per cent of the threshed grain. Every year they worked for about 110 days on the puszta and of this, harvesting proper occupied only 12–15 days. They spent 18–20 days threshing, 30 days on root crops and 50 days on scything here and there. The value of the produce they earned during this period 'per scythe', in other words per couple, was roughly 300–500 pengős. For the reaper must have a partner, whom he himself paid, generally with 300–350 kg of wheat. But he could employ his wife in this capacity; she cooked for him and sometimes had to carry the lunch she had prepared at home some four or five hours' walk out to the puszta and home again. For the sharecroppers got their food from home and were supposed to return home also for a night's rest; they did not receive lodgings on the puszta. They did not go home. At night they lay down under the ricks or stooks, or if the weather was wet and cold, under the carts, or in the barns and sheds.

Naturally they did not sing—particularly not while they were harvesting. Those who mention singing reapers simply did not tell the truth. It is just as impossible to sing while scything as it is while climbing a rope. When they went in procession from one field to another they might well have sung, but they did not. They wiped away the sweat and coughed the dust out of their throats. When the harvest was complete they sometimes sang if they were given wine, but this was very rare. At most the girls crooned away.

Only one folk custom was in fashion among the harvesters. From the first swathe felled by the scythe they made a chain and bound the wrists of the farm manager with it. What did this imply? They did it smiling and with obvious delight, and all of them came to the ceremony. The custom remained in force, but with a slight change: they came to slip on the right arm of the manager a pretty little chain composed of three or four heads of corn.

At very rare intervals we had day-labourers also at Rácegres. They had been unable to find places in the gangs of seasonal labourers or sharecroppers. They too came from the neighbouring villages, whose population was being increasingly released from the land by the call of the 'free world'. Among them were old men of seventy who threw out their chests with pathetic make-believe when they applied for work. There were also ten-year-old girls, on whose shoulders the hoe looked as big as one of the poles used for carrying haycocks. Whenever did these folk get up in order to be at work at sunrise, which really meant at the first crack of dawn? For they too were forbidden to stay there at night. The puszta sucked in folk at dawn and ejected them at dusk like a huge factory. The amount of day-labour varied practically every week. In autumn there was less than in summer, in winter less than in autumn, and it was more or less a rule that there was always less this year than last. Meanwhile prices rose higher and higher. 'Oh, the expense, the expense!'— my childhood was filled with echoes of this cry. The men received an average of 65 kreutzers, the women 45. They worked a month for the price of a pair of boots.

Among the day and seasonal labourers there were some who still possessed a little piece of land at home, a tiny souvenir of their former property which was always being parcelled out in minute pieces as a result of the increasing population. They clung to their land with maniac fury, as is customary with family relics. Even the last ribbon of land could be wrested from them only by auction. They were proud of it and in the meantime filled the air with complaints. Of their homes, the villages wedged in between the big estates and now swelling dangerously, they talked as if of shoes that pinch. They caught their breath, found it impossible to move, yet all the same were proud of them. 'It's all very well for you,' even they said to the farm servants, 'what problems have you got with food and taxes?' The eternal argument that went on among the haystacks concerning which was better off, the farm servant on the puszta or the landless and small peasant in the village, later grew into a nation-wide debate, even among the so-called competent authorities. They twisted it round, asking which was less badly off, though they knew that in this form it was still a minute difference of degree. The villagers were more eloquent, but they would not have changed places with the people of the pusztas. Even at that time the farm servants listened oafishly to the

259

complaints and praise of their own lot. They understood the world less and less.

Here and there could still be found tobacco-workers, with half-shares in tobacco-fields. They were an odd, secretive race, and even the people of the pusztas ostracised them. They were Bohemians, and pariahs. Their work demanded a special kind of skill and a complete disregard for life. They inherited sickness together with their craft. They were yellow and wizened, like the plant which in its long garlands decorated the eaves of their hovels and the ceilings of their rooms, where they lived even more overcrowded than the farm servants. Four-year-old children did their share of the work, and even the dying punched the leaves to make festoons of them. They did the hardest work of all and in the meantime they drank and sang and, not caring a rap for the opinion of the outside world, carried on love-affairs with the most outrageous openness. In most places they were excluded on moral grounds, because they would not take orders. Even at religious processions their youths, lean, short of stature and glistening-eyed, formed a separate band, like a pack of wolves. Their girls were pleasant and friendly— only too ready to make friends, poor Carmens from the banks of the Sár! 'He's been down among the tobacco-workers,' was a moral judgement long after they had disappeared from the district. In our area they were some three pusztas, or ten kilometres, away. On Saturday evenings the young drivers would sometimes visit them, one with a sheaf or two of maize, another with a little bag of flour that would just go into their pocket. They took this either as a gift or in payment, and returned with stories of huge orgies in which the whole settlement had taken part.

CHAPTER SEVENTEEN

The 'summons'. Those who leave the puszta. The people of the pusztas in the village

All Saints' Eve, October 31st, was the great dividing-line among the dull week-days; it was an exciting and real festival and the turning-point of the whole year. This was the day when the estate notified which farm servants were to be retained and which dismissed at the New Year. It was then too that new hands were engaged. This was the day of the 'summons', or as the graveyard humour of the puszta had it, of 'trouser-rattling'. Later the law altered the date for removal to April lst, because by that time the mud had dried on the roads and the loaded waggons could move along more easily.

Early in the morning the whole puszta gathered in strict social rank in front of the office, all shaved and in their Sunday best, a poplar-forest of trembling souls. In front stood the technicians: the smiths and stokers led by the chief mechanic. Then came the wheelwright and his associates, then the coachman, granary overseer, transport-manager and farm foreman, each with his own host of workmen. Next came the shepherds, cowherds and horseherds, then the watchmen, estate swineherds and finally the farm servants' swineherd, who looks after the farmhands' pigs and whose pay is deducted from theirs. Like any other review, this one was silent. Who knew who would be staying on? The men enter the office white-faced, as if they are going to a duel. Sometimes a wailing can be heard as somebody pleads for mercy. First the overseers go

261

before the authorities and if they are approved, they immediately join the tribunal; they then take part in the examination of their underlings, normally in the role of accusers.

With the farm servants, the scene was a brief one, like every great decisive act. The dialogue started with an ancient formula. 'If my person and my honour find favour, my intention is to remain.' Such was the nation-wide formula spoken by the applicant standing stiffly at attention before the tables that had been pushed together. Here the members of the tribunal sat like a court of law, with the estate manager in the middle (he appeared most frequently for this occasion on the puszta). The members of the tribunal looked at each other. Each made his observations if they were unfavourable. The employee received advice and warnings about his future behaviour. But the farm servants took these with a light heart. Those considered worthy of abuse or correction, even 'in their own interest', would be kept on for at least another year. It was not customary to give praise, on educational principles.

They do not speak a word to those who are given their cards; the action is sufficient. When this happens, the farm servants do not utter any intelligible sentence—there is no traditional text for this scene. The actor is thrown back on to his own ingenuity; he struggles hard to say something with trembling lips, and gazes at the floor. 'I've got seven children, sir,' he finally gulps out. He receives no answer. At most the foreman, who perhaps feels something in common with his underlings, says 'You should have behaved yourself!' The victim repeats what he has said once or twice. Then at a sterner command he makes his way out, weeping, in silence, or with curses on his lips. His behaviour depends entirely on his nerves, as it does at the scaffold. Having been dismissed, he takes immediately to the road and tries that same day to go the rounds of the neighbouring pusztas, in case they can take him on. What happens if they cannot? Not even the writer knows this.

Does he evaporate and disappear into thin air? At all events he is not seen again on the puszta.

Then it is the turn of the new arrivals who have asked for their cards from their former employers on the previous afternoon. The service-book contained no space for the character of the farm servants. But the estates had their own methods of noting undesirable elements. Usually they put secret marks on the contract. For example, if there was a dash before the name, this implied that the person is quarrelsome; if the name was underlined, the holder cannot be recommended for employment. The gradual arrival of newcomers continued for the next few evenings.

The restlessness which pervaded the puszta for weeks before the 'summons' enveloped our house too. My father wanted to leave every year. In the autumn the main outside work was over and he, like the rest, was confined to the puszta and slept in a bed every night; it was then that a strange vagrant instinct awoke in him and he felt he must move, like a migratory bird. He could not find his place anywhere. Every evening he bemused the family with his day-dreams and on Sundays he almost always asked the manager for leave of absence. He went the rounds of relations and friends, sometimes taking us with him. Was he looking for a better job? I would not say so. In the houses of relatives and countless friends, he would relate in a happy and confident tone how much he was esteemed and what a good job he had; why, on holidays when his hands were clean, even the manager stopped to shake hands with him, for he...
I listened enchanted, even when I discovered his tendency to exaggerate. In my own mind I approved his words and, seeing his delight, would have liked to help him as he talked. He did not overemphasise matters: he was simply incapable of complaining. This was how he defied the ocean of wailing and groaning, and wanted to rise above it. If, however, he had to

mention his troubles, he would blush, stutter and burst out laughing in his torment; then finally looking either to the sky or to the ground, he would bring it all out in one breath, but his very next words would be to console not himself, but his audience, and then he would put on a sorrowful expression. I have never discovered this trait among his relations, but later I was astonished to find it in my elder brother and then in myself. These excursions never bore any fruit. Once he was offered a job at the electricity works in Fehérvár. He set out rubbing his hands to have a look at it; the result was that he nearly brought back with him the stoker from there, because he had 'so fallen in love with the life of the puszta.'

The gentry often changed. The count and his family leased the puszta, then for a year or two after it had run out, he himself took it over. Then he leased it again and yet again took it back with all its old equipment, carts, machines and animals —and naturally farm servants too, for they were just as much part of the puszta equipment as the former.

Each new era was worse than its predecessor, this being a characteristic of eras in general. Under the count and his family, the farm servants were treated with patriarchal rudeness, but a great deal was overlooked; in other words supervision was not very strict. The tenants were impersonal, stiff and cold, not only in their contacts, but also when they should have shown some understanding. Their method of discipline was to dismiss offenders politely but with immediate effect. They kept to the contract in every minute detail, and insisted on their employees doing the same. From that time onwards, the farm servants could not 'acquire' a single grain of corn or leaf of maize beyond what was prescribed. There was order. The farm servants were delighted at the return of the count and even agreed to a reduction of their payment in kind in the hope that they would be able to make up for it with their acquisitions. This practice came to an end once more with the succeeding tenant, nor did he increase payment. Such was progress.

Those who could escaped. With the despair of drowning men, the farm servants now began to look even beyond the villages to the towns. Budapest! In their imagination the capital gleamed afar like a wonderful fairy palace shining high above the curse-ridden morass of the pusztas. Something which had previously been unimaginable began to occur ever more frequently: a man failed to return from military service to his 'safe place'. The old folk who had managed to scrape together a little money or half an acre of land somewhere hurried to abandon the sinking ship, particularly when the news got around that the master of the Öttöd estate wanted to make an inventory of the property of one of his departing foremen; he then prosecuted him on the very logical grounds that he could not have saved enough of his wages for even a quarter-plot of land, not even in thirty years!

On one occasion when the puszta changed hands, my mother's parents began to calculate; they soon decided that if they moved to a village and grandfather could devote his time to beekeeping, they would earn as much as was promised in the new contract. At that time they had served on the puszta for thirty-six years. They had a little money too. It was nowhere near enough to buy a house, but one morning grandmother went out alone into the maizefields, to meditate in that great wilderness like the prophets of old. At night she returned with the news that they were buying a house. 'Grandmother bought that house with her hoeing': such was the saying that later went round the family. It contained a little flattery and a little scorn, but had a basic ring of pride too.

The plan itself was enough to cause both a celebration and a revolution in our midst. Grandmother went the rounds of the nearby villages and viewed at least two hundred houses, giving each a thorough examination. She brought back specimens of the thatch, the well-water and the earth in the garden or court-yard, like Árpád's envoys of old. At home the whole family inspected and debated these specimens. We knew exactly how

265

much was needed to make up the price of any of the two hundred peasant houses. Where could it be obtained? My father offered to get a loan from his parents. It was rejected with a single glance. It was the Junkucz family, with whom they had been close friends for years, who gave it to them without asking— indeed in spite of their refusal to accept it.

Grandfather wanted to move to the pleasant, well-ordered community of landed peasants at Sárszentlőrinc. There was a house there that we had marked down; all of us had looked at it several times. Grandmother was willing to accept this plan. Then one of her daughters moved to Cece and immediately ran into serious trouble, as was the rule in her family. Her husband contracted a fatal disease and the doctors gave him up, merely prophesying a long period of suffering for him. This event decided their choice, however much grandfather grumbled, perhaps for the first time in his life. 'What, live among those dumb-clucks!' He had a poor opinion of the inhabitants of Cece, although he had only once been there to a fair. That was enough for him to establish that they were selfish, profiteering and cruel. 'Whatever sort of folk are they who don't even sing at fair-time?' The people of Cece certainly did not sing, they were ashamed to raise their voices for no purpose. But with her keen powers of detection, grandmother discovered in Cece a smallholder who had an apiary, neglected and tumbledown though it was. She immediately contracted with him for grandfather to look after the bees in return for a modest supply of corn. 'At any rate that's half the flour I need for baking,' she said on her return. At the New Year they emigrated to Cece.

As soon as one entered the village, the arrangement of its streets and houses disclosed its history, rather like the weather-beaten furniture in a family house. To the left and right of the broad main street neat little streets opened out. Almost every one of these made a dangerous bend after the first couple of yards, and turned into a narrow alley, then with a sudden twist ended in a *cul-de-sac*; or if not, it ducked under a gateway and went on to its hidden goal. The wanderer would suddenly find himself in the yard of a house. The inhabitants would then guide him through the beds of potatoes to where the street suddenly appeared again at the end of the garden, like some souvenir. Then it would open out into a square and later diminish to a street once more, until it met another house squatting comfortably in the middle of it, its windows casting a suspicious gleam on all comers. It is much easier for the traveller to find his way around Paris than around Cece. For Cece is a 'free settlement', which means that the extensive grounds of the old private houses were divided and built on by the heirs just as their desires and feelings towards each other dictated. If the brothers or brothers-in-law liked each other, they built their houses to face each other; if they were at loggerheads, then they turned their backs. After five hundred years of this characteristically Hungarian method of town-planning, the result was that after a good feast the descendants of the mettlesome Petchenegs would wander round half the night, desperately pleading to the stars to find their way home.

The original inhabitants, Calvinists, descended from three or four families, live in this peculiar ant-hill, which is a warm and life-giving spot perhaps because of its very lack of order. It grows ever larger in accordance with its own strange laws. With stubborn and miraculous persistence it dissects and engulfs the five hundred and thousand acre estates of the former landowners, who were not protected by entail. Their noble names, aristocratic tastes and love of splendour are now proclaimed only in dignified distichs on their magnificent tombstones, if one can push aside the waist-high weeds from them in the neglected cemetery down by the duck-pond. At a proper distance from the old ant-hill, new little houses form a protective belt; newcomers from the surrounding pusztas

267

have built here their mud-hovels of one room and kitchen, situated in the middle of a tiny yard.

These yards are neat and clean, unmarred by sheds, rusting ploughs or steaming dung-hills. At most a single hen stalks around in them, tied by a piece of string. It is enough to make one weep as one glances over the low fence of maize-stalks into these miniature yards and sees the shining, model cleanliness of sheer poverty. Here live the Catholics, who greet one first in the street and borrow flour, people at whose door even the gipsy does not knock unless he is on the verge of suicide. There are also some Catholics at the bottom end of the village; though they are better off, they too must have been new settlers at one time, for they have not been able to mix with the original Petcheng settlers to this day. The village lives its life in completely separate strata—and this includes both economic and love-life. It becomes united at most when there is a dance in the solitary ancient monument, the barn in the big inn-yard, where Petőfi once came to act. Of this, however, the folk of Cece know nothing. Obviously they do not want to know of it, because however much I stressed it, they did not think it anything to be proud of.

It was typical of grandmother's enterprising spirit that she bought a house, not in the landless peasants' row down at the Catholic end of the village, but up on the ridge in the very middle of the ant-hill. With the boldness of a military strategist, she broke through and encamped right in the middle of the enemy, and what was even more surprising, her plan succeeded. What battles did she fight with the old, black, tenacious peasant women who ruled the roost in the neighbouring Calvinist houses? I cannot say, but after a single year she had won respect. The unctuous, sly old women knocked at her door to ask her opinion and advice. Grandmother treated them somewhat high-handedly. She greeted them first in the street, but never stopped for a little neighbourly gossip; knowing her nature, I could not imagine her doing this anyway.

She always had work to do, even more than on the puszta. This was certainly one reason for the respect she acquired. The richest peasant's wife in the street discovered in her a kindred spirit and tried to learn from her. She was a patient, soft-spoken woman, far more sensible than those around her, and her name, which I mention here in gratitude, was Mrs István Pordány. In exchange she would help out now and again with a little flour and milk, for in Cece grandmother did not keep a cow. She even sent her sons across if men were needed to do some heavy work.

For this was where my grandparents began to make their real home, in Cece, towards their seventieth year. The house was a dilapidated, miserable little peasant hovel, with rotting thatch and cracked mud walls. (They collapsed fifteen years later in the year when my grandfather died, as if they had made a gentlemen's agreement to last that long.) In summer the water in the well dried up, and in winter it rose to the brim. On the day they moved in the fence collapsed into the desolate yard.

My father succeeded in obtaining from somewhere a wire-bending apparatus, and during the course of one winter the old folk made a beautiful wire fence. They thatched the roof with reeds. Grandfather built a superb apiary and planted vines in the garden, while grandmother put so many roses in front of the house that the porch became transformed into a tunnel of flowers. What they had been preparing to do all their lives now became apparent. In the middle of the trackless jungle of dirt, dust and dung, a tiny paradise blossomed forth. The peasants gazed in astonishment over the stylish wire-fence (the street, which twisted like a trampled worm, was somewhat higher than their yard), and automatically touched their hats if they happened to catch sight of Philemon and Baucis inside; the old couple trotted around swiftly and were always kind to each other—it seemed that now, childless again after so many years,

269

they had released their great affection for each other, the affection which at the time care and work had obscured.

We were always astonished how grandmother had ever found this house in the first place. Even after the tenth visit we managed to find it only after being guided by the villagers through the mass of tiny lanes. As soon as I stepped through the gate I got lost and staggered back again after tramping through half the village: true, I always lost the way in every village amongst the dispiritingly similar houses. At first I even got lost in Nebánd; after passing the fifth house, this strange world made my head whirl and I screamed for help to lead me back home.

Grandfather returned the peasants' greetings with a cautious glance. He was suspicious of them. Perhaps he had learnt in his childhood that they must regard him as a vagrant, a nobody, a mere farm servant. But they did not. Cece accepted my grandparents—an event without precedent either before or after them.

Why? First of all, I believe it was on religious grounds. In that district all the farm servants were Catholics. In Cece, to the Calvinist 'nobility' who had multiplied and developed into a healthy peasantry, 'Papist' implied not merely a religious sect, but a social stratum or caste. Now grandfather's folk were Calvinists and at the end of their surname they had a historic -y, which was guaranteed to increase respect. What had distinguished them on the puszta made them one with the natives here. Grandfather was only so much of a Calvinist as was implied in that district—as opposed to the church-going Catholics, it meant first of all a spirit of enlightenment and freedom. He did not attend church. He possessed a remarkably well-balanced spirit, and was simply not concerned with notions of God or death. He read. His mind, which only now had a real chance of spreading its wings, manifested astonishing independence. As I recall him now, I am amazed at it. Let one scene serve as proof.

He kept one festival, which was Good Friday, the great Calvinist festival, and this too, of course, was traditional. For seventy years grandfather had fasted on Good Friday, out of respect for his forebears. And this he did up to that Good Friday when I happened to be staying with them and pointed out his inconsistent behaviour. 'If you are not religious, why do you keep this one feast, grandad?' piped up the Satan who happened to be temporarily lodged in my adolescent heart. Grandfather looked at me for a moment. 'You're right,' he replied. It needed only a moment for him to shake off the habit of years, the ancient tradition of his father, grandfather and greatgrandfather. He went into the pantry and munched happily at a piece of bacon. That is the kind of man he was.

He was almost elected a presbyter, but in spite of this he was not attracted to his co-religionists. If he had a little spare time, he would stroll through the maze of paths and lanes to where the landless peasants lived. It was a kind of shore where he could feel the wind and waves of the puszta, if only in the laments of the shipwrecked. He called on those with whom fate had once cast his lot, out there in the place of tribulation. What did he seek among them? After all, he was not talkative and he soon grew weary of idle gossip. Yet he would spend half the day there, shyly leaving behind—for the children—a bag of gherkins or kohlrabi, a piece of pumpkin, a round of new bread or whatever he had happened to take out of the larder without grandmother's knowledge, but with her silent agreement; in other words there was a touching complicity between them. He would come back shaking his head. He did not normally say anything about his adventures, but grandmother knew sign language very well. At most he would say, 'You're a fine woman, mother.' Grandmother knew that this too was not praise but thanks; it meant heartfelt gratitude that they were able to live some kind of human life, not starving and begging like

271

those whose fate might have been theirs. She would turn away and quickly get down to work. But after the death of her husband, when she was in her eighties, the tears welled up in her old eyes and trickled through the maze of dry wrinkles whenever she recalled these words, as she did ever more frequently.

CHAPTER EIGHTEEN

The future of the people of the pusztas.
The landless peasants

The people of the pusztas were gradually diminishing, although their birth-rate was far above that of any other social class. Even in those days the driver's wife would have five or six children, of whom four on the average would reach the age of two. And even these were a burden. In the old days the farm servants insured themselves against starvation in old age by bringing up as many children as their bodies could bear. One of them at least would get on in the world, and they surely might hope to end their days with one of them. But this calculation of theirs went wrong too. Once upon a time the estates did not concern themselves with the size of the farm servant's family—the larger it was, the more cheap labour they had on hand. Now they took note of it, for to them too children were a burden; they brought trouble and unnecessary expense. The tenant of the B. estate objected to the high cost of maintaining the school under his patronage, quarrelled with the schoolmaster and finally decided to close it, or rather to make it superfluous. He would engage only childless farm servants and after a couple of years of enthusiastic campaigning reached his goal: the school was forced to close down owing to the lack of pupils. 'What use are all those children?' he would say as he waved away prospective farm servants. What use indeed? Of the driver's four children, only one at most could stay on the puszta—or perhaps not even one.

The rejected farm servants withdrew to the edges of the puszta, dragged out a miserable existence among the landless peasants in the villages, and waited the call to work, if not for a lengthy period, at least for a couple of weeks or a month. They knew no other trade; where else could they look or turn? What can a driver do in the world apart from the job he knows? No skilled workmen or industrial labourers ever came from their ranks, chiefly because apprenticeships would have cost money, if only for a new suit. Moreover during their apprenticeship, boys did not earn, while if there were a chance of day-labouring, they could do so freely from the age of ten. The only place for this was the big estate. So for years on end they kept their swollen eyes on the estates. But machines made labour increasingly redundant. In the district covered by this book there was a village where 4,200 people were employed in 'agriculture' on 5,600 *hold* of land. In the 'theoretical commune' of the 38,000 *hold* estate which embraced the village, the population was 3,300, exactly 613 less than it was thirty years before. This village is Ozora, and my figures can be checked against the census returns.

In Canada, given proper machinery, areas of 100,000 acres can be ploughed and reaped by a handful of mechanics. There they have no need whatever of farm servants. Did this future await the Hungarian peasantry? If economic production and not the availability of labour is accepted as a guiding principle, then the Hungarian pusztas would be denuded. In a society where cells, like cancerous growths, strive for independence, the large estates naturally had but one end in view, like any industrial, commercial or financial concern they were out to make a profit. Whoever would reproach them for this would have to break a whole chain of interconnected links, even if he affirms that we have but one mother earth and that she is sacrosanct—more sacrosanct and more ancient than private property, which has more recently been created a god. There were some estates which had given up the outdated idea of exclusive

274

cereal crop production, and devoted themselves to intensive agriculture, with establishments for dairy-farming and pig-fattening. Did they require more employees than the former? At first perhaps they did—up to the time when machines could perform the work more cheaply, swiftly and efficiently, indeed, up to the time when machines were no longer aids but rivals to the labourers, and truly serve the aims of 'profit' and not 'development'.

The 'speed of development' and 'the wind of progress' for the moment blew keenly over the pusztas, breaking in through the farm servants' windows and scattering like chaff the folk who in the course of a thousand years have never been able to take root.

In the smallholder areas of Hungary the density of population fluctuated between 80 and 100 per square kilometre. Fejér county, the most productive district of Transdanubia, was half occupied by large estates. There the density of population was 57 per square kilometre. But even this was too great and uneconomical, and it was rapidly decreasing. If all the work were to be performed by machines, half this number would suffice. In the official report on the census of 1930, we can discover four or five times on each page the explanation for the decrease of population in some districts: 'decrease in the number of agricultural employees', 'decrease in the number of farm servants', 'decrease in the number of farm servants through removal to towns to find work', 'migration of indigents owing to difficulties of obtaining employment'. Can we guess the future? This cannot be calculated and perhaps it is no longer a literary or political problem, but an economic one and therefore improper. Let us then confine ourselves to objective observations. Once an old herdsman, who had gone into envious raptures over the happy state of the factory workers, told me his reflections on the matter; if the gentry were to see fit, not a soul need remain on the puszta. 'Not even a puppy,' he added, 'at most there would only be the flies and the gnats in the meadows.' This naive observation might well be extended to the whole of Hungary. To console the old man I told him that it was true of the factories also. 'Ah, well, that's life,' he said finally, with a sigh of relief, unburdening himself of a problem which appears to grow more difficult as one ponders on it.

In the swollen villages the people were like a flood held back behind a dam. They grew ever denser and more numerous. The landless peasants from the villages would gladly have flooded the pusztas in their millions in search of a 'safe retreat', while at the same time the people of the pusztas were anxiously trying to discover a tiny hole in their horizon through which to escape into an atmosphere which, if not more humane, was at least not devoid of humanity, away from the 'safe retreat'. Their chances grew less and less.

The natural road away from the pusztas led only downward. The farm servants knew this and if they had to move, it was with anxious hearts that they prepared to go. They felt that the slippery slope awaiting them led to a greater and gloomier depth than they had yet experienced, whose bottom could not be perceived by human eye. All their lives they had been filled with affectionate yearnings for the villages, and when they lay open to them, they started back in terror. Absolutely nothing lay in store for them—the legendary end of the world. Ten or twenty kilometres from their old home on the puszta lay a land so foreign that it might have been a different planet, snow-bound and frigid, where entirely different beings existed. They found no home in the villages.

It was the fate of the seasonal and monthly labourers that awaited them, if they had known what this was. But one had to be born to this too, and it took one's whole life to get used to it. The people of the pusztas staggered around in the new atmosphere; they were clumsy and helpless. Even the landless peasants looked down on the first generation of them in the village. The 'newcomers' asked somewhat naively to join the harvesting gangs. Usually they were rejected, for according to the old hands they did not even know how to reap. The truth was that they could not stand it.

Where was the time when the people of the pusztas could remove to their own piece of land! Where was the old dream of the little house at the end of the village! Now it was rare even for the foremen to achieve this objective.

Nor was the example of my mother's parents in Cece repeated. For a very long time it was only the landless peasants in the village who accepted the puszta folk, and they were by no means as delighted to see them as the people of the pusztas had been in their case. And what did this matter? What did the landless peasants count for in the village? It was remarkable if the villagers returned their greetings. It was a strange world. It seemed as if three completely isolated tribes lived in the villages, foreign to each other even in the languages they spoke. The landed peasants expressed themselves before the notaries, priests and teachers, if it was absolutely necessary, in halting, involved, impossible sentences. The landless peasants also stumbled over their words, but twisted their sentences differently when they spoke to the former, again only in cases of the utmost need. To the intelligentsia they too used a separate language. And the intelligentsia themselves spoke differently to the landed and landless peasants. All this had to be learnt, and it was not easy. It was so difficult to speak that members of the different strata meeting in the street and forced to greet each other merely raised their hats; words, even a simple 'Good day!', were stifled in their mouths. The people of the pusztas shivered. They would willingly have crept back to their old world, rather than rise from it. During the year they made solemn vows, murmured and grumbled, but when the time of the 'summons' came, they withdrew their heads beneath the water like frogs.

The stories told by those remaining on the puszta about their fellows who had succeeded in making their way up in the world were like the legend of the little swineherd who won a kingdom and a princess. They were fairy-tale heroes, with one important difference: they did not usually return. Everybody disowned the people of the pusztas; this is the first toll extracted from those who leave their world. Or is it the first test to prove the flexibility and adaptability of the mind? The son of a farm servant who in Budapest develops into a postman or policeman strides with a haughty and majestic air in front of the farm servants' dwellings during the Christmas holidays; he notes whom to greet first and indeed whose greetings to return. He visits his home more and more rarely and finally breaks away completely. If he were not to disown his past, he could never achieve that small personality which a postman must acquire in society, and would for ever remain a puszta servant. The people of the pusztas knew this and gazed on the empty bragging of those who had undergone the transformation with the humility properly due to heroes. Of the six unusually gifted Szabó boys, one engaged himself to a landed peasant, then to a butcher in Fehérvár and finally became a shop assistant. The second, after trials and tribulations which might have come out of a fairy-tale, became a tram-driver in Pécs. The son of the chief carter at Almamajor became a railway porter, and what a gentleman he was! He sometimes visited his home. The carters stood around him in a circle, and with shining eyes stared at his splendid uniform. Was it possible? It was unbelievable.

The second husband of one of my maternal aunts went blind in one eye, and since at home they refused to regard him as a whole human being, either for work or for pay, he set out heroically into the world with his one eye. He became a rent-collector for the stalls in the Lehel Market in Budapest, and at the same time our family benefactor. He never returned among us again. From the moment he stepped out of the East Station in Budapest, he seemed suddenly to become aware of some dreadful conspiracy stirred up against him, and regarded his birth-place with disgust. When he talked of anything pertaining to the countryside, he did so with the implacable, indeed pathological hatred of a Coriolanus, and began to bang the table. Yet out of the kindness of his heart he would smooth the path of his relatives, including my own, who hankered after Budapest.

After the departure of my mother's parents, my aunts slipped away one by one, taking with them their husbands and ever-increasing brood of children. They migrated to other pusztas, but at least they had stirred themselves and tried to better their lot. We were now the only family to remain in the old home, and we grew increasingly restless. Messages came from the relatives who had been swept away. They came quite frequently from various directions, all full of encouragement, but each of them awoke in my father plans and day-dreams for life. Once again he wanted to educate himself, and puzzled his head over further examinations. He was reminded of his adolescence. My mother enthusiastically fanned the flames. The rent-collector and his family painted the life of Budapest and the blessings of civilisation in tempting colours. One travelled to work by tram, and the water came from the wall. The only thing that restrained my father from departing immediately was the proposal from Ozora that he should be his own master and become a carrier or lease an inn. By now grandfather had left Nebánd, and it would not have been a bad idea to take his place there. We left Rácegres when we were dismissed.

Once again there was a change of management. The lease ran out and the count's family again took the puszta into their own hands. As was now the rule, wages were reduced all along the line. In addition, even we should have had to share our dwelling with another family. Was it that the new officials could not see the obvious value of my father's work? And his origins? In addition they offended him. The cup was full, but it needed a powerful nudge from my mother for it to run over.

At midday my father calmly and even smilingly recounted at the family table the rude and quite unnecessary insult he had suffered, but by the time we had reached the soup, he was burning with desire to revenge himself as quickly as possible. He washed and shaved, and then boxed the ears of one of the farm officials. He finally brought to a full stop the first great chapter of our life.

Our horizon, like the stage when the gong sounds, suddenly became flooded with light and opened out. The roads which wound off to the four quarters of the earth suddenly acquired meaning and interest, for at last we should be using one of them, but which? For the time being my father did not wish to work on a puszta; he was tempted by the thought of freedom. He gave himself a breathing space to gain information and to study. He would like to have another look round in the world. He decided to go up to Budapest, take another couple of examinations on operating milling machinery and Diesel motors, and in the meantime try to get into a factory to taste the life there. Of course he would not take the family on this adventure; we should hide ourselves in some village meanwhile. He immediately started to study. He might have been preparing to set out on an exotic voyage of discovery, and we would glance at him with devotion and pride, like wolf cubs at their sire as he goes off to find prey.

My mother's parents wanted us to move in with them for this period. My father's relatives received his plans with astonishment; they were scared and horrified of Budapest, which to them was a sink of iniquity. They would much rather have borne the shame of my father sinking to the level of a swineherd at home than his becoming a factory worker. They would sooner have agreed to his emigrating to America, for they felt it to be less foreign and distant than Újpest. And they were quite right: one could return from America, but never from

Újpest. In the plan they sensed the pushing, restless spirit of my mother's family which now, look you, had even seized hold of János. All of a sudden arms, hearts and even purses were thrown wide open, as if we had to be rescued from a fatal disease or spell. My mother rightly feared this aid. The family lurking in the black depths began to move feverishly and wound its tentacles round us like a gigantic octopus. The relations could not suppress the plan to go to Budapest, but they were indomitable in their insistence that we move to Ozora. So it was in that direction that we started off from the puszta, with four waggons up to their axles in mud. But as had happened years before with my mother, now too we stopped half-way. We rented a one-roomed lodging from a butcher in Simontornya.

Unfortunately we had practically no money. What my parents had scraped together over the years in accordance with grandmother's instructions my father had lent to one of his brothers-in-law and never got back. We had only what we got for the smallholding we had liquidated. But my father refused to touch this; he intended to use it on some suitable scheme to build the future. He put it into a separate little book and carried it around with him everywhere, so that if the suitable scheme materialised it was always at hand.

We left Rácegres with light hearts. We shed a few tears, not only as we bid farewell to our old friends one by one, but from general emotion. But our tears were soon dissolved in bright smiles and by the time we reached the fields we were on the verge of singing. We faced the future with laughter and confidence, the future which for the present gleamed on the two church towers of Simontornya and on the roof of the old castle keep which still remained intact. My father good-humouredly floundered in the mud from one cart to the next. He was in a joking mood. Once upon a time he had said to a farm official, 'If ever I get out of this rotten hole, I shall forget it so completely by the time I reach the second poplar that I'll never look back at it.' This occurred to him now, and he tried to keep his promise. He did not look back, but kept asking us how much of the puszta could still be seen.

But when we reached the village and the houses began to crowd together along the sides of the metalled road, our happiness evaporated and even he became silent. I was sitting on the second waggon, which was piled as high as a haystack, nursing a broody hen in my lap. I was gripped by sudden terror, as if I were on a boat amidst dangerous rocks, and I scarcely dared to look down. I gazed at the grey wintry sky, the bare tops of the trees, the last familiar signs of a world that had disappeared. Fortunately we had no need to pitch and toss for long, for our new lodging was at the end of the village in the landless peasants' quarter. As soon as we arrived my mother put up the beds, swept out the room, lit a fire and put us to bed, though it was still light. She accustomed us to the new house in the way used for animals—by sleep.

Father left a couple of days later, and my brothers and sisters returned to their schools. I was left alone with my mother. I should have gone to the elementary school at Simontornya, but even after the end of the Christmas vacation we kept postponing my admittance from day to day. For weeks we got to know the village through the window. We were scared and simply ate apples.

My father wanted to put the money he had got for the cows and pigs to immediate use and as a first proof of his resourcefulness bought a cartload of apples on the day of his departure. Someone convinced him that he could get twice their price in the spring. He bought them without seeing them, and forgot to mention them... One day we found this load of apples, half of which were already rotten, and we had to eat these immediately. We spread the rest out in the room, to keep an eye on the bruised ones so that we could eat them in time. The apples vied with each other in going bad, and so did we in eating them up. In one month we had finished off the whole cartload. In the meantime we sewed, read and told stories; never had we been so happy. If anybody knocked at our door, we huddled together in fear. Yet both of us had been in villages before—in Ozora and Cece—and I had spent months in Varsád. But then we had been guests, and we could still feel the puszta and home beneath our feet. Now we were strangers, vagrants and nobodies. When anyone looked at us, it felt as if they wanted to stare us out of the world. We dared not appear in public.

Mother sent me to the shop in the middle of the village for some cotton. I had to cross the iron bridge over the Sió, over which not so long ago we had driven to Nebánd, proudly and triumphantly galloping along with an infernal clatter of metal plates, axles and wheels. Now I slunk over it in humiliation. For hours I dawdled outside the shop, not daring to go in, and finally I returned home saying that there was no cotton, they had sold out. My mother understood not only the lie but the reason for it and the utter helplessness of spirit too. 'All right, my boy,' she said with the gentle complicity of comprehension, 'perhaps there'll be some tomorrow.' Next day we set out together, hand in hand. 'Was this the place?' she asked. I saw that she was undecided and found it difficult to go inside. In the end we opened the door with its tinkling bell and went in. We brought out the cotton smiling, as if it were the prize for some heroic deed. We were puszta folk, and only now did we realise it truly.

We were indeed mere puszta folk, without any special characteristics and without the little authority we had enjoyed on the puszta. One day the wife of the old herdsman, Mrs Kosaras, turned up at our door. They had left Rácegres years before. We were overjoyed to see her. On the puszta Aunt Kosaras would at very most have called my mother 'my dear', but here she at once used her first name. They embraced each other and my mother was glad at her familiarity. In the following days the whole Kosaras family came and visited us, and we them.

When we first came back from visiting them, silently walking along the steep, slippery road, I suddenly realised that we were no longer people of the pusztas, but just such landless peasants and 'burdens to others', as they were.

One or two of the streets in Simontornya had the atmosphere of a town rather than a village. Around the Catholic church, the post- office and the old castle, in which once upon a time King Matthias had kept his uncle, Mihály Szilágyi, under guard, there lived tradesmen and Jewish shopkeepers and educated folk. There were the Franciscan monastery, the gendarmerie barracks, the savings bank and the brothel. The peasants gradually gave up their old houses and withdrew to the outskirts of the village. Unfortunately they could not get far away, since on all sides a great estate hemmed in the community, sometimes so closely that one stepped straight out of the garden of a house on to the count's land. The people, pressed in on every side and frittering away their labour at ever cheaper rates, pushed up in their anguish the tall chimney of a leather factory and its workshops, to which a new floor was added every year. The village expanded upwards into the air.

The landless peasants occupied the hilly river-bank, the slopes of the Mózsé hill, from which the Turks once fired at the castle. They camped out in miserable hovels and mud-huts, no whit more comfortable than that besieging army of old. The Kosaras family lived there and so did we, at least until grandfather from Nebánd (we still called him that, though he was now living in the chief town in the district) came to visit us. It was not our poverty that incensed him, but our social degradation. I could not understand either. Were we living in poverty? We did not notice it. Even now the little room lives in my memory as a warm nest of happiness and hilarity. But grandfather grumbled. 'This is no place for you,' he said, restlessly trotting round in his huge boots, for he could not take proper strides in the free space left in the handkerchief-sized kitchen. He immediately began to look for new lodgings.

We moved a few hundred yards nearer the centre of the village, and once more to a butcher's. But here we had the yard too, with a hen-house, cowshed and all. The butcher merely had his shop in the room which looked out on the street. Grandfather wanted to pay the rent. Shyly he pulled out his wallet, which was the size of a brief-case. 'You'll accept it, won't you, from me?' he asked, licking a banknote. 'No, not even from you, father-in-law,' replied my mother. 'Then you put it away, my boy,' said the old man, growing red, and pressed the money into my hand; it was 50 koronas, the yearly rent of the lodgings. At a glance from my mother I gave it back to him. The old man grew even redder, stared dumbly at the ground for a moment and then began to swear. But miraculously it was not my mother's behaviour that he commented on in his own peculiar fashion, but his own children who had been responsible for it. As he went, he left a message for my father to give up his efforts in Budapest and take up some work at home; grandfather would lend him as much money as he needed. 'It's disappearing anyway,' he added, hinting at his children and their husbands, whose attempts and failures to get on in society he continued to finance. At that time there was a craze in the family for inn-keeping; this, they considered, was the easiest step on the upward road. The innkeeper, even in the worst part of the village, was almost one of the middle class. The sons and sons-in-law who had worn themselves out with harness-making, tailoring and the peculiar crafts of the puszta thought that they knew most about this trade; all that was needed was a little money, nothing more. Both the men and their wives were good wine-drinkers.

At first my father visited us every month, then later every Saturday. He found life in Budapest more and more distasteful. He passed his examinations, but now his plan was to find a better job on one of the pusztas. Grandfather's message stimulated him. Why should not he too choose an easier life? One Sunday morning he turned up with two horses. He had bought

285

them in Budapest, where they cost half as much as he would be able to get by selling them in the village...

One of them, it turned out when the first bargaining began, was spavined. My father himself pointed this out triumphantly. It could not pull, and so for the time being was not worth a farthing to us. The veterinary surgeon recommended us to make him walk as much as possible, without harness. This was my task.

First of all I walked him in the yard, holding his halter. Then I trotted him, my only friend, round the market-place. I befriended him and played with him like a dog. Did he also like this life? Very soon he became more faithful to me than a dog, and we could read each other's thoughts.

Every day we walked two or three times through the village. I went in front and he followed me; there was no need to lead him. We walked in the middle of the road, keeping at a respectable distance from other folk. The first time I climbed from a fence on to his back, he looked round in surprise. He saw that I was properly seated and then nodded and started off. I clung to his mane with a beating heart. I sat on his back until we found a suitable place to dismount or until I fell off. Then he would stop immediately. Not only was he an excellent horse, but he had a fine soul. I believe he would have pulled a cart for me. I did not betray him. In silent and friendly conspiracy we went roaming through the fields, secretly finding good pasturage here and there among the crisp spring crops. His coat began to shine and he grew so fat that I could hardly sit him. But I became more and more accustomed to him. When my mother was told of my foolhardiness, I displayed my knowledge to calm her fears. By then we could gallop, and indeed we jumped over a feeding-trough, the horse whinnying happily. Thanks to him, I never became really friendly with the children in the village; at most I knew the landless peasants' children. I went to school regularly, and despite the gloomy prognostications of my father's relatives who expected my spirit to fail in the stricter atmosphere of the village school, I proved to be an excellent pupil. Thanks to the horse, I was very little affected by family affairs. I have only a dim recollection of the great family gathering one Sunday when, in the foggy clouds of cigarette and tobacco smoke after lunch, my father was finally persuaded by his brothers-in-law to make up his mind. He would not return to Budapest, but find work at home. They did not give him any money, but were willing to stand surety for him if he bought any necessary equipment on credit. At first he was reluctant, but after a cleverly-worded persuasive remark, he accepted the plans with all the more enthusiasm, himself colouring the details of the dreams evoked by the rest. Feverishly and impatiently he started on the great adventure of freedom—and after a few experiments, with equal feverishness and blind passion escaped once more to bury himself for ever on the puszta. He, the mechanic, intended to open an inn—on the eve of the Great War.

My future was also considered during the discussion. One of my father's brothers generously offered to look after me, so that I should not stand in the way of the great enterprise. If necessary, he was prepared to adopt me and send me to school—'if you deserve it,' added my aunt, who already had some fillings in her teeth. How does one 'deserve' anything like that? I was ten years old. My glance fell for a moment on my mother. She was silent, and only I knew what her silence meant. But the next moment my eyes were on the window. It was growing dark outside, and I racked my brains about how to escape for yet another little trip with the horse. I was living in a different world.

I used to go visiting with the horse, causing no little surprise in the landless peasants' quarter where I instinctively made my way. I went to see the Kosaras family and other old friends from the puszta. I felt at home here. My tongue was loosened, for here they knew who I was. Or did I go that way because

I could still feel that I was somebody there? It is difficult to renounce one's princely rank.

It was a grim neighbourhood. The former people of the pusztas had become vagabonds, and lived as sub-tenants of even older vagabonds. The landlord and his tenant alike suffered the same pangs of starvation. They lived in the same room, and here there were more families in each room than on the puszta. If there was a cowshed, they lived there too, indeed there was one place where a family had made itself a home out of the old hen-coop they had brought from the puszta. I found all this very ingenious and idyllic: it breathed the air of the puszta.

This was the situation everywhere. I roamed with the horse over to the next village, and to Cece, for on the way to grandmother's, I could go through two villages. In the middle of the villages I would urge my friend the horse to gallop, while at the top and bottom ends we would amble along, curiously turning our heads from side to side. The outskirts of every single village, even the most prosperous, were poverty-stricken and filthy; it looked as if when the village had been assembled, it had been compelled like a dumpling to dip itself in the musty sauce of poverty. Nearly everywhere I found an acquaintance or two. In some places the people of the puszta lived in even greater squalor than in Simontornya. Or was it merely that my brain began to see light and look around in the world? The more villages I visited, the darker became the picture. But just as it was only later, with a mature mind, that I became acquainted with the love life of the puszta, so too the world of the landless peasants really opened up for me only years afterwards, when I revisited my old haunts in search of what I remembered. In the meantime the picture had developed sharp outlines. I was more taken aback by some of its details than by those deadly pale, quivering, shrivelled servants' faces which I had once known as full of smiles, but now glanced at me, as at everything else, with the maniac look of drowning men. For most of them could not even talk sensibly now. The filth had got into their throats, and they croaked and swallowed; if they thought a helping hand was being extended towards them, they wept and shrieked in chorus. They had changed a great deal. Uncle Leperdi, who had once assisted in my education with his powerful hand, called me 'sir' and burst into tears when I asked him why he did not use the familiar form any more. What had happened to them? Uncle Pali Czabuk, who once had made me repeat my lessons to him every afternoon, thus cheering his loneliness, for he was a widower, had simply disappeared. Nobody knew whether he was alive or dead, and if dead, where he was buried.

CHAPTER NINETEEN

Those who emerge. The second and third generations. The way into society

How many were there who emerged into the pure, free air and the realms of free thought in order to carry news of the life led by those who remained below? Perhaps not one. Just as the labourer finds it impossible to speak in front of the land-owner and merely waves his arms—if he can even do that—so social classes too can communicate something intelligible to each other only with a great deal of stammering and various motions of shoulder and fist. It was very rare for someone to rise from the puszta to a higher intellectual level, and he took with him nothing of the spirit of the puszta. Nor could he. The raw hide of the animal does not undergo more immersion, tanning, pounding and scraping to become fine morocco than does the boy from the puszta who through some unexpected miracle reaches secondary school and becomes a member of visible society. This, however, I have already mentioned in my introduction. Let us take a longer view of the problem. What percentage of the college students in Hungary came from the millions of farm servants and landless peasants? It would be difficult to express in thousandths. This too is a species of *numerus clausus*, indeed it is a true one, although the most militant opponents of the *numerus clausus* have never mentioned it in so much as a single word. I knew of no farm servant who had sent his son to secondary school.

The vine-dresser from P. had his son educated as far as he could, up to the third year of his secondary-school course, by which time the boy had instilled into him the dream of a better life. He bore it like an open wound, ready to stab him with pain at the slightest touch. Occasionally the landlord would find a free place somewhere for the son of his butler or head coachman. It was rumoured that the curate at M. was the son of a watchman. I asked him about it, cautiously feeling my way, but at the first suggestion he protested violently, with a red face. When a secondary school was established in the market town of D. which was almost contiguous with the puszta of T., the puszta foreman and the granary overseer both sent their sons there. But these were not ordinary labourers and they would have been insulted if they had been called farm servants.

Any efforts of the farm servants to educate themselves were regarded with disfavour. Even the overseers disapproved of such attempts. Those discovered reading were regarded before the First World War as presumptuous, and after it quite simply as Communists. They had their own views of anyone who made use of the simpler gifts of civilisation too. A driver from K. puszta was dismissed because one November he put on gloves to turn the steering-wheel of the seed-drill. 'Ah, now, in my time...' the farm officials would shake their heads if they saw a labourer in braces. When the girls began to wear high-heeled shoes on Sundays, the wives of the middle class expected the collapse of the moral order and despaired of being able to distinguish between the servant and the lady of quality. Among the farm servants, anyone who was not sufficiently coarse and vulgar, and who did not curse, was suspect. Why be so affected? They were afraid of aristocratic tendencies, which in their view implied softness, untrustworthiness and a bent for thieving—a curious twist of mind, for after all they themselves were gentlemen.

It was at most the third or fourth generation of the farm servants' descendants who had the opportunity to equip themselves intellectually. Some member of a family which had been swept away into a village would be carried on by the current into a city. The more resourceful instinctively sought for servants' employment. They avoided day-labour as far as possible, for they knew this already at home. Their minds were set on such jobs as that of office or school porter, or similar posts in the lower ranks of the public service. Those who succeeded followed the example of their masters and frequently had their children educated. But what did these grandchildren and great-grandchildren know of the life of the puszta, and what could they have done, if they happened to retain a spark of loyal y to the family tree, that sense of duty levied by inheritance? (And in such circumstances we cannot rid ourselves of it, for its encouragement to the fray is backed not by unjust privilege, but by justice itself.) Uncle Hajas's son became a messenger for one of the district courts in Pest, and his son in turn was a law student. Uncle Hajas knew this only by hearsay; he had only a photograph of the student and set it up proudly on top of the dresser. We are a little too quick to allege that many folk are proud to recall their peasant descent, like the magnates their ancestors. I do not believe that Uncle Hajas's grandson often mentioned his grandfather. In my experience such grandfathers usually become transformed, in the atmosphere of the drawing-room, into jovial old landowners, and not infrequently acquire noble names as well.

I know very few cases of such prodigiously rapid advancement as that achieved by both sides of my own family. From Rácegres nobody within living memory had ever been to secondary school. My uncle was the first to do so from Nebánd, and nobody followed his example. Yet there was no family group —and this applied particularly to the foremen and overseers— of which one or other branch was not seized by the desire to go up in the world. How far could they rise? And what did the community vegetating below gain from their advancement? And what did those who advanced gain for themselves?

With the persistence of insects, mothers and grandmothers pushed and prodded their offspring into the light of the sun. They themselves remained to the end in the dank gloom, from whose slime they sucked in the strength which they transformed into honey-sweet sustenance for their successors. Was the transformation too swift? The second generation staggered and blinked in the blinding light up above; it became drunk with the rich, free air and soon lost the ground from under its feet. Oh yes, it certainly developed... Like a plant transferred from the Arctic to the Equator it began to dwell and shine, but this very sudden and boisterous radiance was a warning that it was devouring itself. Driven on by feverish credulity, it grew by leaps and bounds, ever higher and further from its roots. The boys 'made good' in the world. The impetus they acquired hurled several of them far beyond their old limits, and the higher they were hurled, the more dangerous it became, for it was all the more foreign to them. Once their fathers had lived in the secure alliance of a close-knit community; now their sons found themselves on an equally slippery soil. They tried to hang on, they stumbled around, and thrown completely off balance, restlessly hastened on the fulfilment of some secret punishment. If not on themselves, then on their sons. They were not attractive, though they were certainly innocent in all respects. They had become traitors, but traitors to what? They themselves did not know; such matters never crossed their minds. Yet their nature was the restless, self-consuming nature of the traitor, or at best the exile.

When my grandparents had made their bid, the aggressive fever suddenly died away in our family. My father's parents had one of their sons educated. The rest they tried to raise to the level of village craftsmen at least, and spared no efforts to do so. Of their numerous grandchildren, six boys reached secondary school, but only two finished their studies. The second generation came to a halt, while the third began to disintegrate and was in danger of sinking even lower than the place from which their ancestors had risen. True, the times deceived them also. The world was no longer the happy hunting-ground seen by the old folk. All this occurred when my own fate was in the balance.

I got my report at the end of my fourth year in the elementary school with the customary remark by the teacher: 'Something should be done with this boy,' a remark which is so fitting for every fourth-year pupil. Grandmother in Cece pricked up her ears. Then, since nothing happened for weeks, apart from random after-dinner projects, she suddenly appeared at our house one day. Even as she was unwinding her head scarf, she admitted that her visit was on my account. Suspecting the worst, I disappeared outside to the horse. Even in those days I found it difficult to be in the room when my future was being discussed.

My mother, of course, needed no encouragement, but my father had no particular respect for book-learning and school. Just then he was entranced by the butchers' life: they sat in a cart the whole day long, travelling from puszta to puszta; they bought a calf, sold it by weight and made five pengős on the deal and had the hide into the bargain. As for himself, he had neither the strength nor the faith to try this career now, but my elder brother and I were destined for it. But grandmother stood firm. She wrote to the uncle who not long before had been willing to adopt me. She drew blank, as she did with another uncle who lived in a town where there was a grammar school. She despaired at this lack of enthusiasm, and especially at mine. She dictated the begging letters to me, for though she was a voracious reader, only her nearest relatives could make anything of her handwriting. Day by day and with considerable reluctance I scrawled the complicated sentences in the style of

Jókai, all about my unquenchable thirst for knowledge and my exceptional intellectual gifts, which it would be criminal to leave by the wayside, for some day I should be the bright star of the family. I felt no thirst for knowledge at all. 'Well then, what would you like to be?' she asked me one afternoon, pausing for a moment in the middle of our tiring joint labours, which had lasted since midday. 'A groom,' I replied frankly, and immediately dragged her off to the yard to prove my ability. Grandmother examined the horse and a week later sold him. She herself took him to the market at Dorog and solved immediately the problem which had been beyond the powers of the most famous horse-expert in the family. At grandmother's command the fastidious, beautiful steed showed his paces and pulled magnificently; it was no trouble at all to foist him on to the first peasant for almost as much as my father had once hoped to get for him. Then she went off in a rage, taking with her the price of the horse under some pretext. I was entered for the fifth class in the elementary school.

In my misery I gave myself up to study, and very soon to the study of prayer-books. The opposing ideas of my two grand-mothers broke out in me at the same time, and I became a religious fanatic as well as an omnivorous reader. I set up a chair in front of the narrow little window and, kneeling on it, studied the lives of the saints for hours on end until in the dusk the letters began to dance before my eyes. Then I shut my burning eyes and in my trance I saw angels flying and Mary's blue skirt rustling. By now I had to work at home when school was over. It took three or four shouts before I raised my head and, shaken out of the world of marvels, sleepily stumbled around among real objects, dropping everything I held in my hands. I would escape into the loft or up trees so that I could devote myself to my passion in peace. I acquired the reputation of being workshy and lazy. Even my father began to realise that I was more suited to intellectual work.

I got up at dawn every day to serve at low mass. At school religious instruction was given by monks, who knew the religious fervour of my father's family and the deep-rooted heresy of my mother's. They gladly guided my soul, which was exposed to so many dangers, along the right road. I got the books from them, and I was supposed to read them to my mother. So I did. I talked enthusiastically to her about the Virgin Mary—my devotion, as I now recall it, was chiefly concerned with worship of her. My mother listened suspiciously and perhaps a little jealously to my ardour. Yet in the Virgin Mary I worshipped my dear, beautiful mother, who suffered so much, yet always smiled, even through her tears. It was I who carried the Sanctusbell in processions; with an ethereal smile I would walk at the head of the procession, glancing from time to time at the Maytime clouds behind which reigned Mary with her lively, warm gaze. Sometimes I even thought I saw her there. I too looked down from the heights on the people who fell to their knees in adoration on each side of me when they heard the sound of the weighty bell. I too walked a little among the clouds in my ample surplice with its smell of incense.

My maternal grandmother, who was unswervingly Protestant in matters of faith, was delighted to hear of my spiritual transformation. She stood me in front of her and began to ask me questions in a friendly way. I seized the opportunity with fervour, and heatedly began to explain the mystery. Only at the end of my missionary sermon did I feel that I had been sitting an examination, and that grandmother had been curious not so much about my arguments as about my ability to do something which at the time was unknown to me. She decided that I should be a priest, Catholic or Calvinist, whichever was possible.

It was she who accompanied me to the fifth class examinations, and when the usual declaration was made, this time from the lips of a good father, 'Now as for this boy...', grandmother immediately took him at his word. The father stroked his chin

296

in confusion, and did so for two weeks, for from then on we visited him every day. The result was a letter of recommendation in Latin to the Cistercians in Pécs. Grandmother got another one from the Calvinist minister to the college at Pápa.

She took matters into her own hands. She knew by now that she could not count on the family. During the previous few years the retreat on one or two sectors of the front had developed into virtual panic. My father's mother was ill and had given up the leadership, while her followers were dropping from the besieged walls with bloodstained heads. One or two bastions still held out, but they were beginning to shut themselves off from those who followed after, and to seek peace with their superiors. My elder brother no longer attended secondary school and my mother had to put her foot down in order to get him a suitable apprenticeship. Would she succeed in getting me, the last of all, into the fortress? Grandmother collected all her strength and wits. Her plan was touching in its cunning, and naive as that of Ulysses.

I do not know what battles were being waged at that time in the higher regions of the denominations. When they reached us, the waves clashed together with rumblings and wild frothings which sometimes covered whole counties. Almost every village was half Calvinist and half Catholic. In the pulpits of the churches built at opposite ends of the main street, the priests and ministers shook their fists, sent messages and uttered threats with all the wrath of Pázmány and Alvinczi.* They enflamed their flocks and guarded them jealously. A grim battle was fought over the newborn children in mixed households, as to which fold they would enrich. The lambs hummed and hawed and nodded their heads, not really understanding what it was all about. Grandmother did understand it. One day she set out with the letters of recommendation and my reports. She

* The two main protagonists during the Reformation of the Catholic and Calvinist causes respectively.

297

selected one or two of my best drawings and even made me copy out in my best hand one of my pieces of doggerel that had come to light, for at that time I had begun to write whole poems in great secrecy. Unfortunately I was not 'discovered' in either Pápa or Pécs. Grandmother everywhere offered my intellect for sale, quite cheaply, in return for free education and board. She even went to the Lutheran school at Bonyhád, but it was no use. The battle was grim, but not as grim as that.

She returned in fury. She had her own opinion of religious sects in general. Another September approached and with it the sixth class of the elementary school. Everybody, including myself, had given up hope for my future. The whole summer I felt what the calf displayed in the market must feel. I whimpered, and now felt released.

Grandmother, however, like a good fencer who is conscious of his own worth, was merely spurred to further effort by this failure. At the very last moment she once again tempted Providence. But this was the gesture of a card-player who has lost his money and asks to play on what little credit he has. She still had a plan. If I got very high marks, they would take me in at Veszprém from the fifth form of the grammar school free of charge, as a theological student. In other words, I should be a burden to my family only for the first four forms. The promise was a verbal one, but grandmother had a blind faith in the favourable signs.

One of my father's elder sisters lived in the chief town of the neighbouring district, where there was a grammar school. She agreed to take me in as a boarder, but charged as much as if I had been staying outside the family. 'The rest is up to you,' said grandmother, when my belongings had been packed, and she gave me a lengthy lecture, as is customary on such occasions in novels. 'Of course you're not going to be a priest,' she said, 'but you may as well study to become one.' I understood that I should have to tell lies, but was not indignant. I nodded, frowned and then nodded again. Before I said good-bye, she called me aside and told me not to worry, because my future was assured. She had put the price of the horse, all eighty koronas, into the savings bank in my name. When I had finished my studies, I should have the right to draw it out to lay the foundations of my career. Though I should do better not to touch it until I got married. 'Until then you can get along under your own steam,' she said. Seriously and with no little ceremony, I kissed her hand. I felt myself to be a man, and understood the game I was to play. The money for my board was not assured for even six months.

At first I suffered cruelly in that little market town, as if a new layer of skin was stripped from me every day. I had to undergo a painful process of moulting in external appearance too. Up till then, my mother had made all our clothes, even those for us boys. But the fine aristocratic suit in which I was launched into my new life was made by a tailor—the cheaper one at the bottom end of the village. At home I dare not appear in it or even try it on in public; I thought it a ridiculous, clownish outfit. But just how ridiculous it really was only came to light in the town. My schoolmates wore short trousers. Mr Keszler had made my trousers short too, but in such a way that they looked like long trousers cut too short. The two legs ended exactly a hand's breadth above my ankles. For a fortnight my soul was in torment, while I poured out my grief on a postcard to my mother. But what could be done? They were the only trousers I had fit to wear in town. After much calculation, I got another pair, which were about a couple of centimetres shorter and if anything even more ridiculous than the first pair.

I wrote again, and was able to return the first pair, but Mr Keszler treated them as cautiously as if he were cutting into human flesh. They did not emerge very much shorter after the next round either, this time owing to my mother's express wish. She wrote a gentle letter explaining that the trousers were meant to last for several years, and I was to resign myself to wearing them; I should soon grow into them, and in about two years' time nobody would have such a fine pair of trousers as mine. I saw that at home they did not understand my struggles in the world, then sighed and myself sheared off the superfluous cloth. Then I stitched up what was left, making use of the knowledge for which I could still thank grandmother. This was my first independent action and the first sign of defection. Afterwards I walked around happily and vastly relieved.

My attitude to study was like that of the impoverished patient to expensive hospital treatment: now that I was there, I tried to get the most for my money. Or was it like going out to day-labouring? I found my task easy, and saw to it that I did not fall by the wayside. I did what they required better than was necessary—what was this compared with hoeing or tying up vines? Here in the town nobody knew me, and I breathed more freely than in the village. In the unfamiliar streets there was something of the unbridled freedom of the puszta; later I was often reminded in the great capitals of the world of the fields at home. Only occasionally was I overcome by that feeling of depression which still visits me at times—that the folk around me will one day perhaps realise that they have accepted me and put up with me in their midst by mistake; then they will grab me by the ear and lead me back to the stables of Rácegres where I belong. At these times I grew thoroughly despondent. But then the head of that hydra-like spirit inculcated into me by my grandmother would begin to whisper, 'Hold on and reinforce your position!' I could make the burden on my mind disappear only if I drew myself up to my full height and stood out among the others. As yet I did not suspect why I was doing it, but I studied hard and diligently. Soon I became a good pupil, only to become all the worse later on, when my spirit rose in revolt against oppression. For the time being, however, everything appeared to get off to a good start. And then the puszta dragged me back once again. It dragged me back and let me go again, but I do not know whether it did not bind me to it then with an even stronger secret thread.

In the class there were other boys from the puszta, from more or less the same social class as mine. Both of them were dressed in clothes like mine, an outfit which the poor imagine to be the fashion of the gentry. This is how we recognised each other. One wore the image of my trousers, and to make matters worse, in corduroy; the other wore stockings, but with blue stripes like women's. We avoided each other in terror, like mock-ghosts in a melodrama. Sharing the views of the class, I regarded them as impossible figures and no doubt they thought the same of me.

We would loiter on the fringe of some more distinguished group, happy to penetrate it even though it meant playing some servile role. I blush to recall the enthusiasm, the garrulity, adulation and presents with which I sought to win their favour. When the ball rolled far away, I would gladly run after it; I thought it natural that in piggy-back games, where one boy rides on the back of another, I should always be the horse. I tried hard to be an excellent horse. I had some friends already. There were the sons of a tax commissioner, who had obviously been told by their parents to pay me some attention; my uncle was a step ahead of their father on the civil service ladder. Once they invited me to their house. I stumbled into a troop of girls, but managed to stand my ground. Aunt Homonnay stroked my head as if I were a dog that had strayed in from the fields. Fate caught up with me during a geometry lesson.

This was taught by a friendly young teacher. I was sincerely fond of him. I would gaze at him from the heights of happiness if he stopped by me as he walked between the desks. I can still smell the scent of his clothes. He was a tall, blond youth, who fell in the war a year later.

I was standing at the blackboard with ruler and compasses, drawing the figure for that day's lesson with all the confidence of a good pupil. I drew a straight line between the points B and F. 'Tell us what you are doing,' said the master to me.

'I am drawing a straight line between points bee and aff,' I replied. The master smiled and raised his head. 'Between what?'

'Between points bee and aff,' I repeated. My pronunciation was somewhat dialectal.

'Not aff, but eff.'

'Yes.'

'Say eff.'

'Aff,' I said clearly and unmistakably.

'Not aff! Say it properly.'

I was silent. I knew that at home we talked in dialect, not using the sound *ő*, which later I found most attractive, and pronouncing *e* sometimes quite closed and sometimes almost as open, as *a*. If in commoner words we used the customary variations heard on the puszta, mother would correct us, but it was only the form of the word she corrected and not the vowels, because she pronounced them like everyone else. Grandfather would sometimes taunt us, because he spoke in the Great Plain dialect, but then we also laughed sometimes at his pronunciation.

'Well then, say it!' My tongue went numb. All of a sudden I hated the way I spoke.

'What is it?'

'Aff,' I blurted out at length, hardly audibly, with my last remaining strength. The class roared.

'Where are you from?' asked the teacher.

I did not answer.

'From the puszta!' shouted someone.

'*Bregócs!*'

This is the word used by the people of the puszta to make fun of their own kind. It is not known in the villages. Only one of my puszta schoolmates could have said it, to increase the general amusement.

The teacher put a stop to it. He pronounced the correct *e* clearly to me two or three times. But his efforts to make me imitate him were of no avail. Then he explained that I must learn it without fail, otherwise how was he to know what letter I meant?

'You will learn the correct pronunciation by tomorrow,' he said, losing his patience, 'and report to me.'

All afternoon I walked up and down among the willows on the banks of the Kapos, practising. Sometimes I thought I had mastered it. I gasped and croaked, and squeezed my throat with my face turned up towards the sky.

The first thing I did next morning was to test myself. I wanted to cry. A despairing croak came from my throat and seemed to hang in the air like an avenging spirit.

I did not report before the lesson and now it was not only that unfortunate sound, but every other one, that refused to come to my lips. After a good deal of persuasion, punctuated by roars of approving laughter from the class, the young teacher finally grew angry and sent me out of the room. I do not remember what his last words were. 'A silly idiot who doesn't even know how to speak,' he may well have said, 'has no place in the class.' Did I infer from this that I had been expelled from the school for ever? This is how I explained my behaviour later on. Today I do not think so; I was not quite so simple-minded. But I do remember the inexpressible weariness that suddenly overcame me.

Without a word I went out of the room and even before I had shut the door I had decided to go home. But my puszta background did not mean that I did this immediately without giving some thought to the problem. I wandered about the streets until school was over, taking a walk to the station where, with a great deal of difficulty, I succeeded in finding out from the various notices on display how much it cost to go to Simontornya and when the train went. Then I went to my lodgings and had my lunch calmly, as if nothing had happened.

On the pretext that I needed some exercise-books, I asked my aunt for the price of the ticket. I packed up what I could and hid the bundle in the bushes in front of the gate. At eleven o'clock that night I was standing on the platform of our home station, Simontornya.

But why did I not go home to my parents? Why did it suddenly occur to me as I walked along the dark, muddy road that the best plan would be to go to the Szerentséses? By morning I had reached Hegyempuszta.

But in the meantime the Szerentsés family had moved from there to Csojjános, near Vajta. It was after lunch when I discovered them, but unexpectedly they still had some food to offer me.

They vere not surprised at my arrival, nor did they ask me much apart from the usual family questions—least of all did they ask how long I wanted to stay. One more or less did not matter in the least to them. 'You can sleep with Jóska,' said Aunt Malvi. My behaviour gave nothing away; I was happy and talkative. That afternoon I was picking potatoes with the girls and in the best of good humour we pelted each other with the stunted and rotten ones. Only in the evening did something cross Uncle Mihály's mind: 'They said last year that you were going to be sent to grammar school,' he said. 'I've finished now,' I replied. My plan was to get work on the puszta as a half-rate labourer when the New Year came.

Four days later one of the bachelor members of the more distinguished side of the family, a waiter, came to fetch me. He looked me up and down as if I were a robber and a murderer, then, full of the importance of his mission, hurled one word at me, 'Pack'! The bundle was exactly as I had brought it. We set out, but not towards Simontornya. 'Your mother doesn't know anything about this,' he said, when we were walking among the houses in Vajta. There we got on the train and set off towards Szekszárd. At Kölesd-Tengelic, the third or fourth station, without any premeditated plan, I got off the train, bareheaded and without my coat. I walked calmly out of the station. My cousin caught me up by the lavatory and dragged me behind it. I hid my face in my hands as he began to rain sharp, dry blows on my bare cropped head. Then the engine whistled, whereupon he grabbed me by the collar and with a dash hustled me on to the now moving train. I did not resist. I went where I was taken.

Of course, I have not told the whole story. Even so I have taken on too big a subject. Wherever I got hold of 'material', I found my hands entwined by threads from a thousand directions: how can I possible tie them now into a pleasing bow to finish off? Usually the reader expects to find at the end of works which lay bare the most distressing problems some guidance or proposal for their solution. This quietens his awakened conscience, even if he only feels that all is not lost, for after all, if someone has been able to reveal the problem, there will undoubtedly be others to solve it. The sense of community which has aroused his conscience at the same time lulls him into idleness. I dare not soothe him into cheap suppositions. I myself am not credulous. I can see the size of the problem and I can foresee its consequences too. The life of a people is at stake. What is the remedy? This concerns the reader as much as the author, for after all the former now knows as much as the author. As for those who feel this book to be incomplete because it has no solution, and await a continuation of it, I expect them to continue it. It is to them that I dedicate my work.

Born to a poor peasant family living on the Hungarian *puszta*, Gyula Illyés became one of the great figures of populist literature between the two world wars, and one of the celebrated writers of the post-Liberation scene. He was hardly more than a child when he attached himself to the Hungarian Red Army. After the fall of the Hungarian Soviet Republic (1919), he emigrated, and after spending a considerable period in Paris, he returned as a pioneer of surrealist and expressionist leftist poetry. Back in Hungary (1926), he joined Mihály Babits, the unofficial poet laureate, and became the associate editor of *Nyugat* (The West), the most distinguished literary magazine of the time. In his poems of the 1920s, the *Nyugat* traditions were blended with those of the contemporary French schools. Later, in the 1930s, as a key figure of the left-wing of the populist movement, he succeeded in adopting this heritage as part of his ideas. When, after Babits's death, the increasing pressure of Fascism made the further publication of the *Nyugat* impossible, he founded a new periodical entitled *Magyar Csillag* (Hungarian Star), which provided much-needed publication space for persecuted writers.

Illyés is the author of numerous volumes of poetry, several novels and plays, and is an excellent translator as well. His work has been growing in stature and scope since the 1930s, his poetry has gained profundity, his prose subtlety and his works a deeper meaning. He is among the Hungarian writers who are most popular abroad. His drama, *The Favourite*, was produced in Paris, and his selected poetry, which has appeared in several languages, has achieved two editions in the French alone. Illyés is internationally recognized as an important writer; in 1965 he received the Grand Prix of the International Biennale of Poets at Knokke-le-Zoute, an honour previously conferred on St.-John Perse, Giuseppe Ungaretti and Octavio Paz.

Illyés has been especially active as a translator in the last fifteen years. His translations of Eluard, Aragon and other French poets rank with the greatest Hungarian translations, as do his interpretations of Hugo's romanticism and his rendering of the robust realism of Burns, Villon and Ben Jonson.

In the last fifty or sixty years, Illyés has exerted undisputed influence on the literary scene. He is among those poets for whom public and private life are inseparably interwoven, and for whom literature is a kind of battlefield on which the poet, the representative of his people's aspirations, wages his battles for the present and for the future. At each historic stage of the recent past, he took an active part; many worshipped him, many attacked him, many disagreed with his views, but later some of these same critics proved that Illyés was both loved and hated, he was everything but neglected or unnoticed. The Western reader has long forgotten the public poet, and only the major historic tragedies such as the last war make him realize for a few fleeting moments what great service a poet can render his people. Illyés is such a poet and writer, and his work is enriched by that special Central European characteristic, whereby for him serving his people is serving mankind. To be Hungarian as Illyés thinks of being Hungarian is tantamount to what Dante, Shakespeare and Goethe meant by being part of humanity. This all-embracing human attitude, this world-view runs through his works and raises Illyés into the ranks of the greatest Hungarian writers. In fact, if we follow the destiny of his writings in the West, we may add: he is among the great living figures of world literature.

It was about the life of farm servants in his home county bogged down in the quagmire of medieval life that Illyés wrote this book, in which he managed to blend elements of poetic prose, autobiography, sociological study, ethnography and the political pamphlet into an artistic composition of great beauty.

Having grown up in the stagnating, semi-feudal world of great landownership, the writer is able to present various aspects of this life. The leading motif is the description of the dehumanised life of farm servants in the shadow of the manor-house. Memories from childhood, tales told by people, the actual paragraphs of hypocritical statutes, and the chill figures of statistics expose this world, which—up till 1945—tolerated physical punishment, took it for granted that farm managers could order the pretty peasant girls into their beds, reluctantly made a law that no more than one family was to live in one room but never enforced it, and used the rod to drive the farm servants to work from two in the morning to late at night.

The *People of the Puszta*, a book which can perhaps be best described as a lyric sociography, is a memorable contribution to Hungarian literature, a work of lasting value, a document from a period that is past, and an ardent expression of love for one's country. It also furnishes valuable information on the development of a great literary personality.

This book by Illyés was first published in 1936. By now the *People of the Puszta* has appeared in over twenty-two editions, and the number of copies runs into several hundreds of thousands. French, German and Chinese editions have raised a Hungarian triumph into a world success.